LIVING PORTRAITS
SPEAKING STILL

a collection of Bible studies

CREST BOOKS

The Salvation Army National Publications

Alexandria, Virginia

Published by Crest Books, Salvation Army National Headquarters
615 Slaters Lane, Alexandria, Virginia 22314
(703) 299-5558 Fax: (703) 684-5539
http://www.salvationarmyusa.org

Printed in the United States of America

Composition by Jennifer Williams

Library of Congress Control Number: 2003117099

ISBN: 0-9740940-1-3

CONTENTS

FOREWORD

THE BIBLE IS AN AMAZING BOOK; ITS FORMATION NO LESS THAN EXTRAORDINARY. Thirty to forty authors penned its words using three languages (Hebrew, Aramaic, and Greek) over a period of 1,500 years—sixty generations. No other book in history comes close to equaling these remarkable characteristics.

The conditions in which the Bible was written vary as widely as do the backgrounds, personalities, and professions of its authors. From the king's palace in Jerusalem (David and Solomon) to a Roman prison cell (Paul), from the quill of a well-educated priest (Zechariah) to that of an uneducated fisherman (Peter), from Babylon (Daniel) to Rome (Peter and Paul), from a murderer (David) to a physician (Luke) comes the Word of the Lord.

Despite wide differences of time, language, and circumstance, the Bible presents a united, progressive revelation from God to all who will listen. William Ellery Channing sums it up well: "The incongruity of the Bible with the age of its birth; its freedom from earthly mixtures; its original, unborrowed, solitary greatness; the suddenness with which it broke forth amidst the general gloom; these, to me, are strong indications of its Divine descent; I cannot reconcile them with a human origin."

WILLIAM W. FRANCIS

A Portrait of Sovereignty

This first series of portraits reveals the exploits of prophets such as Malachi and judges such as Deborah and Samson as they witness to the God who is all powerful, all righteous, and who demands and deserves the worship of the people He has made. We begin with John, the gospel writer and disciple, who further uncovers the drape of the Great I AM as He is evidenced in His Son, of whom the prophet Isaiah spoke.

ONE

JOHN: THE ETERNAL DECLARATIONS

WILLIAM W. FRANCIS

Commissioner William W. Francis is the International Secretary for the Americas and the Caribbean. He is the author of *The Stones Cry Out* and *Celebrate the Feasts of the Lord* (a Crest Books publication) as well as a frequent contributor to *The War Cry* and other Salvation Army publications.

Of all the sixty–six books of the Bible, the Gospel of John is a favorite for many. Throughout his singular work, John alone records the eight cryptic declarations of Jesus that begin with the phrase, "I AM . . . ."

1: Jesus Said, "I AM . . ."

KEY TO UNDERSTANDING THE DISTINCTIVE CONTENT OF JOHN'S gospel is an appreciation of the author's unique relationship to Jesus. A comparison of the gospel accounts of the women gathered at the foot of the cross (Matthew 27:56; Mark 15:40, 16:1; John 19:25) reveals that John's mother, Salome, was likely Mary's sister, making John and Jesus first cousins. Crucial to this deduction is John 19:25, which lists the same group of four women named by Matthew and Mark, substituting "[Jesus'] mother's sister" for "the mother of Zebedee's sons" (Matthew) and "Salome" (Mark). It is therefore likely that these three references describe one person—Salome, John's mother, and Jesus' aunt.

John's gospel is different from the synoptic gospels (Matthew, Mark, and Luke). Its uniqueness is doubtless due to his close relationship with Jesus. Not only was John likely Jesus' cousin, but he was also a member of the "inner circle" of disciples that included Peter, James, and John (see Mark 5:37, 14:33 and Matthew 17:1). At the conclusion of his gospel, John clearly states his purpose in writing. He declares that his words were "written that you may believe that Jesus is the Christ, the Son of God, and that by believing you may have life in His name" (John 20:31).

The Gospel of John is noted for what it omits and for what it includes. More than ninety percent of John's record is unique to his gospel. For example, of the eight miracles recorded by John, six are found only in his gospel.

Written in the last decade of the first century, John's gospel does not include stories that were well known by that time. He omits a description of Jesus' birth and the first thirty years of His life, as well as His baptism by John the Baptist and His temptation in the Judean wilderness. John does not mention the institution of the Eucharist or Jesus' struggle in Gethsemane. The "Great Commission" and the account of Christ's ascension into heaven are also absent.

John includes accounts that are not contained in the other gospels. The marriage feast at Cana (2:1–11), the coming of Nicodemus to Jesus at night (3:1–15) and Jesus' profound conversation with the woman of Samaria (4) are recorded only by John. It is John alone who recounts the raising of Lazarus from the dead (11), the washing of the disciples' feet at the Last Supper (13:1–17), and Jesus' teaching about the Holy Spirit (14–17). John's gospel brings the disciples to life. Thomas speaks (11:16; 14:5; 20:24–29); Andrew (1:40,41; 6:8,9; 12:22) and Philip (6:5–7; 14:8,9) are described in such a way that they become for the reader recognizable personalities.

John also provides details not found in the synoptic accounts. For example, he meticulously records that there were six stone water pots at the wedding in Cana of Galilee (2:6), that the bread the boy brought to Jesus consisted of barley loaves (6:9), that there were four soldiers gambling for Jesus' seamless robe (19:23), that the exact weight of the myrrh and aloe used to anoint the dead body of our Lord was 75 pounds (19:39) and that Jesus prepared breakfast for His weary disciples on a charcoal fire (21:9).

Most striking among the statements that only John records are the occasions when Jesus uses the self-revealing phrase, "I AM . . . ." Eight times Jesus uses this phrase with a sentence structure that conspicuously parallels God's direction to Moses. In the midst of the burning bush, God said to Moses, "I AM who I AM. This is what you are to say to the Israelites: 'I AM has sent me to you'" (Exodus 3:14). This series will ponder Jesus' startling assertions:

I AM the Bread of Life (6:35,48,51)
I AM the Light of the World (8:12, 9:5)
I AM the Gate for the Sheep (10:7,9)
I AM the Good Shepherd (10:11,14)
I AM the Son of God (10:36 KJV)
I AM the Resurrection and the Life (11:25)
I AM the Way and the Truth and the Life (14:6)
I AM the True Vine (15:1,4,5)

1. Why is John's gospel unlike that of Matthew, Mark, and Luke?

2. Why does John selectively limit his narrative—elaborating on some items while ignoring others?

3. What did Jesus mean by calling Himself "I AM"? "I AM" what or who?

4. What was John's target audience that made the reference to "I AM" necessary and applicable?

2: The Bread of Life

Then Jesus declared, "I AM the bread of life. He who comes to Me will never go hungry, and he who believes in Me will never be thirsty" (John 6:35).

EIGHT TIMES DURING HIS FINAL YEAR OF EARTHLY LIFE, JESUS STARTLED HIS LISTENERS by using a mysterious phrase beginning with the words "I AM . . . ." Only the Apostle John records these cryptic, self-revealing declarations in his gospel. John vividly describes the occasion when Jesus made His first pronouncement: "I AM the Bread of Life." It was in spring—Passover time— one year before His death that Jesus "crossed to the far shore of the Sea of Galilee . . . and a great crowd of people followed Him because they saw the miraculous signs He had performed on the sick" (John 6:1–2).

John sets the stage for Jesus' declaration by meticulously recounting the only miracle recorded in all four gospels: the feeding of the five thousand. The apostle provides details that enliven the scene, noting that it was the spring of the year (4) with "plenty of grass" in the area (10), and it was to Philip from nearby Bethsaida that Jesus posed the seemingly absurd question, "Where shall we buy bread for these people to eat?" (5).

After Jesus fed and addressed the multitude, He retreated to the nearby hills known today as the Golan Heights. His disciples sailed back to Capernaum. When a storm almost capsized the boat in the middle of the lake, not only did Jesus come to the disciples' rescue by walking on the water, but "immediately the boat reached the shore where they were heading" (21).

Word spread swiftly through the nine villages surrounding the Sea of Galilee. By foot and by boat the people followed Jesus to Capernaum (22–24), where they cornered Him in the synagogue (25 and 59). Jesus ignored their shallow questions and bluntly challenged their motivation: "I tell you the truth, you are looking for Me, not because you saw miraculous signs but because you ate the loaves and had your fill. Do not work for food that spoils, but for food that endures to eternal life" (26–27). With these piercing words Jesus moved the conversation from their desire for physical nourishment to their need for spiritual sustenance.

Jesus' popularity had soared that day. The multitudes followed Him (2). Some in the crowd considered Him a prophet (14) and a number were ready to make Him king (15). Others asked the right questions: "What must we do to do the works God requires?" (28) and "What miraculous sign then will You give that we may see it and believe You? What will You do?" (30). After Jesus described the spiritual bread that He offered, the crowd pleaded, "Sir, . . . from now on give us this bread" (34). The throng's approval plummeted when Jesus declared that He alone was the bread they were seeking.

Jesus proclaimed, "I AM the Bread of Life. He who comes to Me will never go hungry, and he who believes in Me will never be thirsty. But as I told you, you have seen Me and still you do not believe" (35–36). It did not take long for the fickle crowd to turn on Jesus. The Jewish leaders "began to grumble because He said, 'I AM the bread that came down from heaven'" (41). Some asked, "Is this not Jesus, the son of Joseph, whose father and mother we know? How can He say, 'I came down from heaven'?" (42).

The crowd came looking for bread, and Jesus offered them Himself—the Bread of Life. The cost of discipleship was simply too high for many to pay. Jesus illustrated the sacrificial cost with an unforgettable, startling metaphor: "I AM the living bread that came down from heaven. This bread is My flesh, which I will give for the life of the world. . . . I tell you the truth, unless you eat the flesh of the Son of Man and drink His blood, you have no life in you. . . . For My flesh is real food and My blood is real drink. Whoever eats My flesh and drinks My blood remains in Me, and I in him" (51–56). Sadly, this discourse ended with many followers leaving Jesus.

"'This,' they concluded, 'is a hard teaching. Who can accept it?' . . . From this time many of His disciples turned back and no longer followed Him" (60–66). Thankfully, the story does not end here. It was Peter who had the right answer. Peter did not always act in the proper manner, but he never failed to answer Jesus' questions correctly. "'You do not want to leave, do you?' Jesus asked the Twelve. Simon Peter answered, 'Lord, to whom shall we go? You have the words of eternal life. We believe and know that You are the Holy One of God'" (67–69).

Jesus' penetrating question resounds throughout the ages to all who would follow Him. His faithful disciples must ever follow Peter's example and respond: "We believe . . . we know . . . we gladly receive and follow the Bread of Life."

SOMETHING TO THINK ABOUT

1. What is the connection between Jesus' miraculous feeding of five thousand and His referring to Himself as "the Bread of Life"?

2. Why did such a huge crowd follow Jesus? What did they want?

3. What did people discover that made it difficult to follow Jesus?

4. What makes it so hard today for people to follow Jesus? What is holding you back?

3: The Light of the World

When Jesus spoke again to the people, He said, "I AM the Light of the World. Whoever follows Me will never walk in darkness, but will have the light of life" (John 8:12).

SIX MONTHS AFTER DECLARING "I AM THE BREAD OF LIFE," JESUS RELUCTANTLY journeyed from Galilee to Jerusalem. It was the last time He would attend the Feast of Tabernacles before His death. He urged His brothers to attend the feast without Him, explaining "for Me the right time has not yet come" (John 7:8). However, two verses later, John notes that Jesus changed His mind: "After His brothers had left for the feast, He went also, not publicly, but in secret" (7:10). Jesus not only changed His mind. He attended the feast in disguise.

The occasion provided the setting for three of the eight "I AM" proclamations. During this seven-day festival, Jesus declared "I AM the Light of the World" (8:12 and 9:5), "I AM the Gate for the Sheep" (10:7-8) and "I AM the Good Shepherd" (10:11,14).

This celebration was one of the three Jewish Feasts of Obligation. God commanded that "three times a year all your men must appear before the Lord your God at the place He will choose: at the Feast of Unleavened Bread, the Feast of Weeks, and the Feast of Tabernacles" (Deuteronomy 16:16). All males within a day's journey of Jerusalem (about twenty miles) were required to attend.

The Feast of Tabernacles (*Sukkot*, in Hebrew) celebrates the forty years that the children of Israel wandered in the wilderness, living in booths or tabernacles. The feast was a time of magnificent pageantry and thunderous rejoicing. Rabbis say that "he who has not seen the Feast of Tabernacles does not know joy."

Water was the important element in the celebration of the feast. Each morning a white-robed priest drew water from the Pool of Siloam in a golden pitcher. He carried the pitcher of sacred water on his shoulder as he proceeded up the vast Temple steps. The crowd opened a way for the priest to walk through the expansive Court of the Gentiles and into the Court of the Women. Levites standing on both sides of the fifteen steps leading to the Court of the Israelites intoned Isaiah 12:3: "With joy you will draw water from the wells of salvation." The priest paused on each step. Reaching the top, he passed through the giant Nicanor doors and proceeded straight to the altar. After ascending the ramp to the top of the altar, the priest poured the water and a flask filled with wine into silver vessels that hung over the altar. As he poured the water and wine, the entire congregation chanted Psalm 118:25: "O Lord, save us; O Lord, grant us success."

The daily water libation symbolized a memorial, a prayer, and a forecast. Water represented a memorial to God for His provision in the desert, a prayer that God would again give water for the next harvest and a forecast of the days of the Messiah.

It was on the last day of the Feast, *hoshana raba* ("The Great Day of the Call for Help"), that "Jesus stood and said in a loud voice, 'If anyone is thirsty, let him come to Me and drink. Whoever believes in Me, as the Scripture has said, streams of living water will flow from within him'" (7:37–38). Could it be that the priest carrying the final water libation heard His shout?

Later that same day, Jesus again startled the crowd. John records that "When Jesus spoke again to the people, He said 'I AM the Light of the World. Whoever follows Me will never walk in darkness, but will have the light of life'" (8:12). On the last day of the feast, Jesus boldly proclaimed that He alone was the light of the world. Jesus was the light, and to His followers He gives the light of life. Jesus not only stated the fact that He is the light of the world, but He went on to explain why the world needs the light. Whoever follows the light will never stumble, for he or she will "have the light of life" as a beacon in a dark world.

The important verb in Jesus' proclamation is "follow." The Greek word is *akoluthéo*. Of the seventy-seven times this word is used in the New Testament, only once does it signify following someone other than Jesus (Mark 14:13). Every other time, this word describes following Jesus. *Akoluthéo* carries five primary meanings. It describes (1) a soldier following his captain, (2) a slave accompanying his master, (3) a person accepting a counselor's opinion, (4) a citizen giving obedience to the laws of a city or state, or (5) a student following a teacher's line of argument. All five meanings apply to the believer following the Light of the World. Christ calls us to follow Him as His soldier and recognize Him as master, counselor, judge, and teacher. As the Light of the World, He calls His followers to become "sons of light":

> *You are going to have the light just a little while longer. Walk while you have the light, before darkness overtakes you. The man who walks in the dark does not know where he is going. Put your trust in the light while you have it, so that you may become sons of light* (John 12:35–36).

Children of Light—let your light shine!

SOMETHING TO THINK ABOUT

1. Why did Jesus attend the feast without calling attention to Himself?

2. Given the obvious references to water, the "living water" comments make sense. But why "light of the world"?

3. How can Christ satisfy the deep, longing thirsts of your life?

4. How can we live and minister as "children of light"?

4: The Gate for the Sheep

> *Jesus said again, "I AM the gate for the sheep.... I AM the gate; whoever enters through Me will be saved. He will come in and go out, and find pasture"* (John 10:7,9).

THE APOSTLE JOHN RECORDS THE REMARKABLE EVENTS THAT UNFOLDED DURING the Feast of Tabernacles celebrated in Jerusalem six months before Jesus' death (John 7:14–10:21).

This feast serves as the setting for three of the eight "I AM" proclamations.

The coming of Jesus was the coming of light into the world—light that inevitably brought judgment. The Light of the World exposes the false shepherds of Israel who do not love the sheep. Jesus shines the divine spotlight on the blind guides (Matthew 23:16) who earlier that day threw one of the "sheep" out of the fold (John 9:34).

The picture of the Judean shepherd with his sheep is woven into the language and imagery of the Bible. From the first shepherd-king, David, and from Moses, the great shepherd, to Jesus, the Good Shepherd, the shepherd embodied the essentials of authentic leadership. It is therefore not surprising that Jesus frequently used vivid metaphors of sheep and sheep herding in His teaching.

The shepherd continues to be the most familiar figure of the Judean uplands. Judea's twenty-mile-wide central plateau stretches for thirty-five miles from Bethel to Hebron. While the rough, stony terrain makes farming difficult, it provides an adequate environment for tending sheep.

The shepherd's life is hard. No flock ever grazed without his watchful guidance. He is never "off duty," and must constantly watch, guard, and nurture his flock. Since grass is invariably sparse, the sheep are bound to wander into dangerous terrain. The ground dips sharply on either side of the central plateau to the desert on the east and the coastal plain on the west, and sheep are constantly in danger of falling into one of the many ravines. Without protecting walls, the sheep require safeguarding from the perilous landscape.

Besides protecting his sheep from physical danger, the shepherd in biblical times had to guard the flock from wild animals, especially wolves. In addition, thieves were always ready to steal the sheep. In Jesus' day and today, a shepherd must possess constant vigilance, fearless courage, and patient love.

At the close of the Feast of Tabernacles, Jesus employs these well-known pastoral images to illustrate His relationship to His followers: "I tell you the truth, the man who does not enter the sheep pen by the gate, but climbs in by some other way, is a thief and a robber. The man who enters by the gate is the shepherd of the sheep" (10:1–2). The Jewish leaders did not understand the meaning of the story. Jesus plainly applies it to Himself: "I tell you the truth, I AM the Gate for the Sheep" (10:7).

In the allegory of the good shepherd (10:1–6), Jesus speaks of two types of gates. He uses the word for the "winter" gate in verses two and three. During the cold season, the sheep were kept in communal pens. A strong wooden door protected the sheep at night. Only the appointed guardian had the key to the door.

In verses seven and nine, Jesus chooses a word that describes the "summer" gate—the field sheep pen. Since good feeding grass was scarce in summer, the shepherd constantly led his flock to the best feeding areas, often miles from home. The summer pen was composed of a primitive stone enclosure in an open field. A space in the wall served as the gate. This was the only access to the sheep pen. At night, the shepherd slept across the opening. Sheep could not come in or go out except over his body. Literally, the shepherd was the door.

Jesus changed the word for "door" to underscore the fundamental truth that through Him alone His sheep find access to God. As the Apostle Paul affirmed, "Through Him we have access to the Father" (Ephesians 2:18). Jesus opens the way to God.

As the gate to the sheep pen, Jesus provides secure passage for His followers to "come in and go out and find pasture" (John 10:9). To come in and go out unmolested was the Jewish way of describing an absolutely secure life. The leader of the nation was a person who could bring his people in and out safely (Numbers 27:17). The obedient person is blessed when he comes in and blessed when he goes out (Deuteronomy 28:6). The Psalmist is sure that God will keep him in his going out and coming in (Psalm 121:8). With Jesus the pathway to God and from God to service is unmolested.

Jesus concludes with this remarkable statement: "The thief comes only to steal and kill and destroy; I have come that they may have life, and have it to the full" (John 10:10). Literally, the phrase "have it to the full" means "to have a superabundance of something." Jesus' sheep enjoy a superabundant life. Only His sheep can truly say, "It just does not get better than this!"

SOMETHING TO THINK ABOUT

1. Who are the sheep John is referring to?

2. Behaving like sheep has a negative connotation in our society. How was this a common metaphor to John's first audience?

3. How is Christ a "door"? Is He a door for protection, admittance, or both?

4. How does Christ provide a superabundance of life "to the full"?

5: The Good Shepherd

I AM the good shepherd. The good shepherd lays down his life for the sheep. . . . I AM the good shepherd; I know My sheep and my sheep know Me (John 10:11,14).

THE METAPHOR OF JESUS AS THE GATE TO THE SHEEP PEN HAS BEEN STRETCHED TO the breaking point. It gives place to yet another that has been waiting in the background. Jesus Himself is the Good Shepherd (John 10:11–18). Jesus alone fulfills this long-awaited prophecy:

> *This is what the Sovereign Lord says: "Woe to the shepherds of Israel who only take care of themselves! Should not shepherds take care of the flock? . . . I Myself will search for My sheep and look after them. As a shepherd looks after his scattered flock when he is with them, so will I look after My sheep. . . . I Myself will tend My sheep and have them lie down. . . . I will search for the lost and bring back the strays. . . . I will shepherd that flock with justice"* (Ezekiel 34:10–16)

9

He tends His flock like a shepherd; He gathers the lambs in His arms and carries them close to His heart; He gently leads those that have young (Isaiah 40:11).

He who scattered Israel will gather them and will watch over His flock like a shepherd (Jeremiah 31:10).

In John 10:11–18, Jesus contrasts the good and the bad, the faithful and unfaithful shepherd. In doing so, He reveals the essence of His nature, the ultimate sacrifice He will pay for the sheep and the eternal relationship His flock will enjoy. Jesus chooses three precise words to enlarge and illustrate His role as divine shepherd: an adjective (good), a noun (life) and a verb (know).

Good: "I AM the Good Shepherd"

Jesus defines His nature as good. The Greek language has two words for "good." The common word is *agathos,* meaning "inwardly good; of a good constitution or nature." The second, more expansive word for "good" is *kalos.* Besides connoting inward goodness, *kalos* means "good in appearance; beautiful; aesthetically satisfying and pleasing." Jesus said, I AM the good [*kalos*] shepherd." He is not only morally good, but good in every way—totally good, inwardly and outwardly. *Kalos* is goodness in the superlative. For example, *kalos* is translated "choice" in describing the wine that Jesus had transformed from water in Cana (2:10). One can appropriately translate John 10:11, "I AM the choice shepherd!"

Life: "The Good Shepherd Lays Down His Life for the Sheep"

Three Greek words distinguish varying qualities of life. The basic word is *bios,* from which we derive "biology." *Bios* denotes "the period or duration of earthly life; life in its earthly manifestations; life as opposed to death." The second word is *zoe,* from which comes the word "zoology." *Zoe* is a step up from *bios.* It connotes God's gift to man, animating him both physically and spiritually—the absolute fullness of life. The third word is *psuche,* giving us the word "psychology." *Psuche* refers to the inner man; his personality; man's individual distinctiveness.

Jesus uses the word *psuche,* underscoring the consummate truth that He would soon "give His life [*psuche*] as a ransom for many" (Matthew 20:28). The ultimate sacrifice for mankind's sin was not just any life. Atonement required the sinless blood of the God–man—the Good Shepherd, Jesus Christ.

Know: "I know My sheep and My sheep know Me—just as the Father knows Me and I know the Father"

While the Greeks had many words for "know," John pairs two distinct types of knowledge in his writings. The first word, *ginosko,* means "to know through experience; to perceive through the senses; knowledge that results from an active relationship between the one who knows and the thing known; entering into knowing through firsthand or personal interaction." The second word, *oida,* means "to know intellectually; to gain knowledge by observation [versus experience or the senses]; to know about something without necessarily standing in any personal relation or connection with it." Jesus uses *ginosko* four times in verses 14 and 15. He underscores the truth that He and the Father know their "sheep" in the same way in which they know each other. It is a knowledge based on personal encounter, rather than intellectual understanding. The Good Shepherd knows His sheep intimately.

On other occasions the Apostle John contrasted the two levels of knowing. In his first epistle, he declares, "And we know [*oida*] that the Son of God is come, and hath given us an understanding, that we may know [*ginosko*] Him that is true, and we are in Him that is true, even in His Son Jesus Christ. This is the true God, and eternal life" (1 John 5:20 KJV). Clearly, knowing about Jesus should lead the seeker to one day intimately know Him. To know [*ginosko*] Him is to know the truth and to gain life eternal!

SOMETHING TO THINK ABOUT

1. What qualities are desired in a shepherd?

2. What makes Jesus the perfect shepherd?

3. How is Jesus "good" in all He is and all He does?

4. If Jesus is the Good Shepherd and "He knows us" so well, are there things we wish He did not know? Is it possible to hide sin from Him?

6: The Son of God

What about the One whom the Father set apart as His very own and sent into the world? Why then do you accuse Me of blasphemy because I said, "I AM God's Son"? (John 10:36).

THE GOSPEL OF JOHN IS UNIQUE AMONG NEW TESTAMENT GOSPELS. JOHN ALONE includes events not recorded elsewhere, and he omits events recorded in the three synoptic gospels. For example, after recounting Jesus' proclamations as the "Gate for the Sheep" (10:7,9) and the "Good Shepherd" (10:11,14), John is silent regarding the two-month interval between verses 21 and 22 of chapter ten. During this time Jesus went north to Caesarea Philippi and was transfigured (Matthew 17:1–13; Mark 9:2–13; Luke 9:28–36).

Jesus returned to Jerusalem for the Feast of Dedication, also known as the Festival of Lights. Today, we know it as Hanukkah. Held on the twenty-fifth of *Kislew*, the festival celebrates the Jews' victory over the heathen Syrian ruler, Antiochus Epiphanes.

Known for his love of the Greek culture, Antiochus IV (Epiphanes) reigned as King of Syria from 175–164 B.C. In 170 B.C. he launched an attack on Jerusalem, achieving a swift, decisive victory by slaughtering more than 80,000 men, women, and children. Antiochus attempted to destroy Jewish culture and religion. The Temple was pilfered. Circumcision was outlawed. All known copies of the Law were destroyed. The Temple courts were turned into brothels. Swine were sacrificed to the Greek god, Zeus, on the altar.

Six years after the Syrian conquest, Judas Maccabees led a rebel force that defeated Antiochus in 164 B.C. The day following his victory, he cleansed the Temple. The eight-day Feast of Dedication commemorates this cleansing by priests under the leadership of Judas Maccabees. In Jesus' day, the Feast reminded the Jewish people of their deliverance from their enemies.

John describes the events of Jesus' appearance at the Feast of Dedication, less than five months before His crucifixion (John 10:22-39). The setting was Solomon's porch, a roofed portico covering the southern end of the Temple. Solomon's porch was always filled with people—Jews and Greeks. The only business permitted was that of the infamous money changers (Matthew 21:12-17). People came there to pray and meditate as they strolled through the multi-columned plaza. Rabbis walked and taught with their disciples. It was not surprising that Jesus was walking on this occasion. As John points out, it was a cold, wintry day (John 10:22).

The Jewish religious leaders seized this opportunity to ask Jesus the question of the hour—nay, of the ages: "How long will You keep us in suspense? If You are Christ, tell us plainly" (24). Jesus answered that He had already told them. Two considerations also had placed His claim above question and beyond doubt.

First, His deeds: "The miracles I do in My Father's name speak for Me, but you do not believe because You are not My sheep" (25-26). Jesus' miracles fulfilled Isaiah's prophecy: "Then will the eyes of the blind be opened and the ears of the deaf unstopped. Then will the lame leap like a deer, and the mute tongue shout for joy" (Isaiah 35:5-6).

Second, His words verified His claims. Jesus said, "My sheep listen to My voice; I know them, and they follow Me. I give them eternal life, and they shall never perish; no one can snatch them out of My hand" (John 10:27-28). Both Greek verbs (listen and follow) are in the present tense, indicating continued action. The eternal security of believers is assured if they are consistent in obeying and following Christ.

Jesus now comes to His supreme claim. For the first time, He makes His claim clear: "I and the Father are one" (30). The Jewish leaders again took up stones to stone Him as they had previously done two months before (see John 8:59). Stoning was the normal punishment for blasphemy: "Anyone who blasphemes the name of the Lord must be put to death. The entire assembly must stone him. Whether an alien or native-born, when he blasphemes the Name, he must be put to death" (Leviticus 24:16).

Since Jesus' "hour had not yet come," He used a typical rabbinic tactic. He answered their outrage with Scripture, responding, "Is it not written in your Law, 'I have said you are gods'? If He called them 'gods' to whom the Word of God came . . . what about the One whom the Father set apart as His very own and sent into the world? Why then do you accuse Me of blasphemy because I said, 'I AM God's Son'?" (John 10:34-36). In quoting Psalm 82:6, "You are 'gods'; you are all sons of the Most High," Jesus argues that if Scripture can call human judges "gods," why should one who gives His whole life and service to God, and who was sent from God, be accused of blasphemy for designating Himself "Son of God"? Jesus' further defense was another appeal to the value of his miracles as proofs of God's endorsement. God would not endorse a blasphemer.

Jesus claimed two things for Himself (John 10:36). First, He was consecrated (*hagiazo*) by God to a special task. Second, He had been sent (*apostello*) by God into the world. Jesus did not think of Himself as coming into the world, but rather as being sent into the world for a specific task. His coming was an act of God!

SOMETHING TO THINK ABOUT

1. Why didn't Jesus answer the Pharisees directly concerning His identity and mission?

2. Why didn't the Pharisees understand or see who Jesus was? How about us?

3. Why is the comment that Jesus is the Son of God so pivotal to our faith?

4. What was Jesus' full mission? Was it just salvation—or was there more?

7: The Resurrection and the Life

Jesus said, "I AM the resurrection and the life. He who believes in Me will live, even though he dies; and whoever lives and believes in Me will never die" (John 11:25).

CHAPTER 11 OF THE GOSPEL OF JOHN RECORDS THE CLIMAX OF A SERIES OF "SIGNS" that unify and authenticate the public ministry of Jesus (chapters 2–12). This chapter contains the most striking miracle in John's gospel and the longest account of any miracle in the New Testament—the raising of Lazarus from the dead.

The miracle took place about one month before Jesus' crucifixion. It was the third recording of Jesus raising someone from the dead. He raised Jairus' daughter before the funeral (Mark 5:35), the son of the widow of Nain during the funeral (Luke 7:11–17), and Lazarus after the funeral (John 11). The only negative outcome of the three resurrections is that the gospels give no guidance on how to conduct a funeral. Jesus broke up every service He attended!

Jesus had temporarily retreated from public life (10:40–42), no doubt because He knew the ominous events ahead. This hiatus comes between the controversies in Jerusalem described in chapters 7–10 of John's gospel and the triumphal entry into Jerusalem before Passover (12:12–19).

Jesus had been well received "across the Jordan" in Perea, "the place where John had been baptizing" (10:40). John the Baptist accomplished his mission. He had lived up to his own preaching: "He must become greater; I must become less" (3:30). He had indeed "[made] straight the way for the Lord" (1:23).

The fact that Jesus was generally accepted in Galilee, Samaria, and now in Perea is significant. When it became apparent that the populace would also soon accept Him in Jerusalem, authorities took steps to kill Him. Following the raising of Lazarus, members of the Sanhedrin (the seventy-member Jewish religious council) came to a doleful conclusion: "If we let Him go on like this, everyone will believe in Him, and then the Romans will come and take away both our place and our nation" (11:48).

John begins his narrative by first establishing Jesus' deep affection for Lazarus as well as Mary and Martha, his sisters. John quotes the sisters' urgent message to Jesus: "Lord, the one You love [*philias*] is sick" (11:3). Two verses later, John reveals the depth of Jesus' love for the family by clarifying that "Jesus loved [*agape*] Martha and her sister and Lazarus" (5). The Greek word for "love" in verse three suggests a "close friendship," while the word in verse five signifies a "pure, unselfish love." Jesus had a special love for this family.

One reason for Jesus' love for Lazarus, Mary, and Martha may be that they were a wealthy family who chose to live among the poor. Lazarus had a "family tomb"—a sure sign of first-century wealth. In addition, it was Mary who "poured perfume on the Lord and wiped His feet with her hair" (11:2). Only the wealthy could afford such a lavish display of affection. Since the Hebrew word Bethany means "House of the Poor," many poor families probably lived in this modest village on the outskirts of Jerusalem. The wealthy normally lived within the protection of city walls.

When Jesus arrived in Bethany, Lazarus "had already been in the tomb four days" (17). Lazarus had died around the time the messengers reached Jesus with the news that "the one you love is sick" (3). Knowing what miracle He would perform "for God's glory so that God's Son may be glorified through it" (4), Jesus tarried for two more days to make sure that Lazarus had died. It took Jesus and the disciples two days to traverse the steep, treacherous road from Perea to Bethany, traveling about twenty miles a day. By the time they arrived, Lazarus had been dead for at least four days. Jesus wanted to ensure that everyone understood that Lazarus was dead. Though not taught by the rabbis, a popular belief persisted that the spirit of a dead person hovered around the body for three days. A resurrection on the fourth day would be striking because all hope for natural restoration would have gone.

Characteristic of the sisters, Martha went out to meet Jesus while Mary initially remained in the house (20). After comforting them, Jesus came to the tomb and ordered the stone covering removed. He stood above the entrance, and through a small opening in the side of the inner tomb He called in a loud voice, "Lazarus, come out!" (43). Those nearby were astonished to see Lazarus, still wearing his grave shroud, ascend the few steps from the inner tomb. Jesus' words to Martha now brimmed with life-giving certainty: "I AM the resurrection and the life. He who believes in Me will live, even though he dies; and whoever lives and believes in Me will never die" (25–26).

Throughout the two millennia that have followed, Jesus turns to every person and asks the question He addressed to Martha: "Do you believe [I AM the resurrection and the life]?" May our answer ever be the same as hers: "Yes, Lord, I believe that You are the Christ, the Son of God, who was to come into the world."

1. The Bible records other occasions when someone dead was brought back to life. Why was the resurrection of Lazarus different?

2. How did the Lazarus miracle incite Jesus' enemies to unite to kill Him?

3. Were the Sanhedrin concerned for orthodox religion or for their own personal position and power? Why?

4. Why did Jesus wait so long before going to Lazarus and his sisters?

8: The Way and the Life

Jesus answered, "I AM the way and the truth and the life. No one comes to the Father except through Me" (John 14:6).

JESUS CELEBRATED HIS LAST PASSOVER MEAL WITH THE DISCIPLES IN WHAT IS KNOWN as the Upper Room. Earlier in the day, He sent Peter and John to find and prepare the room. He instructed them to look for a man carrying a jar of water. He would be easy to find. Women customarily transported jars of water on their shoulder. A man carrying water would be conspicuous. They were to follow him to a house and say to the owner, "The Teacher asks: 'Where is the guest room, where I may eat the Passover with My disciples?' He will show you a large upper room, all furnished. Make preparations there" (Luke 22:11–12).

Pilgrims from all over the world thronged Jerusalem for Passover—the Feast of Redemption. The crowd swelled the city's population, transforming its streets into a collage of ethnic sights, sounds, and smells. The celebrants were oblivious to the event taking place in which an itinerant rabbi from Nazareth shared a final Passover—a last supper—with His followers.

Toward the end of the meal, Jesus delivered a farewell to His disciples. His discourse commences in the Upper Room (John 13:31–14:31), continues after the Passover meal (15:1–16:33), and concludes before His crossing to the Garden of Gethsemane (17:1–26). Jesus' colloquy contains some of the most tender words in all Scripture.

Before leaving the Upper Room, Jesus confirmed that His earthly life was ending. He had previously predicted His death on only two occasions (John 7:33–34, Matthew 16:21). At the close of the meal, Jesus revealed the certainty of His departure. "My children, I will be with you only a little longer," Jesus explained. "You will look for Me, and just as I told the Jews, so I tell you now: Where I am going, you cannot come" (13:33). Knowing the disciples' shock and sadness, Jesus comforted them. "Do not let your hearts be troubled. . . . Trust in God; trust also in Me. . . . If I go and prepare a place for you, I will come back and take you to be with Me that you also may be where I am. You know the way to the place where I am going" (John 14:1–4).

Thomas spoke on behalf of the others. "'Lord,' he confessed, 'we don't know where You are going, so how can we know the way?' Jesus answered, 'I AM the way and the truth and the life. No one comes to the Father except through Me. If you really knew Me, you would know My Father as well. From now on, you do know Him and have seen Him'" (14:5–7). Jesus' words reminded the disciples of fundamental truths of their Hebrew faith: the way to God, the truth of God, and the life from God.

I AM the Way

The Hebrew scriptures addressed the way to God and the way people should live. Isaiah declared: "Whether you turn to the right or to the left, your ears will hear a voice behind you, saying, 'This is the way; walk in it'" (Isaiah 30:21). Later, the prophet named and defined the way to God. "'And a highway will be there,' the prophet proclaimed. 'It will be called the Way of Holiness. The unclean will not journey on it; it will be for those who walk in that Way; wicked fools will not go about on it'" (Isaiah 35:8). The Psalmist expressed the prayer of God's people: "Teach me Your way, O Lord; lead me in a straight path because of my oppressors" (Psalm 27:11).

Jewish sages looked forward to the coming of the Messiah. He alone would show the way to God and the way to live. Jesus more than fulfills the prophecy, for He not only points the way, He is the way.

I AM the Truth

For the Hebrew people (and most Eastern cultures), truth was more than a series of correct statements. They connected truth with a person. Statements were true because the people who expressed them were true. The Psalmist reflected on personal authenticity when he prayed: "Teach me Your way, O Lord, and I will walk in Your truth; give me an undivided heart, that I may fear Your name" (Psalm 86:11). Knowing God's way and God's truth results from an undivided relationship with Him.

Many people have told the truth; only Jesus embodies it. Parents, educators, pastors and others can say, "I have taught you the truth." Only Jesus can declare, "You will know the truth, and the truth will set you free" (John 8:32). The truth is a Person—Jesus Christ.

I AM the Life

The writer of Proverbs reflected on mankind's endless quest for a meaningful life. "These commands," he noted, "are a lamp, this teaching is a light, and the corrections of discipline are the way to life" (Proverbs 6:23). The Psalmist also affirmed, "Your Word is a lamp to my feet and a light for my path" (Psalm 119:105).

Yet, even God's words were not enough to give His creation eternal life. In God's perfect plan, He sent His Son—the living Word (John 1:1–4)—so that all who believe in Him might experience a life bursting with joy. As Jesus declared, "I have come that they may have life, and have it to the full" (10:10).

The concluding sentence of the divine promise is all important. "No one," Jesus affirmed, "comes to the Father except through Me" (14:6). He alone is the way to God. He alone embodies the truth. Through Him alone issues fullness of life.

SOMETHING TO THINK ABOUT

1. Why was the planning for Jesus' last Passover so careful and elaborate?

2. In our postmodern society, truth is what we make it. Why is it so essential that Jesus taught that He not only told the truth, but *was* the truth?

3. Why is there no other way to the Father except through Jesus?

4. How can knowing and believing in Christ as the real truth set us free? Free from what? For what?

9: The True Vine

I AM the true vine, and My Father is the gardener. . . . I AM the vine; you are the branches. If a man remains in Me and I in him, he will bear much fruit (John 15:1,5).

THE APOSTLE JOHN IS THE ONLY GOSPEL WRITER TO TRANSCRIBE JESUS' FAREWELL discourse with His disciples (13:31–17:26). His extended address lasted an estimated two hours, commencing during the Passover meal in the Upper Room and not concluding until Jesus and His band of disciples reached the Garden of Gethsemane just before midnight. The final portion of this celebrated colloquy (chapters 15, 16 and 17) contains Jesus' tender words of assurance to His disciples as they walked together from the Upper Room, across the Kidron Valley, to the Garden of Gethsemane.

The Passover meal, known as the *seder* (meaning "order"), usually lasts four to five hours. The sun had set by the time the meal concluded and Jesus bid His disciples, "Come now; let us leave" (14:31). Jesus then led the group of eleven (Judas having departed the meal early) across the Kidron Valley to the western slope of the Mount of Olives.

Well known in Jesus' day for its spacious natural caves, olive trees and presses, the entire area provided an escape for people seeking relief from the heat of the crowded city streets. Gethsemane (meaning "olive oil press") was in reality a section of Jerusalem's first-century "city park." While leading His followers to the comfort and protection of Gethsemane was not unusual for Jesus, the disciples had little idea of what they were to face later that night.

On the road to Gethsemane, Jesus comforted His disciples with some of the most compassionate words found in Scripture.

I AM the true vine, and my Father is the gardener. He cuts off every branch in Me that bears no fruit, while every branch that does bear fruit He prunes so that it will be even more fruitful. . . . Remain in Me, and I will remain in you. No branch can bear fruit by itself; it must remain in the vine. Neither can you bear fruit unless you remain in Me. I AM the vine; you are the branches (John 15:1–5).

It is not surprising that Jesus used an illustration of vines and branches to comfort His disciples. The Mount of Olives was heavily wooded. When Nehemiah restored the Feast of Tabernacles, he commanded the people to "Go forth unto the mount, and fetch olive branches, and pine branches and myrtle branches, and palm branches and branches of thick trees to make booths" (Nehemiah 8:15, KJV).

The disciples understood the metaphor of a vine and its branches. As in Jesus' day, vines continue to grow throughout Israel. Vines require much attention if they are to produce the best fruit. While vines grow quickly and in all directions, it is critical that the soil is clean and full of nutrients. A young vine is not allowed to flower for three years. Each year it is drastically cut back to conserve its life energy. When the vineyard does yield a harvest, branches that have not borne fruit are cut off. The farmer knew well that the vine cannot produce a large crop without drastic pruning.

Beyond a practical understanding of vines, the disciples also grasped the theological implications of Jesus' illustration. The Old Testament often portrays Israel as the vine in the vineyard of God. The prophet Jeremiah recorded God's confirmation: "I had planted you like a choice vine of sound and reliable stock. How then did you turn against Me into a corrupt, wild vine?" (Jeremiah 2:21). The Psalmist praises the One who "brought a vine out of Egypt; [and] drove out the nations and planted it" (Psalm 80:8). The vine became the symbol of Israel. One of the glories of the Temple was the vast golden vine that hung on the front of the Holy Place. The vine was the emblem emblazoned on national coins during the brief period of Jewish independence known as the Maccabean period (164–47 BC).

Jesus referred to Himself as the "true vine" (15:1). The Greek adjective is *alethinos*, meaning true or real; genuine. "True" is one of the Apostle John's favorite words. He used it twenty-three times in his New Testament writings. It is only used five other times in the rest of the New Testament. *Alethinos* means "that which has not only the name and semblance, but also the real nature corresponding to the name." It is the opposite to that which is fictitious, counterfeit, imaginary, or simulated. *Alethinos* means the genuine article. By all criteria, Jesus is authentic. He is true God and true man.

Jesus is the true vine. The symbol of the vine in the Old Testament is always used in connection with degeneration. The point of Isaiah's prophecy is that the vine has run wild. Jeremiah complains that the nation of Israel has "degenerated and become a wild vine." Jesus—the true vine—is the divine regenerator. The Bible tells us that one day, God, the Father, will seat Jesus on the throne of heaven and declare, "I AM making everything new!" (Revelation 21:5).

1. Why did Jesus use the image of the vine and branches to explain His as well as our relationship with God?

2. If Jesus is the true vine, who or what is the false one?

3. How had Israel become a wild vine? How have we?

4. Grapes require a great deal of care and pruning to bear fruit. How does this care apply to us? What fruit are we commanded to produce?

10: The Alpha and the Omega

I AM the Alpha and the Omega, the First and the Last, the Beginning and the End (Revelation 22:13).

JOHN IS THE ONLY GOSPEL WRITER TO RECORD JESUS' EIGHT STARTLING DECLARATIONS that begin with the cryptic phrase, "I AM . . . ." According to the book of Revelation, Jesus' final assertion was His post-ascension pronouncement, "I AM the Alpha and the Omega, the First and the Last, the Beginning and the End." Although authorship of the Revelation is not certain, there is a long tradition that the author, called John throughout the book, is the beloved apostle. He was the author of five New Testament books, including the Gospel of John; 1, 2 and 3 John; and the Revelation. Early evidence suggests that the Apostle John was indeed the author. Justin Martyr (135 A.D.), one of the early church leaders, believed him to be the author, and a document known as the Muratorian fragment (c. 170 A.D.) ascribes authorship to St. John.

If the Apostle John is the author, it is fitting that he would record Jesus' final proclamation, "I AM the Alpha and the Omega." John wrote the Revelation while imprisoned on Patmos, a narrow, rocky island in the Aegean Sea off the coast of modern-day Turkey. Under the egocentric Roman Emperor Domitian (81-96 A.D.), John was banished to the island because of his faith (1:9). Domitian was the first Roman emperor to compel all his subjects (including Jews and Christians) to worship him as a divine son of the gods.

John testifies that it was on a Sunday, "the Lord's day" (1:10), that he heard a loud voice directing him to "write on a scroll what you see and send it to the seven churches" (1:11). When John turned to see who was speaking, he saw seven golden lampstands, and among the lampstands was someone "like a son of man, dressed in a robe reaching down to his feet and with a golden sash around his chest" (1:12-13). John was so overcome that he "fell at his feet as though dead" (1:17). The figure among the lampstands was Jesus, who then placed His right hand on John and said, "Do not be afraid. I AM the First and the Last. I AM the Living One; I was dead, and behold I am alive forever and ever! And I hold the keys of death and Hades" (1:17-18).

First and Last

Jesus' use of the phrase "the First and the Last" is a reference to the self-description of God. He echoes God's pronouncements recorded by the prophet Isaiah: "This is what the Lord says—Israel's King and Redeemer, the Lord Almighty: 'I AM the First and I AM the Last; apart from Me there is no God'" (Isaiah 44:6). A few chapters later, God declares, "Listen to Me, O Jacob, Israel, whom I have called: I AM He; I AM the First and I AM the Last" (Isaiah 48:12).

Alpha and Omega

The expression "the Alpha and the Omega," along with its parallel phrase "the First and the Last," is found four times in Revelation. In two places, the idioms refer to God (1:8 and 21:6), and in two they clearly describe Jesus (1:17–18 and 22:13). In the latter passages, Jesus proclaims Himself as the First and the Last—the Alpha and the Omega (alpha being the first of twenty- four letters in the Greek alphabet, and omega being the last). The phrase "alpha and omega" suggests completeness.

Although John recorded the divine vision in Greek, the phrase has a Hebrew counterpart. The first letter of the twenty-two letters of the Hebrew alphabet is *aleph*, and the last is *tau*. The rabbis had an expression: "Adam transgressed the Law and Abraham kept it from *aleph* to *tau*." They also said that "God had blessed Israel from *aleph* to *tau*." As in Greek, the Hebrew phrase represented God as absolutely complete. He is before time began, He is now, and He will be when time ends.

Beginning and End

John's extraordinary vision concludes with the risen Christ assuring the readers of His immi-nent return. "Behold, I am coming soon!" Jesus promised. "My reward is with Me, and I will give it to everyone according to what he has done. I AM the Alpha and the Omega, the First and the Last, the Beginning and the End" (22:12–13). Jesus affirmed that He was there at the beginning, and He will be there at the end. He is there from birth to death. He is there when we start our walk with Him, and He will be there at the end.

The word for beginning (*arche*) means more than first in a point of time. It means first in the sense of the source of all things. The word for end (*telos*) does not simply mean an end in the point of time. It means the goal. All life begins and ends in God. As the poet F. H. Myers aptly notes:

> *Yea thro' life, death, thro' sorrow and thro' sinning*
> *He shall suffice me, for He hath sufficed:*
> *Christ is the end, for Christ was the beginning,*
> *Christ is the beginning, for the end is Christ.*

Not only is Christ coming soon, but He assures His followers that when He comes He will reward every man according to his work. This is indeed good news. The best is yet to come!

1. How is Jesus first and last at the same time?

2. How does alpha and omega suggest completion—of life, ministry, worship?

3. How will people be rewarded for their faith? Will there be judgment for lack of faith? Why or why not?

4. How is Christ both the object and goal of our worship?

Two

Judges: Apostasy and the Covenant–Faithfulness of God

A. Kenneth Wilson

Major A. Kenneth Wilson, a third generation Salvationist, is the assistant editor in chief and national literary secretary at National Headquarters in Alexandria, Virginia. A frequent contributor to *The War Cry,* Major Wilson also penned *Fractured Parables.*

Hollywood would love to claim first rights to the idea—the solitary hero avenging the oppressed, punishing the guilty and restoring law and order. But the Lord thought of it first and recorded some of those events in the Old Testament Book of Judges. While the stories from Judges often border on the heroic, the flagrant rejection of the Lord's authority makes the book a sad catalog of sin and wasted opportunities.

1: Here Comes the Judge

THE PEOPLE OF ISRAEL KNEW WHAT GOD EXPECTED OF THEM, though they never seemed to get with the program. God asked them to worship Him in holiness and truth and to trust in His provision. They had plenty of history to be convinced of God's care, since He had rescued them from four hundred years of bondage in Egypt, guided them through forty years of wandering in the desert and finally brought them safely to their homeland and inheritance. All they had to do in return was possess the land and completely drive out the Canaanite tribes who lived there. They could do that as long as Israel had a great leader empowered by God, like Joshua. Without that leadership, they were in serious trouble.

Joshua, Israel's general and successor to Moses, summoned the people for a solemn convocation at Shechem just before they separated and went to their homes across Canaan. He wanted to make sure the people's hearts were in line with the Lord's expectations while reminding them of all the Lord had done for them over the years (Joshua 24:1–12). He further refreshed their collective memories of their complete victory over Jericho and the other nations—all the other "ites"—who were powerless to stop the Hebrews' march homeward. The Lord was fighting for Israel, winning cities and homes they did not build, vineyards and orchards they did not plant (14).

Joshua told them: "Fear the Lord and serve Him with all faithfulness. Throw away the gods your forefathers worshipped . . . and serve the Lord. But if serving the Lord seems undesirable to you, then choose for yourselves this day whom you will serve, whether the gods your forefathers served . . . or the gods of the Amorites, in whose land you are living. But as for me and my household, we will serve the Lord."

They answered, "Far be it from us to forsake the Lord to serve other gods! It was the Lord our God Himself who brought us and our fathers up out of Egypt, from that land of slavery, and performed those great signs before our eyes. He protected us on our entire journey and among all the nations through which we travelled. . . . We too will serve the Lord, because He is our God" (14–18).

Joshua further warned that God would not tolerate sharing their hearts or their worship of pagan fertility gods. Nor would He overlook their breaking solemn vows of spiritual fidelity. If they broke their promises, God would be as hard as He had been compassionate.

A Broken Promise

The people pledged that day to love and serve God alone as each went home to possess his inheritance. They did well throughout Joshua's lifetime. But after he died at the age of 110, new generations that did not recall his influence or know firsthand of the Lord's provision became as wicked as the pagans that they were to have driven out. "The Israelites did evil in the eyes of the Lord. They provoked the Lord to anger because they forsook Him and served Baal and the Ashtoreths. In His anger against Israel, the Lord handed them over to raiders who plundered them. He sold them to their enemies all around, whom they were no longer able to resist" (2:11–14). The pattern of sin and deliverance became a perpetual cycle. The people forgot the things of God, willingly "prostituted themselves" to other gods and pagan practices, placing themselves in the path of God's righteous anger. Judgment came from without after the values of the Israelites had rotted from within. Raiders from the surrounding nations plundered anything of value with impunity.

Israel was charged, by God's decree, to drive the pagans out of the land, to avoid a corrupting influence. But they did not do it. As in a marriage between a strong Christian and an unsaved spouse, rarely does the stronger help redeem the weaker. Usually the weaker brings down the stronger. Not driving out the pagan influence would be like having your doctor report after cancer surgery that "We got eighty percent of the tumor. We could have gotten it all but it was too much trouble. Live and let live, I always say." You would no more tolerate such malpractice than God accepts such "mal-worship."

When invaded and oppressed, the people begged for the Lord's intervention. Because of His great compassion for His people whose only claim to redress was His own unchanging covenant with them, He sent special people—judges—to deliver the people and to enforce the laws during those dangerous days. They were not kings and had no right of dynastic succession. Some served for many years, while others like Shamgar record no duration of appointment, since his entire career is contained in one verse in the Bible. Some were eager to do the Lord's work. Others were disappointing failures who squandered their God-given opportunities.

Unfortunately, as soon as a crisis passed and one judge died, the people slid back into their old habits (18), becoming worse than they were before, creating continuing cycles of rebellion, apostasy, prayer, repentance, and deliverance. You would think they would learn from their history. Instead they were doomed to repeat it. They didn't choose to forget, for that would take as much effort as learning. They just decided to forget to remember. That takes no effort at all.

The Book of Judges reiterates the basic theme, "There was no king in Israel" and "everyone did that which was right in their own eyes." So rather than enjoying freedom in God's provision, there was anarchy, corruption, persecution, and confusion. Whenever we fail to make God the Lord of our life, and instead chose to do what seems right "in our own eyes," we run the same risk of sliding away from truth—right into trouble.

SOMETHING TO THINK ABOUT

1. How had the Lord provided for the people of Israel in the past? What did the Lord require in return?

2. What did the people do that so angered God? How about us—what have we done?

3. Why did the people continue to make the same bad choices that got them into trouble in the first place?

2: The Nephew and the Southpaw

AS LONG AS THE PEOPLE OF ISRAEL HAD A STRONG, GOD-ANOINTED PERSON LEADING them, like Moses or Joshua, they remained reasonably obedient and marginally faithful. But after Joshua died and new generations came along that knew little or nothing of the Lord's history, Israel became as pagan as the pagans around them. "The Israelites did evil in the eyes of the Lord. . . . They provoked the Lord to anger because they forsook Him and served Baal and the Ashtoreths. In His anger against Israel the Lord handed them over to raiders who plundered them" (Judges 2:11–14).

The Israelites also intermarried with the Canaanites—specifically contrary to the Lord's instruction. "Did evil" is a remarkably understated commentary on Israel's precipitous moral, ethical and spiritual slide as they willingly worshipped the Canaanite fertility deities with their bizarrely obscene practices (3:5–8).

As a result, the Lord allowed the king of Aram to invade Israel and keep them in subjection for eight years. Other than name and location, we know nothing of this oppressor. But if he was like every other of his type throughout history, there was at least one thing that would grieve all concerned—taxes. He may have designed the original "1040 Extremely Short form": Line 1) Enter your name; Line 2) Enter your address; Line 3) Enter your financial worth—cash, stocks, bonds, real estate, cattle, etc.; Line 4) Send Line 3.

The One they had ignored, disobeyed, abused, taken for granted, and treated with contempt was the One they begged for help. Poverty rearranges priorities in a hurry.

The Lord Sends a Deliverer

Hearing their anguished pleas, the Lord sent a deliverer—Othniel son of Kenaz, Caleb's younger brother—the nephew of a legend. Uncle Caleb, along with Joshua, was sent by Moses into Canaan to spy out the land. He advised Moses to immediately take the land just as the Lord had promised (Numbers 13–14). When the rest of the spies came back with a negative report, the people panicked and lost faith in God, refusing to attack. As a result, that whole generation was doomed to wander in the wilderness for forty years, never entering their homeland—except for Caleb and Joshua.

It is difficult to be the nephew of a legend—people expect so much from you. Rather than remain in his uncle's shadow, perhaps Othniel learned to live by the witness of Caleb's unshakable faith in God. Scripture records that "the Spirit of the Lord came upon him," giving him true charismatic leadership—not creativity, good looks, intelligence, diligence, wealth, or cunning—but the Spirit of the Lord—that made him a blessing to his friends and dangerous to his enemies.

The Lord gave the king of Aram "into the hands of Othniel, who overpowered him," furnishing Israel forty years of peace and prosperity (Judges 3:10–11). But soon after Othniel died, "the Israelites did evil in the eyes of the Lord, and because they did this evil the Lord gave Eglon king of Moab power over Israel" (12). They went right back to their old ways until they were invaded and occupied again. And when times were hard, this time for eighteen years, "the Israelites cried out to the Lord, and He gave them a deliverer—Ehud, a left-handed man, the son of Gera the Benjamite" (15).

Scripture notes that he was a lefty—a significant detail to us lefties who make up twenty percent of the population. Usually left carries a negative connotation—out in left field, left behind, two left feet. In this case, Ehud's being a southpaw worked to Israel's advantage.

The Bible says that Ehud was sent to deliver Israel's tribute—extortion money—to Eglon who "was a very fat man" (17). If I were to cast him in the film version, he would probably look like a combination of an elderly Orson Welles and Jabba the Hutt from Star Wars. When he went to meet the portly potentate, Ehud came armed with an eighteen-inch, double-edged dagger strapped to his right thigh under his clothing. After Ehud presented the money he leaned over to the king and whispered, "I have a secret message for you." Being greedy, Eglon eagerly hoped that the message would bring some great personal profit.

When the two had retired to the king's private quarters with no attendants or guards present, Ehud came closer. "I have a message from God for you." As the king rose from his seat, "Ehud reached with his left hand, drew the sword from his right thigh, and plunged it into the king's belly. Ehud did not pull the sword out, and the fat closed in over it" (21–22). Eglon was so fat, Ehud couldn't get the blade out!

People would expect a weapon to come from the right side and be on their guard. Since lefties were rare, probably making him ineligible for military service by sword fighting backwards and so avoiding the customary pat-down by the king's security people, Ehud got close enough to personally dispatch Israel's oppressor. Ehud made his escape while Eglon's attendants waited outside. By the time they realized something was amiss and broke down the door, they found Eglon dead, Ehud gone, and Israel in command of the fords of the Jordan River that led into Moab.

When the Moabite army of ten thousand men came out to face Israel, they were killed to a man (23–29). The Bible says on "that day Moab was made subject to Israel, and the land had peace for eighty years" (30)—until they forgot and did evil again.

Before we berate them for their spiritual amnesia, we must ask how many shallow promises we have made to God that were forgotten as soon as the crisis passed. We all have done it. We need to remember all the Lord has done and continues to do for us.

"Praise the Lord, O my soul, and forget not all His benefits—who forgives all your sins and heals all your diseases, who redeems your life from the pit and crowns you with love and compassion, who satisfies your desires with good things so that your youth is renewed like the eagle's" (Psalm 103:1–5). We need to remember all the Lord has done so He can break the repeated cycle of sin, repentance, deliverance, disobedience, sin, repentance, deliverance—so we can live lives that are holy and free from the enslavement and oppression of sin. Good news for both right-handed and left-handed alike.

SOMETHING TO THINK ABOUT

1. What did that evil mentioned in Judges 3:12 involve?

2. What was so unusual about Ehud being left-handed?

3. Why did the people continue to forget how the Lord delivered them from oppression?

4. What promises have you made to the Lord in times of crisis, that were forgotten once the crisis passed?

THE LORD NEVER USES THE WORLD'S STANDARDS WHEN HE RECRUITS PEOPLE TO DO exceptional things for Him. The world chooses those who demonstrate great skill; God wants those with willing hearts. The first two of Israel's judges were unusual—one the little-known nephew of a famous war hero, the other a left-handed warrior from the smallest and perhaps least significant tribe of Israel. The next two may appear stranger yet for their odd choice of weapons. But the Lord always has a way of doing things contrary to our expectations.

Even though he is mentioned in only one verse of Scripture, Shamgar still made a significant contribution to the people of Israel. Judges 3:31 reads, "After Ehud came Shamgar son of Anath, who struck down six hundred Philistines with an oxgoad. He too saved Israel." Maybe Shamgar doesn't need a lengthy biography since there are never any ordinary or insignificant people where the Lord is concerned.

Anath must have been quite a father to have raised such a son who would agree to save the whining Israelites. He must have taught his son to stand for God and what was right regardless of the cost. Shamgar, we are told, killed all of the Philistine oppressors armed with nothing more than a pointed stick used to "encourage" a balky team of oxen. To use a modern weapon would be impressive, but a crude cattle prod—incredible. Perhaps as Shamgar stood to face the taunting Philistines, he may have thought that six hundred to one was a fair fight.

When taunted by the Philistine invaders, Shamgar may have answered, in a Clint Eastwood paraphrase, "You don't think the three of us are just going to let you walk out of here, do you?"

"Three—I see only one of you," jeered the Philistines.

"Me, God and this giddy-up stick!"

When the dust settled, no one was laughing.

The next judge as recorded in chapters four and five advanced God's equal opportunity program for women as He sent Deborah and Jael "to serve and protect" Israel.

Perhaps at or near the same time that Shamgar was fighting the Philistines, Israel returned to its familiar pattern of moral and spiritual chaos. In this case the people were oppressed by Jabin, a king of Canaan. Jabin, along with Sisera, his general-in-chief, terrorized Israel for twenty years with a huge army and nine hundred charioteers. Going to fight against those iron chariots with bladed hub caps must have been the ancient equivalent of trying to stop tanks with rocks (4:2–3).

The Lord sent Deborah, a married prophetess who was already dispensing justice in her own right, holding court under the palm trees near the towns of Ramah and Bethel in the hill country of Ephraim (4–5). Informed of the Lord's plan to defeat the Canaanite armies by prophetic revelation, Deborah sent for Barak, one of Israel's trusted military leaders. She instructed him to take ten thousand warriors to Mt. Tabor where the Lord would deliver Jabin and Sisera's army and all their chariots into Israel's hands with the same calm assurance as guaranteeing a pizza delivery "in thirty minutes or less."

A Diminutive Warrior

I am not sure if Barak was feeling dread, fear, or just covering all the possible scenarios. He stipulated, "If you go with me, I will go; but if you don't go with me, I won't go" (8). Deborah agreed to accompany Barak and the army, but indicated that the honor for winning the day would not be his—or Deborah's either but would belong to a nomadic housewife, or rather "tent-wife," Jael. Married to Heber the Kenite, a nomadic descendant of one of Moses' relatives, Jael happened to be passing through the Mount Tabor area as Sisera and his army were massing to fight Barak's mobilization. That encampment was no coincidence; it was God's hand liberating Israel (9).

Sisera went out smugly confident of his army's military prowess. But the battle soon became a rout as Jabin's army was slaughtered. Seeing the battle was lost, much like the last stand from Custer's point of view, Sisera abandoned his chariot and his troops and fled as fast as his feet could carry him. Running for his life, Sisera stopped to rest at Jael's tent, feeling reasonably safe from harm since the king of Hazor and the Kenites had friendly relations. Jael went out to meet Sisera and invited him into the tent offering him sanctuary and rest. Covering him with a blanket, she let him relax—and be lulled into a false sense of safety.

"I'm thirsty," he said. "Please give me some water." But instead of water she gave him some milk. And everyone knows the formula for sleep: exertion + warm milk = sound sleep. It was just a matter of time before Sisera was asleep. Unfortunately for him, the nap would be permanent.

Scripture says that "Jael, Heber's wife, picked up a tent peg and a hammer and went quietly to him while he [Sisera] lay fast asleep, exhausted. She drove the peg through his temple into the ground, and he died." I love the eloquent understatement of the King James that says after she fastened Sisera to the floor of the tent with a tent peg through his temples, "so he died" (21).

When Barak and his men pursued Sisera, Jael went out to meet them and showed them Israel's enemy, dead. And from that day Israel became stronger and stronger until they were finally rid of Jabin the Canaanite king (19–24).

Both these stories of deliverance seem strangely anachronistic and almost out of character for God, who blesses the meek and honors the peacemakers. But life then was violent, as a new nation was being forged, built on a relationship with God in a notoriously lawless, immoral, and brutal land. These were the labor pains of a theocracy like none the world had seen before.

Because God used such odd weapons and unusual champions, there could be no doubt that He was the true Deliverer. No one else could take the credit. And if the Lord can do all that with a willing man armed with a pointed stick and a faithful lady with a tent peg, imagine what He could do with us—if we let Him.

SOMETHING TO THINK ABOUT

1. Name some other odd weapons or tools the Lord has used to show His power.

2. Judges 3:31 refers to Shamgar fighting for the Lord armed with only an ox goad. Describe the mental image you have of him and of the fight to liberate Israel.

3. If your life and ministry could be summarized in one verse like Shamgar's, what would you like the record to say about you?

4. Why is it significant that the Lord used women to help deliver Israel from their enemies?

4: Gideon—the Reluctant Hero

ONE WOULD HOPE THAT ISRAEL WOULD EVENTUALLY UNDERSTAND WHAT THE LORD required—but they never seemed to get it. Once again "the Israelites did evil in the eyes of the Lord, and for seven years He gave them into the hands of the Midianites" (Judges 6:1). Things had been bad before; now they were worse.

Although Israel and Midian were distant relatives (Jethro, Moses' father-in-law, was from Midian), there was a history of bad feelings between the nations. The oppressive occupation forced many Israelites to live as refugees in their own country while the Midianites moved in like an invading swarm of locusts ravaging everything in its path (1–7). You can almost hear Israel's anguished cries pleading for a deliverer. If only their true repentance for sin had been as vocal.

Some men seek fortune; others seek fame—Gideon just wanted to be left alone. But God was going to send Gideon to deliver the people who deliberately rejected the Lord in spite of His constant provision. An angelic messenger came to the family farm where Gideon was threshing wheat in a winepress, keeping it hidden from the Midianites. The angel said to Gideon, "The Lord is with you, mighty warrior. . . . Go in the strength you have and save Israel out of Midian's hand. Am I [God] not sending you?"

"But how can I save Israel?" Gideon asked. "My clan is the weakest in Manasseh, and I am the least in my family."

The Lord answered, "I will be with you, and you will strike down all the Midianites" (14–16).

In a brief moment of panic, Gideon asked to make a sacrifice to the Lord to seal the deal. Gideon asked, "If I have found favor in Your eyes, give me a sign that it is really You talking to me. Please do not go away until I come back and bring my offering and set it before You."

The Lord said, "I will wait until you return." When the Lord calls us, He is patient with our halting faith as He gives us time to consider and commit to His plan. The Lord commanded Gideon to take one of his father's strongest bulls and use it to tear down the neighborhood Asherah pole and the altar to Baal, and use the wood for an altar of sacrifice to Jehovah. This infuriated the pagan priests, who marched to Gideon's house demanding his life.

Wisely, Joash, Gideon's father, said, "If Baal or Asherah have a problem with Gideon, let them take care of it. Do you have to fight their fights for them?" Not wishing to make their deities appear impotent, the priests left in a huff. Gideon's actions earned him a new name: Jerub-baal—"Let Baal contend with him"—because he broke down Baal's altar (25–32). But those exploits were minor compared to what the Lord still had in store. Gideon would deliver Israel from Midian in a great battle.

Confirming the Lord's Call

Since he was not a professional soldier, Gideon asked for a sign to verify what was to happen. "If You will save Israel by my hand as You have promised, I will place a wool fleece on the threshing floor. If there is dew only on the fleece and all the ground is dry, then I will know that You will save Israel by my hand, as You said" (36). And that is exactly what happened. Seeking a double assurance, Gideon reversed the process and again the Lord responded in the affirmative. It is good to pray and seek the Lord's confirmation, but once done it is time to step out on faith and get to work.

Thirty-two thousand men responded to Gideon's call to arms. The Lord said to Gideon, "You have too many men for Me to deliver Midian into their hands. So that Israel won't boast that their own strength has saved them, tell them that if anyone is afraid or wants to go home, they can do so now—no questions asked." When a recount was done, Gideon still had ten thousand men left. Still too many to make the deliverance miraculous (7:2–3).

The Lord told Gideon to take his men down to a stream to drink. "Separate those who lap the water with their tongues like a dog from those who kneel down to drink." Three hundred men brought the water up to their mouths with their hands (5–8). The Lord would defeat the army of Midian with the three hundred who were alert for danger and ready for a scrap. No Las Vegas bookie would cover odds like that—three hundred to innumerable! But with God in the equation, Midian was outnumbered from the start.

While in the Midianite camp on a late night recon patrol, Gideon overheard two men recounting a dream. One said, "A round loaf of barley bread came tumbling into the Midianite camp. It struck the tent with such force that the tent overturned and collapsed." His friend responded, "This can be nothing other than the sword of Gideon, the Israelite. God has given the Midianites and the whole camp into his hands" (9–15).

Now supremely confident, Gideon divided his men into three companies and armed them with trumpets and clay jars with lit torches inside them. While the Midianites slept, Gideon's men surrounded the camp. At a given signal they broke the jars, exposing the torches, blew the trumpets and shouted, "A sword for the Lord and for Gideon!" (16–18).

The Midianites were so rattled, thinking themselves surrounded by superior forces, that they fought each other in the darkness. Those not struck down by "friendly fire" ran for their lives with Gideon's men in hot pursuit.

The key to this account is not that the Lord did such a mighty work with so few men, but that He did such a mighty work with just one: Gideon, in spite of his lack of confidence and fear. He, like Paul, would claim, "I can do everything through Him who gives me strength" (Philippians 4:13). God gives strength to do whatever He needs us to do in ministry for Him and His people. He can work wonders through us, if we are willing and obedient.

1. Why did Gideon feel the need to confirm God's call by a series of tests rather than accepting it as presented?

2. Why did Gideon's army have to be reduced so radically?

3. How would you feel about going into battle with three hundred men against hundreds of thousands?

4. Has the Lord called you to a special work? Will you say yes like Gideon?

5: It Seemed Like a Good Idea at the Time

HAVE YOU EVER DONE SOMETHING THAT SEEMED LIKE A GOOD IDEA AT THE TIME, only to have it end in disaster? What seemed so logical and safe when first considered soon caused nothing but grief? Such was the case for Gideon and for Israel.

Fresh from their victory over the army of Midian with only three hundred soldiers, Gideon's men and volunteers chased the stragglers all the way back to the Midian border. There they captured the Midianite leaders Oreb and Zeeb, who were summarily executed. But no sooner had Gideon returned to resume normal life when some of the men of Ephraim who were not involved in the battle, or even invited to participate, began to whine and complain about being left out of the action.

With great diplomacy and tact, Gideon avoided a major confrontation of wounded egos and returned home to enjoy the peace (see Judges 8:1–21), demonstrating strong statesmanship skill. But the people of Israel wanted to make Gideon king. "Rule over us—you, your son and your grandson—because you have saved us out of the hand of Midian" (22). They forgot that Gideon was only the instrument of God's miraculous deliverance, for the Lord could have used a child to lead Israel had He chosen to do so. Fortunately Gideon remembered his true place in the incident and told them, "I will not rule over you, nor will my son rule over you. The Lord will rule over you" (23). Way to go Gideon! He had his priorities straight and gave the credit and praise where it rightfully belonged.

Opening the Door to Idolatry

Gideon did everything perfectly—almost—for practically with his next breath he opened the door to idolatry, undermining the effectiveness of his previous efforts: "I do have one request, that each of you give me an earring from your share of the plunder." (It was the custom of the Canaanite tribes to wear gold earrings.)

They agreed and each man chipped in a ring from his share of the spoil. The weight of the rings came to 1,700 shekels—680 ounces of solid gold, not counting the other ornaments, pendants, royal robes, and decorative chains the Midianites had on their camels' necks (24–26). Gideon took the gold and made an ephod—like an armor breastplate to commemorate the victory over Midian. He kept it on display in his hometown for tourists to see. Then all who visited the site could remember the Lord's power in battle when they saw this symbol of divine protection.

Bad choice. Gideon wanted to express his thanks and praise to the Lord, but he should have asked the Lord what would be a suitable remembrance. Before they all went off awarding medals and jumping up and down chanting, "We're number one!" as if their team just won the Super Bowl, Gideon should have asked God what He wanted. They should have asked before they made the ephod—not after. The Lord has no need for gold. He owns it already. God doesn't need anything fashioned by man as a reminder of His character and power. The Lord made that abundantly clear generations ago in the law given to Moses (Exodus 20:4–6). What the Lord always appreciates and never tires of receiving are our prayers, our worship, our service—our very lives. He doesn't need things to make Him happy.

They must have forgotten the lesson of Moses and the bronze serpent (see Numbers 21:9). When people, bitten by poisonous serpents, in faith looked up and saw the metal snake and trusted the Lord, they were made well. That was good. But they took what was good to the wrong extreme, for they reverenced the thing, not the One who healed them. They set up entire departments devoted to serpentine maintenance with people assigned to move, polish and display the symbol for all to see. It was not a historic relic like the Liberty Bell at Independence Hall, but an item of sacred worship.

When the people saw the ephod, they worshipped it and not the Lord, for "all Israel prostituted themselves by worshipping it [the ephod] there, and it became a snare to Gideon and his family" (Judges 8:27). Israel sold themselves by going after a cheap substitute for God's eternal love. They began almost immediately to fall away from true heart worship by trying to manipulate God to accede to their terms and control.

Although Midian was subdued and Gideon brought peace to Israel for forty years, he was not able to erase the damage he had done by making the golden trophy. Gideon enjoyed life, had many wives and seventy sons, one of whom was Abimelech—the failure who wanted to be king and would do anything to achieve his goal. And with Abimelech things would soon go from bad to worse. "No sooner had Gideon died than the Israelites again prostituted themselves to the Baals. They set up Baal-berith [the golden ephod] as their god and did not remember the Lord their God, who had rescued them from the hands of all their enemies on every side" (28–33).

We have done this, too, whenever we have begged the Lord to bless the messes we have created, seeking His guidance after the fact rather than before. The Lord would rather hear from us first and point us in the right way than hear our pleas to rehabilitate the disasters we have caused. "Lord help me to do it right the first time because it was Your idea—not mine."

1. Is it possible for well-meaning people to replace a relationship with God with religious service and activity? How?

2. Why did people choose to worship idols rather than the Lord?

3. What can we do in the early stages to keep our plans and ideas from becoming disasters? What should Gideon have done?

6: The Failure Who Would Be King

HISTORIANS CALL IT THE "GREAT MAN THEORY." SIMPLY STATED, SIBLINGS OF STRONG political, cultural, and religious leaders rarely exceed or duplicate the achievements of their parents. Richard Cromwell was not as effective as his famous father, Oliver. Israel's King Solomon, for all his wisdom, was not equal to King David. Even in the early days of The Salvation Army there was concern that Bramwell Booth would not be as effective as his father, General William Booth. Rarely do offspring have the same charisma, vision, and determination as their founding forebears, often opting to maintain and perpetuate an organization or dynasty. They then become entrenched in the parental legend that defines their lives.

Such was the sad tale of Gideon's son Abimelech. After Gideon's death, Abimelech went to his mother's side of the family to enlist support for his political ambitions. Abimelech must have remembered the offer made after the battle with Midian to make Gideon the founder of a mighty dynasty—an offer Gideon refused. Abimelech campaigned saying, "Which is better for you—to have all seventy of Jerub-baal's sons rule over you, or just one man? Remember, I am your flesh and blood." When his brothers repeated all this to the citizens of Shechem, the people gave Abimelech their allegiance (Judges 9:1).

With his brothers' support and seventy shekels donated by the temple of Baal-berith, Abimelech hired goons and thugs to go to the family homestead in Ophrah, ostensibly for a clan planning council to set up a new administration. Once all were assembled, Abimelech had his potential rivals murdered—seventy brothers. Only Jotham, the youngest, escaped. Apparently fratricide didn't offend the Shechemites, for they willingly gathered to crown Abimelech king (6).

The Strange Fable of the Trees

Jotham, perhaps the only one to speak up against making Abimelech king, told a fable, an infrequently used device in Scripture, involving talking trees. Jesus always used parables that were based on real life. Jotham shouted to the people assembled at Mt. Gerizim for the coronation rally: "Listen to me, citizens of Shechem, so that God may listen to you. One day the trees went out to anoint a king for themselves. They said to the olive tree, 'Be our king.'

"But the olive tree answered, 'Should I give up my oil, by which gods and men are honored, to hold sway over the trees?'

"Next, the trees said to the fig tree, 'Come and be our king.'

"The fig tree replied, 'Should I give up my fruit, so good and sweet, to hold sway over the trees?'

"Then the trees said to the vine, 'Come and be our king.'

"But the vine answered, 'Should I give up my wine, which cheers both gods and men, to hold sway over the trees?'

"Finally all the trees said to the thornbush, 'Come and be our king.'

"The thornbush said to the trees, 'If you really want to anoint me king over you, come and take refuge in my shade; but if not, let fire come out of the thornbush and consume the cedars of Lebanon!'

"Now if you have acted honorably and in good faith when you made Abimelech king, and if you have been fair to Jerub-baal and his family, and if you have treated him as he deserves—and to think that my father fought for you, risked his life to rescue you from the hand of Midian (but today you have revolted against my father's family, murdered his seventy sons on a single stone, and made Abimelech, the son of his slave girl, king over the citizens of Shechem because he is your brother)—if then you have acted honorably and in good faith toward Jerub-baal and his family today, may Abimelech be your joy, and may you be his, too!

"But if you have not, let fire come out from Abimelech and consume you, citizens of Shechem and Beth Millo, and let fire come out from you, citizens of Shechem and Beth Millo, and consume Abimelech!" (7–20). Message delivered, Jotham hid from his brother Abimelech. I would, too.

It took three years for Abimelech to reveal his true character. God allowed this to happen so the people would know the mistake they had made by assigning their relationship with God such a low priority. Abimelech soon discovered that taking the throne was much easier than keeping it, for where there had once been admiration for Gideon, there were only rumbles of revolution against his son. In order to get Abimelech's attention, angry citizens ambushed and robbed tourists and traders diverting income from the king.

In retaliation, Abimelech attacked the city of Shechem, driving an estimated 1,000 inhabitants into an interior fortress tower. Abimelech and his henchmen burned the tower to the ground killing everyone inside (43–49).

Having subdued Shechem, Abimelech went to do the same at the stronghold in Thebez where the populace had retreated for safety. This time as he prepared to burn the tower, a woman dropped a piece of millstone from a window. It hit Abimelech in the head and cracked his skull, delivering a mortal wound. Wishing to die as a warrior and not in such a stupid way as being clobbered by a housewife with a stone, Abimelech ordered his armor-bearer to run him through with a sword (51–54).

There are no winners when disobedience and rebellion are given place. Abimelech paid for his arrogance, fratricide, and deception with his life. What a disappointment it must have been to see all the good that Gideon had accomplished undone by his son's sinfulness.

After a period of some forty-five years under several lesser known judges who did what they could for Israel, the nation's spiritual condition slipped down even further than before as they repeated the cycle of apostasy, decline, and spiritual anarchy. They flocked to worship all manner of pagan deities forsaking their first love—the Lord.

We need to cultivate a personal relationship with God ourselves. We can't live on our parents' spiritual merits or those of others, or we may end up as badly as Abimelech.

SOMETHING TO THINK ABOUT

1. Why did Abimelech want to be king?

2. What character traits would be desirable in a candidate for kingship?

3. Which traits, if any, did Abimelech have that qualified him for this high office?

4. Describe the spiritual legacy you wish to leave for your children after you are gone.

7: A Hasty Promise, a Father's Remorse

JEPHTHAH, HAD HE TRUSTED COMPLETELY IN THE LORD, COULD HAVE BEEN A GREAT judge in Israel overcoming adversity, insecurity, and a poor family upbringing. He could have been a leader on par with Gideon but instead is remembered for a poorly considered promise.

Following Abimelech, a series of little-known judges led Israel for forty-five years. After they died, Israel slipped into its customary pattern of idolatry and disobedience. Once again the Israelites did evil in the eyes of the Lord, choosing to worship the fertility deities of the neighboring countries. Because the Israelites forsook the Lord, they were sold into the hands of the Philistines and the Ammonites, who invaded and oppressed Israel for eighteen years (Judges 10:6–8). And once again the people of Israel prayed and begged God for deliverance. What they really wanted was to be rescued and then have God leave them alone so they could do as they pleased without interference.

The Lord replied, "When the Egyptians, Amorites, Ammonites, Philistines, Sidonians, Amalekites, and Maonites oppressed you and you cried to Me for help, did I not save you from their hands? But you have forsaken Me and served other gods, so I will no longer save you. Go and cry out to the gods you have chosen. Let them save you when you are in trouble!" (11–14).

"Okay, Lord. Sure, we have sinned, but now we need You to rescue us," they pleaded. As a sign of good faith they did get rid of their foreign gods—at least for a short time. And when the Lord could no longer bear the sounds of their misery, He helped them.

Desperate for decisive leadership against the Ammonites, the Israelites pledged that whoever launched an attack against their oppressors would be declared ruler. Jephthah took this as an opportunity for advancement and personal revenge. Although he was a brave warrior and the son of Gilead, the great man whose name defined the region, his mother was a prostitute. That made him an outcast among his own siblings (10:18–11:3).

But it is amazing how quickly slavery changed his relatives' minds, for the very people who drove Jephthah away were the same ones who came begging for his aid. In the same way, how many times has someone mistreated you and almost with the next breath asked you for a favor? How many times have we done the same thing to God?

"Didn't you hate me and drive me away from home?" Jephthah asked. "Why do you come to me now, when you're in trouble?"

"Well, times change," they replied. "Be our commander, so we can fight the Ammonites."

"If I do defeat them, will I be your leader or will you treat me the way you did before?" Jephthah further inquired.

Gilead's elders replied, "The Lord is our witness; we will certainly do as you say" (see 6–10).

Judges 11:29 says, "The Spirit of the Lord came upon Jephthah . . . and he advanced against the Ammonites" with strength to do the Lord's work. He should have immediately driven the enemy from Israel's borders without further comment. Instead Jephthah's uncontrolled ego blurted out a foolishly ill-advised vow.

What Was He Thinking?

"If You give the Ammonites into my hands, whatever comes out of the door of my house to meet me when I return in triumph . . . will be the Lord's, and I will sacrifice it as a burnt offering" (30). Big mistake. He made a promise the Lord did not ask of him. Once made, the vow could not be recalled, much like trying to put toothpaste back into the tube.

We, however, live in an era when promises are made to be broken. Sports contracts are routinely broken or merely used as starting points for salary negotiations. God, on the other hand, expects promises to be kept. What are some of the promises you have made to the Lord and not completed? I have made some; you have too.

When Jephthah came home from battle, perhaps he expected to be met by some pet animal that always ran to greet him. The first one to greet him at the door was his daughter, his only child, singing and dancing, welcoming Daddy home (34). As a father, I can only imagine his feelings at that moment. "Oh! My daughter! You have made me miserable and wretched, because I have made a vow to the Lord that I cannot break" (35). Note that even then he did not take responsibility for his actions. "You have made me miserable," he said—as if it was his daughter's fault.

But during this time of moral and spiritual chaos, Jephthah's unnamed daughter seemed to be one of the few who had a correct sense of what had to be done. A promise made is a promise kept— especially one made to God.

"Father," she replied, "you have given your word to the Lord. Do to me just as you promised" (36). She did ask that she be granted a stay of two months to spend with friends to grieve for the future that would never be. At the end of the two months, the promise was fulfilled. Scripture does not say how, and I am just as glad it does not (37–40).

Jephthah led Israel for six years after winning the war with Ammon, but at a terrible personal cost. Imagine what he could have done had he not made such a foolish promise. Imagine what his daughter might have grown up to become or do.

Our flawed judgment shows that no one sins alone or is unaffected by the decisions of others. Sin always influences those around us, especially those closest to us. Jephthah could have been great, but missed the opportunity. I might have had greater respect for Jephthah had he agreed to take his daughter's place, since the problem was his fault—not hers.

Fortunately God made a promise too—not a foolish one, but one made before the foundation of the world that Jesus would offer Himself a sacrifice to pay the price and penalty of sin once and for all. That is a promise I am glad He kept.

SOMETHING TO THINK ABOUT

1. What prompted Jephthah to make such a foolish promise? Did the Lord require it?

2. How would you have reacted if you were Jephthah's daughter?

3. Was she sacrificed? Killed? Would the Lord have her killed just to make a point?

4. How did Jephthah take responsibility (or not) for his actions?

8: Wasted Gifts, Wasted Opportunities

HIS NAME CONJURES UP IMAGES OF STRENGTH, LONG HAIR, AND CRUMBLING TEMPLES with Victor Mature in the starring role. Most recognize at least part of the Bible story even though it may be the skewed Hollywood version. And every kid who has been harangued to get a haircut has referenced Samson and his unshorn locks.

Judges 13:1 says, "Again the Israelites did evil in the eyes of the Lord, so the Lord delivered them into the hands of the Philistines for forty years." They didn't obey the Lord any better than we do. Unfortunately Samson, who was to be God's man to deliver Israel, took himself far too seriously and the things of God not seriously enough.

The Samson saga begins with his parents, a childless couple from the tribe of Dan. One day an angel came to them with an announcement and a warning that the mother must "see to it that you drink no wine or other fermented drink and that you do not eat anything unclean, because you will conceive and give birth to a son. No razor may be used on his head, because the boy is to be a Nazirite, [not a Nazarene—a person from Nazareth] set apart to God from birth, and he will begin the deliverance of Israel from the hands of the Philistines" (4–5).

In due course, "the Spirit of the Lord began to stir him" (25). The Lord was not all that stirred Samson, for it says that he went to Timanah to see a young Philistine woman he wanted to marry—all part of the Lord's plan to provoke a confrontation to one day deliver Israel (14:1–4).

On the way, Samson was attacked by a lion. "The Spirit of the Lord came upon him," allowing Samson to kill the beast with his bare hands. But remember, Samson's strength came from the Lord, not from the long hair. When Samson returned later, he discovered wild bees had made a honeycomb in the lion's carcass. He kept this whole lion–honey episode a secret (6,8–9).

During his wedding festivities, Samson made a wager with his Philistine groomsmen, based on the lion adventure. "If you can answer this riddle within the seven days of the feast, I will give you thirty linen garments and thirty sets of clothes. If you can't, you must give me the same in return. Here it is—'Out of the eater, something to eat; out of the strong, something sweet'" (12–14).

Not wishing to lose the bet, the Philistines made Samson's new wife an offer she could not refuse. "Get the answer to the riddle for us, or we will burn you and your family to death" (15). She nagged and sobbed until Samson told her the answer. As soon as she found out, she passed the solution to the Philistines. On the last day of the challenge, they gave Samson the answer. "What is sweeter than honey? What is stronger than a lion?"

In a rage, realizing that his wife was the only other person who knew the answer, Samson went to Askelon, where he killed thirty Philistines of about the same size, stripped the bodies, and paid the wager. In the interim, Samson's bride was given to another man.

In retaliation Samson caught three hundred foxes, tied their tails together, fastened a burning torch to each pair, and turned them loose in the dry, standing grain of the Philistines. When the Philistines found out that giving Samson's bride away was what set him off, they burned the family alive anyway. From that day on Samson was the Philistines' implacable enemy (15:5–8).

When fearful countrymen turned Samson over to the Philistines, again the "Spirit of the Lord came upon Samson" with such fury that he killed a thousand men armed with only the jawbone of a donkey (9–19). But as his notoriety grew, Samson's behavior became more outrageous, pushing God's influence to the background.

Play with Fire and You Get Burned

The Philistines needed to find a way to control the Israeli strongman. Direct confrontation hadn't worked. Perhaps Delilah, whose name is synonymous with temptation, seduction, and betrayal, might. The Philistine rulers promised 1,100 shekels of silver from each of them if Delilah could discover Samson's weakness (16:4–5). Samson fell for Delilah. During their romance Delilah begged, "Tell me the secret of your great strength and how you can be subdued." "Superman, tell me your secret identity and how we can kill you," seems almost as blunt.

Samson replied, "If anyone ties me with seven fresh thongs that have not been dried, I'll be as weak as any other man." So Delilah tied him up as Samson whispered, "This is not good."

According to the Bible, almost immediately Philistine men hiding in the room jumped out and tried to subdue Samson. He broke the thongs, thrashing his would–be captors. Delilah whined some more as Samson got a little closer to the truth. This time it was seven new ropes. And again Philistines jumped out of the closet and out from under the bed trying to take Samson.

He should have seen the pattern. Every time he confided in Delilah, people started attacking him. By the third time, Samson's inner voice must have been screaming, since he told Delilah that he could be subdued if she wove his hair into the fabric on a loom (6-14). When the men jumped out again, Samson tore up the loom and freed himself without difficulty. Intoxicated by the lure of lust and power, Samson thought he was in control and safe from all harm.

"How can you say, 'I love you,' when you won't confide in me?" Delilah grumbled. "This is the third time you have made a fool of me and haven't told me the secret of your great strength." She nagged Samson until he told her everything (15-17). Imagine his shock reeling from that first punch after the haircut.

One of the saddest phrases in Scripture says that Samson "did not know that the Lord had left him" (20). Samson had been too preoccupied with himself to notice. Blinded, chained, and forced to turn the prison mill wheel, the shamed ex-hero had time to consider his actions as both his hair and strength grew back.

The final chapter in this sorry tale came at a celebration to honor the Philistine god Dagon, and to ridicule Samson and his Lord. In the midst of the abuse, Samson leaned on the temple's two main support columns. "O God, please strengthen me just once more, and let me with one blow get revenge on the Philistines for my two eyes" (28). He pushed, strained, and knocked down the temple, killing more of his enemies on that day than he had killed in his lifetime—and himself.

Even at the end, Samson does not express sorrow for what he had lost, or how he had failed the Lord. He only requested revenge for his blindness. Never does he indicate remorse for wasting his great gifts that were to help Israel. Although he served as judge for twenty years, imagine what he could have done, had his heart been with God.

Whenever we use our God-given opportunities to satisfy our ego, we run the same risks as Samson. If we trivialize the sacred, we set ourselves up for ruin and disgrace, doing whatever seems right in our own eyes since we have no king or ruler in our lives. But using the gifts the Lord has given for ministry, we can have the strength of thousands.

Something to Think About

1. What good things could you do for God if you had Samson's gifts and strength?

2. What gifts do you have that are designed for ministry but do not include super-human strength?

3. How have you treated the sacred things of God as if they were of little significance?

4. If you could do one great thing for God, what would it be?

THREE

ISAIAH: PRINCE AMONG PROPHETS

HENRY GARIEPY

Colonel Henry Gariepy, who retired in 1995 from his position as national editor in chief and literary secretary, is the author of several books and resides in Tom's River, New Jersey. Colonel Gariepy is an avid outdoorsman and continues to contribute to teaching and writing ministries.

Isaiah stands foremost among the celebrated prophets of the Old Testament. He towers without peer for his unsurpassed poetry, profound insights, distinguished statesmanship. The sixty–six chapters of Isaiah make it the longest of the extraordinary books of the prophets. Its position as first indicates the priority accorded it. The book's prominence among the Dead Sea Scrolls and quotes from it by the first century Jewish historian Josephus further witness to its popularity.

1: Prince of the Prophets

ISAIAH HAS PARALLELS TO THE BIBLE AS A WHOLE. THE BIBLE HAS sixty–six books, Isaiah has sixty–six chapters. The Old Testament has thirty–nine books, the first division of Isaiah has thirty–nine chapters. The New Testament has twenty–seven books, the last section of Isaiah twenty–seven chapters. The Old Testament deals with Israel's sin and God's judgment, as does the first section of Isaiah. The New Testament presents the mission of Christ, as does the last section of Isaiah.

Isaiah is the most quoted Old Testament book in the New Testament. It quotes or alludes to Isaiah passages 472 times in twenty-three of its books. Isaiah's poetic passages are marked by majesty, beauty of expression, brilliant word pictures, and polished literary art. He has the largest vocabulary of Old Testament writers, using nearly 2,200 different Hebrew words. He is credited with writing a history of the reign of King Uzziah (2 Chronicles 26:22).

Isaiah lived and worked in Jerusalem from about 750 to 700 B.C., during the stormy time when the Assyrian war machine was on a roll and Israel was in its path. Scholars suggest that he was a relative of King Uzziah. But the prophet's authority came from the highest source of all—he was called and commissioned as an ambassador of "The Mighty God, The Everlasting Father, the Prince of Peace."

A second century Jewish writing, "The Martyrdom of Isaiah," helped form the tradition that Isaiah was believed to have been "sawn in two" (Hebrews 11:37), during the reign of Manasseh (2 Kings 21:16).

The Unity of Isaiah

How many Isaiahs were there? Like Manasseh, scholars have sawed this writer into "Deutero Isaiah," two authors based on the major difference in theme and writing from chapter forty on.

Such fragmentation is not supported by the Isaiah Scroll found in the Qumran caves near the Dead Sea, and thought to have been copied about 100 B.C. This oldest Hebrew text of Isaiah, a leather scroll now in Jerusalem, shows no break between chapters 39 and 40. There is no manuscript or traditional support for the theory of multiple authorship.

Isaiah is identified as the author in 1:1, 2:1 and 13:1. His special title for God, "Holy One of Israel," is prominent in both sections of his book, occurring twelve times in chapters 1–39 and fourteen times in 40–46, but found only six times in the rest of the Old Testament. Twenty-five other Hebrew words or expressions are found in both divisions of the book that do not occur in any other prophetic writing.

The second century Septuagint translation gives no indication of dual authorship. The seeming anachronism of Cyrus named 150 years before his time, as noted by eminent Bible scholar R. H. Pfeiffer, "offers no difficulty to those who believe that God predicted through Isaiah's pen what was to happen two centuries later." Furthermore, it is not plausible that such a peerless writer would disappear from the scene of history. The New Testament refers to Isaiah as one author: Matthew 12:17–21 (Isaiah 42:1–4); Matthew 3:3 and Luke 3:4 (Isaiah 40:3); Romans 10:16,20 (Isaiah 53:1; 65:1); and John 12:38–41 (Isaiah 53:1; 6:10).

Themes and Theology

The thunder of God's judgment can be heard rumbling through these pages. But the divine call to salvation also sounds loud and clear. The Messiah lives within its pages, with more messianic prophecies in the Book of Isaiah than all the other prophets combined. The suffering servant, the One "wounded for our transgressions" and "bruised for our iniquities" is portrayed in immortal words. The prophet, in his sublime fifty-third chapter, takes us to the foot of the cross in his portrayal of the suffering Savior. This "prince of the prophets" also lifts our thoughts to lofty heights, to the Sovereign, "the everlasting God, the Creator of the ends of the earth."

Isaiah is the book of golden texts that through the centuries continue to enrich the life of the believer. When venturing on a journey through Isaiah, we should come with great expectations. It is the book of the true "New Age," God's new age of peace and righteousness. Let us come to this magnificent book with the prayer: "Open my eyes that I may see wonderful things in your law" (Psalm 119:18).

SOMETHING TO THINK ABOUT

1. What is unique about Isaiah's prophecy and style of writing?

2. Why does Isaiah refer to the Lord as "the Holy One of Israel?" Does that speak of a special relationship or point of view?

3. How is Isaiah the most messianic of all the Old Testament books?

4. What makes Isaiah the most prominent of all the prophetic books of the Bible?

2: The Prophet Speaks to Our Day

THE FIRST CHAPTER OF ISAIAH IS A SYNOPSIS OF THE ENTIRE BOOK. IT PRESENTS THE prophet's mission and his message of judgment and redemption. Though he saw "through a glass darkly" that which would later be revealed on Calvary, he proclaims the stupendous message of God as a sorrowing yet loving Father who calls His rebellious children to return to Him.

Isaiah, "prince of the prophets," launches his magnificent manuscript with his byline, commission, and historical context, all in the opening verse: The vision concerning Judah and Jerusalem that Isaiah, son of Amoz, saw during the reigns of Uzziah, Jotham, Ahaz, and Hezekiah—kings of Judah. Quoted in the New Testament more than any other Old Testament author, the prophet does not speak his own words. Rather he proclaims the vision, the revelation direct from God. The four kings he names identify the period of his prophecy with international turbulence, political chaos, and moral breakdown. Assyria's war machine is rolling toward greater conquest, and Israel is in its path. The southern kingdom of Judah had purchased stability by paying tribute to Assyria.

"The Lord has spoken" (2) introduces God as principal speaker throughout the book. The opening scene is as a courtroom. The heavens are called upon as witnesses. Israel is the accused. The plaintiff is God himself. In a blistering indictment He charges: "They have rebelled against me. . . . They have forsaken the Lord; they have spurned the Holy One of Israel and turned their backs on Him" (2,4).

God is speaking to Israel as a father: "I reared children and brought them up" (2). Disappointment marks His message to them. Employing striking imagery, the prophet quotes God as saying that unlike Israel, even domestic animals know their master (3). The Israelites are accused of forgetting and forsaking God.

Total devastation will be the sentence for the apostate nation. "Some survivors" (9) becomes the first intimation of "the remnant," a major recurring theme of this book. God's ultimate purpose for the redemption of man will not be aborted. There will be those who will be faithful and will know His blessings in the age to come.

The Lord through Isaiah denounces their hollow sacrificial systems that are poor substitutes for righteousness (10-15). There can be no gap between our worship and our living. Let us beware that we do not offer empty rituals in place of the moral purity and true worship God requires of us. But in the midst of this dark picture of rebellion and judgment, a note of hope is sounded. God calls His children to repentance: Wash and make yourselves clean. Take your evil deeds out of my sight! Stop doing wrong, learn to do right! God calls the nation to "seek justice, encourage the oppressed" (16-17).

And here, in the book that has been called "The Gospel of the Old Testament," is sounded one of the most compelling invitations of the Bible: "Come now, let us reason together," says the Lord. "Though your sins are like scarlet, they shall be as white as snow; though they are red as crimson, they shall be like wool" (18).

This invitation declares the astonishing fact that God, the Creator of the cosmos, cares for us. He loves us and calls us back to Himself even when we have forgotten and forsaken Him. He has bestowed upon each of His children the gift of reason, and if we will exercise it we will be led to discover His love and His way for us.

The royalty of Isaiah's day wore robes dyed deep scarlet and crimson. In one of the most beautiful statements of the Bible, to His rebellious children of all ages God promises that though our sin be deep dyed as scarlet or crimson, He will make our hearts as white as snow or wool. The Suffering Servant, whom the prophet later identifies as the One "wounded for our transgressions," will be the means of this cleansing. This sublime text and promise has been the gateway for countless prodigal children to return home to their Heavenly Father.

I will thoroughly purge away your dross and remove your impurities (25) is the promise of God to the one who repents and returns to Him. "I will remove all your alloy" is the rendering of the Revised Standard Version. When silver was refined and the dross skimmed off the surface, the refiner could then see himself mirrored in the purified metal. When the Divine Refiner removes the dross of sin from our lives, our purified lives will reflect the very image of God.

The message of Isaiah is poignantly relevant to our day. Are we not living in a time of turbulence, political chaos, moral breakdown? Do we not know something of the ravages of war, the more ominous clouds of a nuclear holocaust, and of a people who have forgotten and forsaken God? But let us hear and heed the dominant note of hope and salvation in Christ.

SOMETHING TO THINK ABOUT

1. How had Israel rebelled against "the Holy One of Israel?" How have we?

2. Who will escape God's judgment? Will any be saved, or will all die in exile?

3. Read Isaiah 1:18. What do you make of God's invitation to "Come, let us reason together" ? Are we encouraged to dialogue or debate with God?

4. How does the Lord still show love and compassion to His people even though they have repeatedly rejected Him?

3: God's New Age—A World Without War

"THE NEW AGE," A MOVEMENT THAT BORDERS ON RELIGION, IS A FALSE BELIEF WHICH has led many astray and posed a subtle challenge to Christianity. But the book of Isaiah proclaims the true new age, God's new and glorious age of the future. Isaiah presents God's new age with a seven-fold repetition of "In the last days" or its equivalent (2:11,17,20; 3:7,18; 4:1,2), wherein universal justice and peace will be the hallmarks.

Hope for a world without war has captured the imagination of peace and political movements throughout the world. The gift of a monument from cold war leader Russia to the United Nations has the classic text from Isaiah engraved on it: "They will beat their swords into plowshares and their spears into pruning hooks. Nation will not take up sword against nation, nor will they train for war anymore" (2:4). This noble passage, also quoted by Micah (4:3), articulates man's deep and immemorial longing for peace. True and lasting peace will come in God's new age. Then and only then will man not train for war anymore.

We have seen man walk on the moon and develop the fantastic technology of our day. But humankind is still unable to learn how to live together in peace. War and violence dominate the headlines of our day. Isaiah's sublime, prophetic vision of the future is the only and ultimate hope for mankind. God has a new age coming. It will be an age of justice, unity, and peace with nations; people bonded together, not by paper treaty, but by faith and love.

From Revolt to Ruin

In contrast, the prophet in these early dismal chapters describes the destruction that will come upon Israel for its sin (2:6–4:1). The pages of history are littered with the wreckage of ruined civilizations. Drunk with their own power and vice, these people forgot and forsook God. "What do you mean by crushing my people and grinding the faces of the poor?" (3:14–15). God holds leaders accountable for the sacred offices entrusted to them.

The very first act of George Bush, Sr., following his being sworn in as President of the United States, was a prayer. As millions of television viewers watched from around the world, he prayed,

"Make us strong to do Your work, willing to heed and hear Your will. Write on our hearts these words: Use power to help people. For we are given power not to advance our own purposes, nor to make a great show in the world, nor a name. There is but one use of power, and it is to serve people. Help us remember, Lord."

Washington is known as a pinnacle of political power, a showplace of marble monuments and thought of by some as the Sodom and Gomorrah of politics. But how reassuring in that moment to see it become an eloquent witness of our motto, "In God We Trust." The true measure of a nation's greatness is not the sum of its possessions or the power of its armaments. It is reckoned in its faith and righteousness and justice. The leaders of Isaiah's day had forgotten that leadership is a sacred trust.

Womanhood and the Nation

We see in Isaiah (3:16–4:1), as in Amos (4:1–3), a blistering judgment upon the luxury-loving women whose degeneration helped lead the nation to ruin. Their haughtiness and coquettishness were repulsive to God. No less than twenty-one items of vanity are listed in verses 18–23. These ornamentations, symbols of their pride, read like a boutique's inventory. But their pride will bring upon them instead of fragrance, a stench; instead of fine clothing, sackcloth; instead of beauty, branding. The loss of men in war will be a further calamity for these vain and lustful dowagers of Israel.

The quality of its womanhood will always influence greatly the character and destiny of a nation. They are called to be the keepers and guardians of the springs of life. Their tenderness and sensitivity are needed to keep the heart of the world from hardness and corruption. May they be faithful to the special purpose God has ordained for them, and may we of the other gender encourage and affirm them in the Lord. In contrast to the degeneration and doom of those who rebel against God, the faithful will come to know the beauty and peace of God's new age.

The Branch of the Lord

The Branch of the Lord (4:2) alludes to the Messiah. The same Hebrew word *tsemach* is used as reference to the Messiah in 11:1 and Jeremiah 23:5, 33:15; Zechariah 3:8, 6:12. From the stump of Israel He will come forth with life and fruitfulness and glory for the new age of God.

SOMETHING TO THINK ABOUT

1. How will the way to lasting peace, which Isaiah speaks of, be achieved?

2. Why was Isaiah critical of vanity and conspicuous consumerism as evidenced by the wealthy of his day?

3. What did Isaiah mean by saying the new branch of the Messiah will come from an old stump?

4: The Song of the Vineyard

YOU MAY NEVER HAVE YOUR NAME IN *WHO'S WHO*, BUT A FAR MORE IMPORTANT BOOK exists for you to be recorded in: the Book of Life. There will be a remnant, Isaiah prophesies, whose names are recorded. This theme is found elsewhere in the Bible: Exodus 32:32; Daniel 12:1; Malachi 3:16; Luke 10:20; and Revelation 5:8. There will be a day of accountability for our life here on earth. May we be found faithful, in the words of the old hymn, with "our name written there, on the page bright and fair."

Those who remain . . . will be called holy. God calls us to be a holy people. The hallmark of the faithful ones will be holiness. Our highest good comes from a holy life. Holiness is an unalloyed love for God, an unreserved commitment to God and an unbroken fellowship with God. The highest privilege and priority for every Christian believer is holiness.

A Love Ballad

The prophet's celebrated parable of the vineyard (5:1–2) is set in the poetic beauty of a song:

> *I will sing for the one I love a song about his vineyard:*
> *My loved one had a vineyard on a fertile hillside.*
> *He dug it up and cleared it of stones*
> *And planted it with the choicest vines.*
> *He built a watchtower in it and cut out a winepress as well.*
> *Then he looked for a crop of good grapes, but it yielded only bad fruit.*

Building a vineyard took great care and provision over a long period of time. Digging in the rocky soil and irrigating the arid ground of Palestine was hard work. Walls had to be built to keep out animals, and watchtowers erected. Then there was the constant hoeing and pruning. Such investment of labor and care created expectation of a good harvest. But the parable states that the Lord's vineyard "yielded only bad fruit."

The ballad of the vineyard is a love song. It speaks of God's love as He went to great lengths for His people which ultimately led to infinite pain when Jesus was crucified on Calvary. They were His "vineyard." He had reason to expect good fruit from them. But when they spurned His love and showed ingratitude, God rejected them. They will become as a deserted vineyard, arid and choked with the weeds of their evil doings. The person who shows contempt for the lovingkindness of God will become a spiritual wasteland, fruitless and doomed for destruction.

Specific Sins and Consequences

Isaiah does not let himself get lost in generalities but deals with specific and representative sins. He pronounces a series of six woes for wrongdoings followed by pronouncements of God's judgments. The first "sin and woe" saying deals with greed, with the acquisition of more than is needed at the expense and impoverishment of others (8). In our country of affluence we do not need to look far to see the same rapacity of the wealthy while many go hungry and homeless and live in deprivation. God, in reproaching this sin, warns that a day of accounting will come when "great houses will become desolate, the fine mansions left without occupants" (9). Let those who are obsessed with real estate and riches take heed.

The second woe of drunkenness (11–14) has become one of the worst curses in our land. Millions suffer abuse, poverty and tragedy from alcoholism. Vast sums of money as well as innumerable lives are squandered on alcohol. Not only the addict but innocent victims among family, friends and society suffer from this curse. Intoxicated drivers kill over 25,000 persons a year on our highways. It is one of the great scourges in our country. "Man will be brought low" (15) by alcohol is as true today as it was in the time of Isaiah.

The sins of Isaiah's day as outlined in the final four woe sayings are up-to-date sins of our day. We too live in a world of deceit and skepticism (18–19), with the lack of moral sense of those "who call evil good and good evil" (20). We have among us the sophisticates "who are wise in their own eyes" (21). We all too painfully witness the perversion of justice with those "who acquit the guilty for a bribe, but deny justice to the innocent" (23).

Each sin Isaiah names has its counterpart in our society and world today. God's mercy for the repentant is everlasting, but so are His judgments upon sin. Impending doom is conveyed in the imagery of the roar of lions, the thunder of waves and a darkened sky (24–30). As the song reminds us, "For times like these, we need a Savior." Let us look to the One who, as the previous chapter prophesied, came as the Branch of the Lord to deliver us from evil and make us faithful and fruitful for our Heavenly Father.

SOMETHING TO THINK ABOUT

1. Why are we called to be holy? Given our capacity to do wrong, is this possible?

2. Who or what is God's vineyard? Why did it yield bad fruit?

3. Why did Isaiah focus on drunkenness as one of the great sins and woes of his day?

4. How have the same sins and woes been duplicated in our society? Can they be corrected or remedied? How?

5: Isaiah's Three Looks

THE SIXTH CHAPTER OF ISAIAH IS ONE OF THE BEST KNOWN IN PROPHETIC LITERATURE. It describes Isaiah's soul-shaking encounter with the glory and holiness of God and the commissioning of this prince of the prophets.

Crisis

"In the year that King Uzziah died" launches this diary of the prophet's encounter with God. Uzziah, also known as Azariah, in his later years was afflicted with leprosy for profaning the Temple (2 Chronicles 26:16–21). His death, circa 740 B.C., was a historical landmark in Israel. It marked the end of a long and prosperous reign characterized by military conquests, agricultural advances, impressive building, mining, and maritime enterprises (6–15). Though appearing outwardly prosperous, the soul of the nation was inwardly corrupt. In addition, the ominous march of Assyria threatened the whole Fertile Crescent, with Judah in its path.

God often speaks to us in the poignant experiences of life. Joni Eareckson Tada testifies: "My paralysis has drawn me close to God and given a spiritual healing which I wouldn't trade for a hundred active years on my feet." Fulton Sheen records in his autobiography: "The greatest gift of all may have been His summons to the cross, where I found His continuing self-disclosure." The turning point in the life of Martin Luther was when his friend, Alexis, struck by lightning, fell dead at his feet. God may come with a deeper clarity and call in crisis. Sickness, adversity, death— crossroads can become spiritual landmarks where we may hear and heed the call of God. "God whispers to us in our pleasures, but shouts in our pains," is the trenchant statement of C. S. Lewis.

The Upward Look

Isaiah, a highly gifted young man of princely descent, comes to the Temple to find guidance for difficult days ahead. Suddenly the resplendent Temple is transformed into the very throne room of God. In his moving spiritual autobiography, Isaiah exultantly exclaims, "I saw the Lord seated on a throne, high and exalted. The seraphims veil their faces as the very foundation of the Temple vibrates before His majestic splendor."

The inspired writer of the Gospel of John, in quoting from Isaiah's prophecy, states that this theophany, this appearance of Deity, was none other than Christ Himself, who came before the stricken gaze of the prophet: Isaiah said this because he saw Jesus' glory and spoke about Him (John 12:41). To the prophet Isaiah was vouchsafed a vision of the preincarnate Christ, enthroned and exalted in glory. No wonder he has given to us this peerless "Gospel of the Old Testament."

The Inward Look

"Woe is me" is the heart cry of Isaiah as he stands before the thrice–holy God. In the light of God's holiness he is overwhelmed with a sense of his own unworthiness. The discovery of God leads to self-discovery. Isaiah confesses, "I am a man of unclean lips and I live among a people of unclean lips" (Isaiah 6:5). When we see our need of forgiveness and cleansing, God can then do something with us.

God's response to Isaiah is immediate and remedial. One of the seraphims touches Isaiah's lips with a glowing ember from the altar. The altar is emblematic of the Cross, the live coal of the Holy Spirit. Both pardon and purity are prerequisites for the servant of God. "Your guilt is taken away and your sin atoned for" is the assuring word that comes to Isaiah (7).

Once cleansed, Isaiah could hear God's voice calling, "Whom shall I send? And who will go for us?" (8). The call of God is always wedded to a task. Isaiah responds, "Here am I. Send me!" (9).

God then commissions the prophet to go and tell. And what a message it would be. He would tell of the Messiah, the One wounded for our transgressions. His message of God's redeeming work and the new age to come resonates through the centuries.

It was not an easy task to which God called Isaiah. He would not be admired or flattered. It was to be a prolonged mission to a scoffing generation who had a fatal immunity to the truth.

God still calls for those who will go and tell the message of His great redemption. He would lead us from salvation to sanctification to service; from pollution to purity to passion. To follow Christ is still a costly business. He calls us not to success, but to faithfulness; not to security, but to sacrifice; not to comfort, but to a cross. But, as with Isaiah, when we give God our all, the rewards are incalculable and eternal.

SOMETHING TO THINK ABOUT

1. Why is Isaiah so specific about the time of his vision "in the year that king Uzziah died"?

2. Describe Isaiah's vision of the throne of God and the sights and sounds he witnessed.

3. Compare that vision to John's in Revelation 4. What is similar? What is different?

4. If you stood before God in all His holiness and power, how would you react?

6: The Promise of Immanuel

PANIC AND TERROR SWEPT BOTH THE ROYAL COURT AND THE NATION AS JUDAH WAS threatened by invasion (Isaiah 7:2). The reign of Ahaz (chapters 7 through 14) revealed a pivotal and fateful point of no return in the history of the Jewish nation. The era of Assyrian expansion marked the last years of Israel as a nation. Dark days of desolation and doom were in store.

"Keep Calm"

Into this darkness God sent Isaiah with a message of hope. The prophet confronts the king as he is inspecting the defenses of his water supply. The prophet's son, Shear-Jashub, who accompanies Isaiah at God's command, is a living oracle. His name, meaning "a remnant shall return," was given as a prophecy and promise.

The prophet's first counsel from God to the king is one of encouragement: Keep calm and don't be afraid. Do not lose heart (7:4). To keep calm in the midst of crisis can be next to impossible. But it becomes possible when we confront the crisis in the confidence and strength of God.

Isaiah makes this point with a pun. Translators have taxed their imaginations in their efforts to maintain the word play in English. Various renditions are given, such as: "No strong trust, no trusty stronghold.... No confiding, no abiding.... If you do not stand by me, you will not stand at all.... If your faith is not sure, your throne will not be secure." Isaiah wants to drive home in memorable words the foundational truth that only if we stand upon the Word of God will we be able to stand in the day of testing and trouble.

Ahaz rejects the prophet's message and the sign offered him during the Syro-Ephraimite crisis that lies upon the nation. In response to Ahaz' obstinacy, Isaiah prophesies that during an invasion the land will be raped, and devastation will overtake the nation (7:18–8:22).

The Sign of the Virgin Birth

But now, in this hour of crisis, the Lord is about to give an extraordinary sign. "Hear now" proclaims the prophet, calling the nation "to pay attention" for God's promise of great magnitude. The context alerts the reader that this is to be no ordinary announcement. Isaiah flings out his immortal words: "Therefore the Lord Himself will give you a sign: The virgin will be with child and will give birth to a son, and will call him Immanuel" (7:14). This was God's statement of His extraordinary provision for ultimate deliverance of His people.

The word *almah,* translated "virgin," is believed by many scholars to foreshadow or prophesy the virgin birth of Christ. Matthew's interpretation of this verse reads as follows: "All this took place to fulfill what the Lord had said through the prophet: 'The virgin will be with child and will give birth to a son, and they will call Him Immanuel, which means *God with us*'" (22–23). Luke's gospel also attests to the virgin birth of Jesus Christ (Luke 1:27).

The doctrine of the virgin birth has been a battlefield of theological controversy over the years. Biologically, a virgin birth is an impossibility. But so was the raising of Lazarus and the resurrection of Jesus. Someone has stated, "The presence of mystery is the footprint of the Divine." In harmony with God's miraculous power, the virgin birth would be but one of a chain of supernatural events in the marvelous life and mission of our Lord.

Immanuel—"God With Us"

Isaiah's prophecy of the coming of Immanuel should have assured Ahaz that God is working out His purposes for man upon earth. In the gospel account, the angel announces Christ's birth to Joseph by quoting Isaiah that Christ will be called Immanuel. Only Christ alone, unique in all history, could fill the glowing meaning of this name "God with us." Christ was the heart of God wrapped in human flesh. From that feeding trough in the cattle shed of lowly Bethlehem, the cry from that Infant's throat broke through the silence of centuries. For the first time on earth, the voice of God was heard from human vocal chords. Immanuel speaks to us of the mighty miracle and marvel of God becoming man and dwelling among us.

Christ was God walking the earth in sandals. This thought of God living and walking the earth in human form staggers the imagination. Yet that is precisely what happened at the Incarnation.

He alone, of all men, could claim, "Anyone who has seen Me has seen the Father" (John 14:9).

How reassuring to know that this radiant title of Christ first presented by Isaiah is God's promise to us today. Christ is still Immanuel to His followers. He is still God with us. We have His precious promise, "Surely I will be with you always, to the very end of the age" (Matthew 28:20). We follow the One Who said, "Never will I leave you, never will I forsake you" (Hebrews 13:5).

And wonder of wonders, you and I can know the reality of Immanuel to a far greater extent than the prophet Isaiah could have ever dreamed, for we can know the reality of Christ in our lives.

SOMETHING TO THINK ABOUT

1. How does Isaiah offer hope to a people facing war, suffering, and banishment?

2. Why is the virgin birth such a controversial topic? Can it be reasoned out or must it be accepted by faith? Or both?

3. Why is "God with us" so essential to the Christian's walk of faith? How is Immanuel still with us?

7: A New Dawning

"NEVERTHELESS, THERE WILL BE NO MORE GLOOM." ISAIAH OPENS THE NINTH CHAPTER with welcome announcement. The gloom and doom of the previous chapters give way to the prospect of a new dawn as Isaiah gives us one of the greatest messianic passages in the Old Testament:

> The people walking in darkness have seen a great light; on those living in the land of the shadow of death a light has dawned (Isaiah 9:2).

In sublime poetic expression the "prince of the prophets" predicts that a great light will come into the world:

> For to us a child is born, to us a son is given, and the government will be on his shoulders. And He will be called Wonderful Counselor, Mighty God, Everlasting Father, Prince of Peace. Of the increase of His government and peace there will be no end (6–7).

Each new Advent season, the immortal cadences of this lofty lyric inspire us afresh in the enduring strains of Handel's "Messiah." Isaiah gives us in this magnificent text a constellation of titles. Its lofty appellations declare the superlative qualities of the messianic king. These exalted titles speak to us of four divine attributes of our Lord: "Wonderful Counselor" declares His omniscience; "Mighty God," His omnipotence; "Everlasting Father," His eternity; and "Prince of Peace," His unlimited and creative bounty on our behalf.

51

Wonderful Counselor

And He will be called Wonderful Counselor. The traditional King James Version separates this designation as two titles, as does Handel in his oratorio, which he based on Luther's translation. But more recent Bible scholars regard the comma between them as an error and render it "Wonderful Counselor." This interpretation of the single title also has the support of the ancient Masoretic manuscript and is further suggested by the parallel structure of the text.

Life is often perplexing, bewildering, complex, problematic, disconcerting. As our Wonderful Counselor, Christ instructs and guides us through our crises and critical periods. This Wonderful Counselor is always available, never away, never too busy. He is always as close as the whisper of a prayer. He is compassionate and tender toward us. To Him we are not a case, but a child; not a problem person, but a person with a problem and potential.

The inspired chronicler John writes: "He knew all men. . . . He knew what was in a man" (John 2:24–25). He fully understands all the subtleties of our emotion, motivation, and subconscious. He is the specialist of the human heart who will always guide our steps aright. We may with confidence bring to Him our hurts, failures, deep needs, and aspirations. For Christ is the Counselor *par excellence*. He is the Wonderful Counselor.

Mighty God

This sublime title speaks of the divinity of Christ. He was the Mighty God in His preincarnate glory and splendor and then in His birth when He split time in two. He was the Mighty God in His ministry and miracles and in His imperishable teachings. He was the Mighty God in His death as our Savior from sin and in His resurrection as He broke the bonds of death. He will be mighty when He comes again in His glory.

Everlasting Father

"And He will be called . . . Everlasting Father." A more exact rendering of this verse would be "Father of Eternity," as it is rendered in the Amplified Bible. It presents the staggering truth that Christ is eternal. He had no beginning. He is the great first cause of all things. He antedates the eons of geological time and the mind-boggling age of the cosmos.

The Apostle Paul, writing centuries after Isaiah, stated, "He is before all things" (Colossians 1:17). Christ is the timeless One who will enable us to so pass through things temporal that we will not forfeit things eternal.

Prince of Peace

And He will be called . . . Prince of Peace. Peace may be both the most sought after and the most elusive treasure. History mocks the efforts of world leaders and diplomats on behalf of peace. This is not only the age of the split atom but of the split personality as well. Man is beset by neuroses and psychoses that undermine his peace from within. But the heart of the problem is the problem of the heart. Jesus, the Prince of Peace, enables us to have peace with God by His work of reconciliation on Calvary. Jesus enables us to have peace within ourselves. He resolves inner conflicts and tensions. And when we are at peace with God and ourselves, then through His grace we will be at peace with others.

To Isaiah was given the prophecy of these magnificent titles of our Lord. But to us has been given the person who fulfilled them. To Isaiah was given the expectation, but to us is given the experience of Christ and the radiant meaning of these titles in our lives.

SOMETHING TO THINK ABOUT

1. "The people walking in darkness have seen a great light." What changes do you think would result by going from darkness to light?

2. Look at the titles for the Messiah. How do they relate to His lordship? His kingship? Our relationship with Him?

3. Why "Wonderful Counselor?" Is He still that and more?

4. What will it take to make the Messiah the Prince of Peace when the entire world seems to be at war with itself?

8: The Branch That Became the Tree of Life

GOD'S ANGER HAS BEEN KINDLED AGAINST ISRAEL FOR HER PEOPLE'S REJECTION OF His Word and gross sins. Four times the solemn refrain sounds: "Yet for all this, His anger is not turned away, His hand is still upraised" (Isaiah 9:12,17,21; 10:4). Sin is its own punishment, consuming and destroying, preaches Isaiah, for surely wickedness burns like a fire. Israel's obstinacy proves fatal. To paraphrase the words of Jonathan Edwards, it is indeed a fearful thing to fall into the hands of an angry God.

The Fatal Lust for Power

Isaiah had prophesied earlier that God would use the Assyrians as His instrument of punishment upon Israel (8:1–10). In one of the literary masterpieces of this book, God through the prophet then pronounces His "Woe to the Assyrian, the rod of My anger, in whose hand is the club of My wrath" (10:5–11). God had sent Assyria against a godless nation (6) but Assyria's arrogance also draws God's wrath and punishment (12–19).

The Assyrian king Sennacherib's lust for power has its parallels throughout history. Hitler's barbaric grab for world power cost fifty million lives in World War II, laid waste the heartland of Western civilization, and spread death and destruction across six of the world's seven continents.

Dictators and tyrants do not change. Their bombast and violence are the same in every age, whether their battles are fought in the eighth century with sword and chariots or in the twenty-first century with tanks and missiles. Sennacherib was but one in an unending line of tyrants with a lust for power. We have known all too well those whose "purpose is to destroy, to put an end to many nations" (7), who have had their ominous list of cities conquered (9), who "removed the boundaries of nations" and "plundered their treasures" (14).

But in the midst of the prophecy of doom comes Isaiah's recurring reference to the "remnant" who will return (20–34). God will subdue "in a single day" the enemy of this remnant who "rely on the Lord." The defeat of Israel's oppressors will be no less spectacular than Gideon's victory or the Exodus (26). This prophecy was fulfilled in remarkable manner. Isaiah records that the angel of the Lord slew in one night with a plague 185,000 troops of the vast Assyrian army (Isaiah 37:36–38; 2 Kings 19:3537). These accounts reveal that God works in history and the course of events are under His ultimate control.

Promise of the Messiah

Isaiah now leads us from the world powers of man, which shall be destroyed, to the Lord, who will set up the eternal kingdom of God. Assyria is likened to a forest that will be cut down (Isaiah 10:33–34). And Judah is as a stump that seems dead. But in this third messianic prophecy of Isaiah, we read: A shoot will come up from the stump of Jesse: from his roots a Branch will bear fruit (11:1). The kingly line of David was nothing but a broken, cutoff dynasty. Only a stump was left. But Isaiah prophesies that from this stump of Jesse, David's father, will come a Branch greater than all that grew before it. Springing up from this stump will be a young sapling, bringing renown out of obscurity, life out of death. Centuries later the Apostles Paul and John would quote from this text as a messianic prophecy fulfilled by Christ (Romans 15:12; Revelation 5:5; 22:15).

Christ's birth in the lineage of Jesse was no genealogical accident. "A shoot will come up." History portrays certain predictable elements under the sovereignty of God. Those who today publish the obituary of God would do well to ponder the divine thread interwoven through the ages. It has not been severed in this so-called post–modern world. God is still on the throne. The Messiah's glorious mission was fulfilled when He was impaled on the tree that "towers o'er the wrecks of time." That Branch has become the Tree of Life for lost humanity.

The Peace of the Messiah

There will be peace between man and nature. Isaiah presents a pastoral picture of an idyllic setting of peace between wild and tame beasts with children (11:6):

> *The wolf will live with the lamb, the leopard will lie down with the goat, the calf, and the lion and the yearling together; and a little child will lead them.*

The new world, ruled by the Messiah, will be one of justice and righteousness (3–5). God's new age will be one where "they will neither harm nor destroy on all my holy mountain" (9). This will take place because "the earth will be full of the knowledge of the Lord as the waters cover the sea" (9).

Isaiah's final brush stroke of his masterpiece of the new age adds a dimension of universal peace beyond description. "In that day the Root of Jesse will stand as a banner for the peoples; the nations will rally to Him, and His place of rest will be glorious" (10).

And miracle of miracles, we can be there. Praise God!

SOMETHING TO THINK ABOUT

1. How did the Lord use the Assyrian Empire as an instrument of His correction?

2. Would the Assyrians replace Israel as God's "chosen people?" Why not?

3. Why is the dynastic house of David referred to as a dry stump? What went wrong?

4. What will the world be like when the Messiah comes to rule? What will be different?

9: The Wells of Salvation

THIS JUBILANT PSALM ON THE THEME OF SALVATION FOLLOWS NATURALLY THE MESSIANIC visions of the prophet and word of God's deliverance from the doom of His judgment:

> *I will praise You, 0 Lord. Surely God is my salvation; I will trust and not be afraid.*
> *The Lord, the Lord, is my strength and my song; He has become my salvation.*
> *With joy you will draw water from the wells of salvation (12:1–3).*

Such joy becomes irrepressible: "Proclaim that His name is exalted. Sing to the Lord, for He has done glorious things; let this be known to all the world" (4–5).

Water is essential to life, as well as refreshing to our thirst. We could not live for more than a few days without it. How wonderful that something so vital has been provided abundantly by God—in the ground, in our rivers and streams and by rainfall. Jesus gives the water of life to our souls. That well was dug deep on a skull–shaped hill. Its healing waters have quenched the deep thirst of humanity, which no earthly spring can satisfy. We have with joy drawn water from that well of salvation, provided by the One who is the "living water" (John 4:10). We, through Christ, have been delivered from God's judgment on sin. Let us also rise up with praise and witness to His salvation and glory.

The Days of Judgment

The next section of the book of Isaiah, chapters 13 to 23, comprise a collection of doom oracles, or so-called "foreign prophecies" on nations that were enemies of the people of God. The first is a remarkable prophecy of the desolation of Babylon, "the jewel of kingdoms" (13:19). After painting a scenario of the horrors of its ruin (13:6–18), Isaiah prophesies that Babylon "will never be inhabited or lived in through all generations" but will be tenanted only by wild creatures (20–22). To this day Babylon has remained a heap of ruins and uninhabited, since its fall was initiated by Cyrus in 539 B.C. Of its haughty kings, the prophet said, "All your pomp has been brought down to the grave" (14:11). Further edicts of doom follow against Assyria, the Philistines, Moab, Damascus, Cush (Ethiopia), Egypt, Arabia, Tyre, and then unrepentant Judah.

The Missing King

Sargon, king of Assyria, is named in the opening verse of chapter 20. For almost two thousand years this was the only mention of Sargon's name in ancient literature. Critics said the Bible had blundered, there was no Sargon king of Assyria. Then in 1842 there was the remarkable discovery of the ruins of Sargon's palace in Nineveh, with treasures and inscriptions showing him to have been one of Assyria's greatest kings. Time and again the spade of the archeologist has amazingly confirmed the accuracy of the Bible.

A Living Object Lesson

Isaiah is commanded by the Lord to go barefoot and half-naked for three years as a sign and symbol of warning against alliance with Egypt and Ethiopia (chapter 20). Isaiah, gifted of mind and sensitive of soul, was willing to become an object of derision to get across the message of God. He became a walking parable, dressed as a captive to dramatize God's message not to trust the powers of this world which in the end leave us captive and ashamed.

The Salvation Army, in earlier days, often resorted to unconventional means to communicate the Word of God. The Army flourished then with souls and growth. May we never become too sophisticated or respectable and, as a result, turn away from any means by which we can bring people to Christ. The unconventional for God has been a hallmark of the Army's passion for souls.

The End of the World

The next four chapters, 24–27, are an epilogue of apocalyptic prophecy to the first 23 chapters. They sum up God's judgments on individual nations with a universal decree of punishment, the whole earth coming under God's judgment for sin: "The earth will be completely laid waste. . . . The earth is defiled by its people. . . . Therefore a curse consumes the earth" (24:3, 5, 6). Man's sin corrupts and contaminates not only himself but his environment. His rebellion against God brings on terrestrial convulsions: "The earth is broken up and reels like a drunkard" (19, 20). The ominous threat of nuclear holocaust renders Isaiah's words more than idle speculation.

But in the midst of the appalling doom emerges songs of praise to the Lord who is "a refuge for the needy in his distress, a shelter from the storm" (25:4). The Lord is praised who ultimately will swallow up death forever. "The Sovereign Lord will wipe away the tears from all faces" (8). This stupendous promise and daring declaration of the prophet was later echoed in the New Testament and had its fulfillment in our Lord's resurrection and triumph over death.

The darker the storm and clouds, the brighter the rainbow. And here in the midst of the darkest passages of this book shines one of the most radiant gems of the prophet: "You will keep in perfect peace him whose mind is steadfast, because he trusts in You" (26:3). The Hebrew for "perfect peace" is *shalom shalom,* the rich term for well-being, fulfillment, abiding peace. In the darkest storm, He gives a calm. When all is turbulent about us, we can hear His voice, "Peace, be still." The words of the song ask: "Peace, perfect peace, in this dark world of sin?" And it answers: "The voice of Jesus whispers peace within."

These passages impart a theology of history. They depict the fragile and temporary nature of tyrants and temporal power and that history's mills "grind slow but wondrous fine." God is sovereign. The course of events are under His control, and He will fulfill His ultimate plan for man. We are reminded in no uncertain terms that there will be a day of accountability and judgment for every person. History is His story and "All this comes from the Lord Almighty, wonderful in counsel and magnificent in wisdom" (28:29). Isaiah's message for us is: "In repentance and rest is your salvation, in quietness and trust is your strength" (30:15). And emerging from the lurid scenes of doom is the lyrical line and the precious promise: "You shall have a song as in the night when a holy festival is kept" (30:29 NKJV). Praise God. In the darkest night He gives a song of hope and deliverance.

SOMETHING TO THINK ABOUT

1. Why did Isaiah focus on the theme of salvation? Salvation from what, for what?

2. What will become of Babylon? What happened to their grand empire?

3. How did Isaiah dramatize his message?

4. How does the Lord pause in the midst of judgment to provide a promise of hope and restoration? Why?

FOUR

MALACHI: A WAKE-UP CALL

A. KENNETH WILSON

Major Wilson's work on features, profiles, and evangelism pieces frequently appears in *The War Cry*. In addition, he writes for other American as well as international Salvation Army publications, often combining humor with a keen eye for how the gospel intersects with history and culture.

Malachi, the last book of the Old Testament, speaks the final word to a wayward people preceding 400 years of silence until John the Baptist came crying in the wilderness, "prepare the way of the Lord." Malachi's ancient message is as relevant as the evening news.

1: How Have You Loved Us?

IT SEEMS FITTING THAT WE MODERN CHRISTIANS STILL REFER TO God as "Father," since the Bible presents a documentary of His dealings with His stubborn children. The book of Malachi chronicles how we, like the people of Israel in biblical times, have not given the Lord the respect and love due to Him.

Malachi's dialogue gives instruction to our post-modern world, in which truth is relative and open to personal interpretation. Because for many there are no absolutes, including the things of God, feelings and perceptions become their reality. God's love is real—sovereign, unconditional and irrevocable. Their perception of it is not.

Evangelical Christians have sometimes found a home in Scripture where it speaks of grace, freedom, and free will, bypassing the parts dealing with obedience and reverence. They are like employees who memorize the sections of the staff handbook concerning salary and days off, while neglecting those covering punctuality, quality of work and attitude. The prophecy of Malachi is not past business that has nothing to do with grace and forgiveness. Like all of Scripture, Malachi speaks of God creating in the hearts and lives of all believers the character of God making us who God is—holy. We are commanded to be holy, "just as He who called you is holy, so be holy in all you do; for it is written: 'Be holy, because I am holy'" (1 Peter 1:15–16). Holiness is to be evident in our nature and behavior, making both heart and worship right with God.

We know very little of Malachi the man except that his name means "my messenger," that the book was written during the period of Israel's return from captivity in the period 450–400 B.C., and that it is a companion to the historical books of Ezra and Nehemiah. Malachi's message of obedience to God demonstrated holy character and not just religious obligation.

The people of Israel were exiled for their flagrant disobedience. Morally and spiritually bankrupt, they pushed acceptance of evil to new depths of depravity until God used the Persians to deliver a collective attitude adjustment.

At the end of their captivity, they returned home with high expectations—that the land would be renewed with crops, cities and residents; that the Temple and the walls of Jerusalem would be rebuilt in even more magnificent fashion than in the glorious days of Kings David and Solomon; that the Messiah would come and usher in a kingdom where Israel would be the focal point of the entire world; and that life would be simple, easy and affluent.

The reality was that the crops were poor and the restoration work was hard. The aspirations of ease, influence and affluence never materialized. Over time those responsible for worship and religious training became careless in performing their assigned tasks, believing that God had stopped caring for them. They reasoned that if He truly cared, they would be the bosses and not the underlings. Their spiritual collapse came with a whiny "It's not fair. We deserve better."

As disobedient as they were, the Israelites were still God's covenant people, and He never reneges on His promises. A covenant is more than a contract. It is an oath that cannot be broken without severe consequences. God made covenants throughout the Bible—with Adam, Abraham, the Levites, and others. To break His covenant would mean that God would no longer be God.

"How Do You Love Us?"

Well aware of the national and spiritual depression, Malachi begins his entreaty by taking God's position, sharing His words in dialogue with the nation: "O how I have loved you" (see 1:2). Not only had God loved them in the past or when their performance was up to par, but "I have loved you and will always love you without reserve or condition." God shows His patience even as His people slide back to the brink of ruin.

Still locked in their self-absorption, the Israelites respond to God's tenderness saying, "How do You love us?" Back in my neighborhood this response would have been, "Say what?"

"Yeah right, God. But what have You done for us lately? How do You love us?" they cried. "If You loved us You would send us the Messiah now. Why are we still subject to the Persians? Why aren't we rich and living in palaces?"

The Israelites try to dictate terms for God's provision—"prove Your love, but do it our way." In response God says, "I love you, and let Me show you the evidence of how."

Malachi did not have an easy task. The days of a prophet standing with authority, giving the message with a "thus says the Lord," were long gone. The former exiles were as hard-headed as their ancestors. Malachi had to present a logical argument to prove what used to be accepted as divine fact. "Take a look at Edom and Esau," He begins (2–4). "Jacob I have loved . . . Esau I have hated." This was not the Lord speaking literally of hatred but of degrees—"I have loved Jacob and Israel and his descendants and have never given up on them even through the darkest times, the deepest depravities or the sternest correction. But Edom, the nation that stood in the way of Israel and rejoiced when Israel was taken into captivity, is no more. They will try to rebuild but Edom will never recover its national power and prestige."

Malachi reminds the people that it was the Lord who brought them home and sealed Edom's fate. In verse 4 God is "the Lord almighty." The phrase in Hebrew is "the Lord of armies" (NIV) or "the Lord of hosts" (KJV). The Lord is a mighty King, not some senile grandfather who would let any misbehavior pass as he spoils his grandchildren.

But rather than appreciate what God had done in terms of love and protection, the Israelites viewed the things of God as punishment. They treated obedience to His commands as obligations done not to please God but to keep their jobs. Their efforts could not earn God's affection—that was given unconditionally—but should have shown how much His love was valued.

Can you imagine a wedding where the groom asks the minister during the exchange of vows, "What is the least I have to do to keep this marriage alive? Remember twenty-five percent of our anniversaries? Say 'I love you' once a month? Forget this 'worse, poorer, sickness' stuff. How about better, richer, and healthy—or until I get a better offer?"

I can hear the Israelites now: "God, what is the least we have to do and still be under Your care? Partially obey, irregularly worship, have selective memory loss?"

Malachi reminds them and us that God says, "I have always loved you," but He is God not just of Israel but of the entire universe. Rather than receive the judgment they deserved, the Lord allowed four hundred years to pass for Israel to contemplate Malachi's message until He did something to show His love for His people. He sent His Son Jesus into the world. And no one asked, "How have You loved us?" again.

SOMETHING TO THINK ABOUT

1. How is it possible for flawed people to "be holy, because I [the Lord] am holy?"

2. How has God demonstrated His love and faithfulness to you in the past? How have you demonstrated your lack of the same at times?

3. How has God corrected you in ways that appeared harsh or painful at the outset but that were really for your own good?

4. What is the least you can do to keep your significant relationships (e.g., marriage, children, friends, family) going? What is the least you can do to keep the relationship with the Lord going? What is the most you can do?

2: Left–overs, Castoffs, and Junk

WINNING NO POINTS FOR BEING POLITICALLY CORRECT OR HARMLESSLY TOLERANT, Malachi addresses the matter of Israel's insult to the majesty and holiness of God. Malachi's comments are directed first at the priests—the professional clergy of the day—for their lack of joyful obedience as they teach Israel how to worship. Had they lived up to their calling, the people might have behaved differently. But in fact they mirrored their congregations—apathetic, skeptical, and unappreciative. True devotion became detached professionalism. They treated the things of God with contempt, justly earning His great displeasure.

"How Have We Shown Contempt?"

Malachi begins with two familiar images of God—Father and Lord. "A son honors his father, and a servant his master. 'If I am a father, where is the honor due Me? If I am a master, where is the respect due Me?' says the Lord. 'It is you, O priests, who show contempt for My name'" (Malachi 1:6).

Predictably enough, the priests respond, "How have we shown contempt for Your name?" Or perhaps, "Huh? When did we ever do that?"

The Lord replies, "You place defiled food on My altar."

And again, "Say what? How have we defiled You?"

For centuries the name of the Lord was never spoken aloud for fear that the mere uttering of it might show disrespect. Instead there were a series of vowels that have come down to us today as "Yahweh" or "Jehovah." But by Malachi's time the name was spoken freely without fear. Where is the terror of things so holy that they cannot be understood or disobeyed? Where is the awe for a holy God that is as far above us as we are beneath Him? If all we have is affection based on happy moods, our worship becomes sloppy and sentimental, depending more on how we feel than on how God does. Shallow worship will not see us through difficult times any more than will rigid obedience and conformity to a list of rules and regulations that soon becomes legalistic and dry. Honor, fear, love, and obedience all fit together in a balanced spiritual relationship.

What did the priests and people do that was so wrong? There was no overt profanity as they offered sacrifices of the proper type and at the appointed times—like clockwork. They knew the dietary laws from Leviticus and never offered anything from the banned list.

God says, "You despise My name."

The word "despise" has a negative emotional charge in English that is not always carried from the Hebrew. In this case "despise" is not a malevolent contempt but rather the holding of something or someone in such low regard that you consider them nearly worthless. God said through Malachi that the priests thought their relationship with God was worthless because they considered His name and altar worthless.

Sacrificing from the Trash

For a sacrifice to be acceptable, animals were to be clean, without disease or defect. Malachi indicates rather that the animals were diseased, crippled and possibly even stolen. God viewed them as unclean because they cost the giver nothing. It is no sacrifice to give what would have otherwise gone out with the trash. Do we do the same with our service and worship to God?

Malachi gave the priests and people a lesson in animal husbandry, where the weak are culled and the best are kept to perpetuate the animal's best traits, since good livestock is of economic value. The people didn't mind sacrificing leftovers, but they wanted to keep the best. But that is what the Lord wants—our best, not the junk. The people wanted to hold on to their possessions, while God wanted to show that He would provide if they trusted Him. Trust became a matter of faith, not a matter of finance.

"You despise My name, you profane it—because you don't think I am worth your best. You turn up your noses at My altar, My worship, My house as if it is beneath you," says the Lord.

"You would not treat an earthly ruler that way. So why act that way to God?" asks Malachi. But the Israelites did not understand the object lesson.

How about a contemporary version of Malachi's message? Imagine a young man trying to impress his girlfriend. She wants to be treated as a special person and he wants to save a few bucks.

Imagine if he calls her collect, has her buy dinner, gas, and the movie tickets. In a rare show of generosity, he stops by a cemetery where there has been a funeral earlier that day and brings his girl flowers that were left on the graveside. Her first indication of trouble comes when she notices the banner in the bouquet that reads "In loving memory." That would certainly fit the Hebrew definition of "despise"—treating someone as worthless, not even meriting a love offering.

"What's the Big Deal, God?"

"Why does it have to be a perfect animal?" whined the priests. "It's just one dead animal, more or less. What's the big deal, God?"

The animal needed to be valuable because sin has such a high pricetag. Sin costs everything we have—life, peace, and our relationship with God. The offering had to be perfect because God was preparing to do something that could only come from His great heart. He was going to make it possible for His people to live free from the bondage of sin. He was going to give His best and most beautiful to pay the cost of sin—His Son Jesus—so we can share in the holy nature of God.

God's name was His reputation, His love, His compassion, His righteousness, His provision, and above all, His holiness—and the Israelites had made His name appear valueless. Malachi reminded them that God commanded them not to have any other gods above Him. Obedience matters. Holiness matters. Malachi stressed that because of the Israelites' poor witness and example, other people would think less of God.

Malachi says that it would be better to close the Temple rather than live a lie. Perhaps the biggest lie is that we think we are doing God a favor by going through the motions of worship, doing less than our best. We have to ask, like Malachi's listeners, "How much is God worth?" That is a far more demanding question than theirs: "What's in it for me?"

A relationship with God is not a contractual arrangement whereby we declare the terms and the Lord pays off. We cannot manipulate God. Malachi indicates that our proper response to God's concern should be, "Isn't there something else I can do to be even closer to You?" God's blessing did not then and still does not equal financial prosperity. Sometimes He grants that, but other times He teaches us trust when times are tough.

I am surprised that the Israelites did not tar and feather Malachi for his scathing rebuke. Rather, I hope they learned that their offerings as well as their motives were flawed and decided to seek the Lord's forgiveness and correction.

Though Malachi's message was first directed at the priests, the rest of us are not off the hook. The Lord deserves and wants the best we have to offer—our work, energy, time, and devotion—or else we make Him sick with our disobedience. Dare we give less than our best?

SOMETHING TO THINK ABOUT

1. Have we ever treated God with contempt? How?

2. What type of sacrifice does God want and require from us?

3. Have you ever given the Lord less than your best? How?

4. Why was the Lord so upset with defective, second-rate offerings?

3: Three Broken Covenants

THE OLD ADAGE SAYS THAT "PROMISES ARE MADE TO BE BROKEN." ONE OF THE HARDEST lessons to learn in life is that promises are made to be kept—not broken. We are tested all the time as we make commitments to church, to work and especially to our families. We try our best but we sometimes fail miserably at keeping true to our word. This section of Malachi is perhaps the most difficult since it deals with the family of God whose members have broken His covenants and dealt wickedly with each other.

Over the course of Scripture, God made many solemn promises, covenants—with the nation Israel. More than binding legal agreements, they were irrevocable pledges of fidelity between the people and God. A contract forges an agreement between two parties to perform some service within certain limits. In a covenant, two parties give themselves to the pledge without limits. God offered Himself entirely to the people and invited them to do the same.

The Israelites made a solemn covenant with God at Mt. Sinai. Less than five weeks later, though, they were dancing around the Golden Calf as if nothing had happened. By the time of Malachi, the Israelites had returned from captivity after their extensive and collective attitude adjustment. So what went wrong? Malachi reminded them that they had broken covenants almost as a matter of common practice. Five times in a span of fourteen verses the prophet refers to violated covenants. Three are described in detail:

- of Levi—between God and the priests (Malachi 2:1–9)

- of the fathers—between the people and God (10–12)

- of the husbands—with their wives (13–16)

All three covenants were broken because the people couldn't keep those they had made with God. The Apostle John conveys a similar idea. "If anyone says, 'I love God,' yet hates his brother, he is a liar. For anyone who does not love his brother, whom he has seen, cannot love God, whom he has not seen" (1 John 4:20). The Lord says, "Don't tell Me that you love Me when you mistreat those closest to you."

Covenant of Levi and the Priests

In Malachi chapter 2, the prophet pronounces judgment on the priests in the name of the Lord. The Lord had a special relationship with His priests dating back from the days of providing them an inheritance in the Promised Land. If they devoted themselves entirely to the Lord's work, He would bless them so well that they would not need to inherit real estate to sustain themselves.

They were to give glory to God and honor His name (2:1). Even as the rebuke was being delivered, the Lord gave the priests opportunity to change their ways. "'If you do not listen, and if you do not set your heart to honor My name,' says the Lord Almighty, 'I will send a curse upon you, and will curse your blessings'" (2).

The priests had the Torah, the law—not just a rule book but the divinely given manual for living in right relationship with God. Armed with that instruction, the priests were called to be mediators between people and God. The priests were to be a window through which people saw God and His unobstructed plan for their lives. They were to be like the old window cleaner commercial that claimed: "glass so clean it seems to disappear."

By now, the priests were fixed on themselves and wanted to hear, "Wow, what a great window!" They were self-aggrandizing, while watering down God's message and showing favoritism to the wealthy and influential. Malachi, speaking for God, rebuked them: "You have turned from the way and by your teaching have caused many to stumble. You have violated the covenant with Levi" (8).

In the New Testament, after four hundred years of silence, you can read Jesus' sharp criticism of the Pharisees, the inheritors of the old priesthood. Jesus decried their empty worship and spoke of them as "whitewashed tombs"—lovely on the outside while inside filled with death and decay; enjoying public acclaim while lacking purity and power.

Covenant of the Fathers

Malachi continues, "Have we not all one Father? Did not one God create us? Why do we profane the covenant of our fathers by breaking faith with one another?" (10). They broke faith with the people of God by marrying unbelievers. The Lord promised to make Abraham a great nation with descendants as numerous as grains of sand on the beach. Quite a promise to an old man with one son born late in life to an aging mother!

These are the terms of the covenant: "When the Lord your God brings you into the land you are entering to possess and drives out before you many nations . . . do not intermarry with them. Do not give your daughters to their sons or take their daughters for your sons, for they will turn your sons away from following Me to serve other gods, and the Lord's anger will burn against you and will quickly destroy you. This is what you are to do to them: Break down their altars, smash their sacred stones, cut down their Asherah poles and burn their idols in the fire. For you are a people holy to the Lord your God. The Lord your God has chosen you out of all the peoples on the face of the earth to be His people, His treasured possession" (Deuteronomy 7:1-6).

This is not a popular section of Malachi's message but one that seems harsh and intolerant. You would think his listeners would have learned a lesson from the exile and the example of King Solomon and his three hundred foreign wives. Solomon's faith did not influence the new spouses for good, but rather, their idolatry weakened him to the point of spiritual uselessness.

The lesson was that they could not accept a "live and let live" attitude with sin any more than with cancer. One kills the body, the other the soul. The priests and the leaders should have remembered and obeyed but instead brought spouses opposed to the things of God into the family and fellowship.

Covenant with Wives and Families

In Malachi's day, multiple marriages were permitted—although not encouraged. The prophet declared that the Lord was tired of the people's crying and pleading as they came to offer their sacrifices, because they had broken their covenant of love with their wives. The Lord witnesses our vows and expects them to be honored.

The men were replacing the "wives of their youth" with younger, more favored women. And we thought we invented the male midlife crisis! Just because a man wants to recapture some of his youthful virility, the Lord will not allow him to replace his fifty-year-old wife with a pair of twenty-five-year-old girlfriends. And the same applies to the ladies, too!

Marriage, the covenant that applies divine "new math" where 1+1=1 ("a man and woman will be united and be one flesh"), is a promise that is meant to be kept—and not just until a better offer comes along. Spouses are not to be tossed aside with the same disdain as tossing a coat over the back of a chair. Malachi points out that the failure to keep family and spousal covenants is a natural by-product of sin. If we cannot maintain intimate personal family relationships, how can we keep faith with God?

All three of these covenants in Malachi's rebuke deal with problems of broken faith between God and His priests, families, and husbands and wives. All three involve violent relationship-breaking acts where there are no winners—only losers. Such is the devouring character of the sinful self that wants to satisfy its own needs regardless of the needs of others. Priests wanted to glorify themselves. Fathers wanted to please themselves. Spouses declared their desires were not being met and demanded their right to satisfy themselves. The emphasis is always on self—I will get my needs met no matter what, regardless of what God wants.

But in truth our greatest need is for God. Nothing else can satisfy—not work, ministry, spouse, kids, church or anything but a deep, intimate relationship with God. As in the time of Malachi, the family still needs leaders, followers, fathers, mothers, husbands and wives to be obedient to the plan and leading of God.

Something to Think About

1. If promises are meant to be kept, how have you kept your promises to God, your spouse, your family, yourself?

2. How can we be a "window" rather than a "door?"

3. Which needs in your life remain unmet? How does God enter into the situation?

4. What have you substituted for God in meeting those needs?

4: "Ready or Not, Here I Come!"

THE PEOPLE OF ISRAEL, HAVING LISTENED TO THE PROPHET MALACHI'S CALL TO GIVE what is best in themselves to God, next complain that the result was not as expected.

"Where is the God of justice?" they demanded. "We followed the rules, we played fair and what has it gotten us? Nothing. Even the pagan unbelievers live better than we do, with big houses and nice things. Thanks, God—for nothing! Show us the money! It is time for You to pay up."

The people of Israel whined, thinking that their unrighteous siblings were getting a better deal than they were. Parents know what that sounds like, and it's not pretty. They wanted the Lord to intervene, not to make things right, but to make things easy.

"Where is the God of justice?" Did they understand what they were asking? Did they really want to get what they deserved?

Malachi tells the people that God has heard their cries for justice and announces, "Ready or not—here I come." God will send His messenger and set things right. Unlike the child's game "Hide and Seek," when the Lord comes, you had better be ready; the "or not" is not something to be taken lightly. Malachi begins by saying that "you have wearied the Lord with all your words" (2:17). We would say, "God is just plain sick and tired of all your talk." I have never fully understood the pairing of illness and fatigue, although I know the feeling. The Lord was sick of words without heart obedience. Activity they had; holy character they lacked.

"You sniff at it," says the prophet. "You treat the Lord like you're turning up your nose at Grandma's funky tuna casserole! You're tired? God is even more tired!"

The people of Israel asked, "Will righteousness prosper? Will sin be punished? Why does it seem that the good people have tougher times than the bad ones?" The questions we must ask if we are going to grow in our service and relationship with God are: "Why am I doing this? Who am I doing this for? Am I serving God for some sort of divine payoff, or just because He loves me and I love Him?"

The scenario between the Lord and the thick-headed people reminds me of my own dad. He, like most parents, often asked rhetorical questions to convey his exasperation and instruction.

"How many times do I have to remind you?" he would ask me, concerning some family chore I had conveniently forgotten. "Eight hundred forty-seven," I casually replied, thinking myself most clever. He failed to see the humor. God has, too.

The Lord Sends His Messenger

Malachi informs the people that God is going to do something drastic. Unlike the government and most churches, He is not going to enact new regulations or programs. He will send a person, His messenger, to straighten things out.

God says, "Behold, I send My messenger." This is where things get confusing, for it seems like there are three messengers. In reality there are two distinct events and personalities. One is the coming of the messenger to prepare the way for God, and the other is the Lord Himself. Malachi, whose name means "messenger," was not the messenger himself but the one appointed to deliver the first word of those who are coming.

"'I will send My messenger, who will prepare the way before Me. Then . . . the Lord you are seeking will come to His temple; the messenger of the covenant, whom you desire, will come,' says the Lord Almighty" (Malachi 3:1).

The first messenger who would prepare the way was John the Baptizer. (See Mark 1:2–3). I call him that instead of John the Baptist to eliminate any possible misunderstanding connecting him with a particular denomination. John would complete the prophecy of the "voice of one calling: 'In the desert prepare the way for the Lord; make straight in the wilderness a highway for our God. Every valley shall be raised up, every mountain and hill made low; the rough ground shall become level, the rugged places a plain. And the glory of the Lord will be revealed, and all mankind together will see it. For the mouth of the Lord has spoken'" (Isaiah 40:3–5).

John was the advance man for the coming of the Messiah, not drumming up business like when the circus comes to town, but making sure people knew that the prophecy they had long expected was coming their way. John knew he was not the main event. "I [John] baptize you with water for repentance. But after me will come One who is more powerful than I, whose sandals I am not fit to carry. He will baptize you with the Holy Spirit and with fire" (Matthew 3:11).

The second messenger, according to Scripture, will come quickly—not in terms of speed but in terms of suddenness. Once things begin to be revealed by John the Baptizer—the first messenger—pay close attention, for the pace will pick up dramatically.

The second use of the "Lord Almighty" in Malachi is not *Adonai* but the rarer *ha–Adon*, the literal use of the word "Lord." This is the same "Lord" used by Peter in Acts 2:36, when he declared on the Day of Pentecost that the messenger is Jesus: "Therefore let all Israel be assured of this: God has made this Jesus, whom you crucified, both Lord and Christ" (Acts 2:36).

The Messenger of the New Covenant

Jesus Christ, the one promised by Malachi, would be the messenger of the new covenant—to replace the one broken by Israel for generations. He would make a new pledge, not written on tablets of stone like those their fathers broke, but written on the hearts of believers (see Jeremiah 31:31); not sealed with the blood of bulls as in the days of Moses (see Exodus 24), but by His own blood for the payment for our sin.

Malachi reminded his hearers that in their eagerness for God to adjust the balance of power in their favor, the terms of the old covenant had to be paid. They wanted to see a financial benefit, but what they had was a national debt of disobedience. The old covenant had to be paid and it was—in full—for all people, for all time. The cross set the balance sheet right. Sin is punished, but grace enters as divine credit in place of sin debt.

Malachi warns his listeners that the Messiah will come and will clean them like the refining of precious metals or like powerful bleaching soap (3:2-4). He will not come to reward disobedience and leave you as foul and rotten as before. Ready or not—here He comes to do the deep soul cleaning. But better to have Him do that than judge, for that will be much more severe (3:5).

Today as in Malachi's time, silversmiths purify the ore as it melts under great heat. Little by little the impurities are skimmed off as they rise to the surface. Only when the refiner can see his face in the gleaming liquid metal is it pure enough to be poured and fashioned. When we are heated by the fire of the Holy Spirit, Christ skims away the impurities of our lives so that the reflection of His holiness and character can be seen in us.

I don't have much silver, but I do recall when my grandmother came after me with a bar of Lava soap. She scrubbed until she nearly took the skin right off! The Lord's "soap" scrubs all the way down to clean the heart, motives and thoughts. Then and only then will our sacrifice and worship be acceptable and pleasant to the Lord. But if they are not cleaned up, Malachi 3:5 says that judgment will fall against four groups in particular:

· Sorcerers—those who try to manipulate God to conform to their terms, not His.

· Adulterers—those who demand to have their selfish needs and desires met even if means breaking covenant relationships with God and each other.

68

· Perjurers—those who lie to ruin others and advance themselves.

· Those who defraud and oppress—who harm those without the means to fight back.

Sins against the weakest members of society have always been particularly offensive to God, since the Lord is as concerned about our morals and relationships as He is with our piety.

Malachi delivered his announcement and believed by faith what he would never live to see, that all would end just as God promised. What Malachi spoke of before the start of four hundred years of silence smothered the land, Jesus completed. That silence was gloriously broken by a torrent of angelic singing witnessed by poor shepherds on a Bethlehem hillside.

"Don't be afraid. I bring you good news of great joy and you are hearing it first. Do you remember the words of old Malachi? He was right. Today in the City of David is born to you a Savior; He is Christ the Lord. Glory to God in the highest!" (See Luke 2:8–14).

Way to go Malachi! Your divine telegram of good news has been delivered and the Messenger of the new covenant has come!

Something to Think About

1. As far as your relationship with God is concerned, have you ever thought, "What's in it for me?" What is in it for you?

2. What does God need to change in you to make you the person He intended you to be?

3. What is the new covenant? How is that one different than the old?

4. Since God has no needs as such, what could you give Him that would be truly pleasing?

5: Will You Rob God?

"OKAY, MALACHI," THE ISRAELITES SAY, "WE HAVE SUFFERED THROUGH YOUR LONG harangue about our covenant breaking, greed, unacceptable sacrifices, and the rest of our long list of sins. Do you have any good news for us?"

"I've good news and bad news," Malachi says. "The good news is that God loves you, in spite of how shabbily you have treated Him."

Malachi goes on to share the permanence of God, who remembers His covenants even when we don't. The fact that God never renegotiates His promises is all that kept the Israelites from being toasted like a replay of Sodom and Gomorrah! How thrilling to know that God sees us with delight, not as failures or as inadequate. The fact that He loves us is good news. But that He likes us—that is almost too wonderful to express. God has to love us—that is His nature; but to like us, and to want to spend time with us—that is truly amazing grace.

Malachi delivers God's message: "Return to Me and I will return to you" (3:7). The act of returning also required repentance—to do a 180° turn and go back the way you came. But the Israelites had forgotten God's instructions. Seeing God as the problem rather than admit their need for restoration, they demanded more information. "How are we to return?" they asked. "We haven't gone anywhere."

Malachi responds to their question with another. "Will a man rob God? Yet you rob me" (8).

"Say what? How can we rob God? We can't even see Him!"

"You do it," Malachi explained, "by robbing God of the tithes and offerings justly due Him." That is the bad news. As long as Malachi was railing against inadequate sacrifices and broken covenants, the people tolerated him. But messing with their money was way too personal.

The problem was not the tithes and offerings. Scripture records that the Lord "owns the cattle on a thousand hillsides" (Psalm 50:10), meaning that His abundance makes even the wealthiest rancher a pauper by comparison. If we used the same analogy today we'd probably say that God's plenty makes Microsoft look like the corner deli!

Not a Matter of Finance, but One of the Heart

Robbing God was not a matter of stewardship or finance, but of the heart—indicating a lack of faith in God's ability to provide, a lack of obedience to His commands and a lack of reverence, thinking God unworthy of their tithes or worship. The lack of giving was symptomatic of their contempt for God and how far they had drifted from Him. Their situation may have also been prompted by ignorance, caused by an unmotivated priesthood that never taught the people how to obey and how to worship.

Tithing, the principle of giving one tenth of your money to support the Lord's work, is not an investment program to receive divine blessings. It is an act of worship for the building of God's kingdom. The Israelites did not see that the issue is not that God takes ten percent but that He gives us the other ninety percent to use as we see fit. Along with those who refuse to give at all are those who give legalistically or begrudgingly. They think they are buying a heavenly lottery ticket, anticipating a big payoff. Malachi warns them to worship on God's terms and to stop trying to manipulate Him.

We may not consciously ask, "What is the least I can give and still have the Lord's provision, or at least keep Him off my case?" Yet our financial support is the last thing we give to God and the first thing we take back when we feel we are not getting what we deserve. But it's good that we don't always get what we want. The Lord always shows us a better way—His way.

Rather than announce the immediate demise of all concerned, the Lord issues a challenge through Malachi. "'Bring the whole tithe into the storehouse, that there may be food in My house. Test Me in this,' says the Lord Almighty, 'and see if I will not throw open the floodgates of heaven and pour out so much blessing that you will not have room enough for it. I will prevent pests from devouring your crops, and the vines in your fields will not cast their fruit. Then all the nations will call you blessed, for yours will be a delightful land'" (Malachi 3:10–12).

This is one of the few times that God gives a challenge to obey and see the fruits of it. Israel knew the danger of provoking Him, as they recalled their ancestors who spent years wandering after God led them out of Egypt, all because they tried His patience.

The faithful minority who feared and loved the Lord wrote all this down in a book of remembrance. They understood the concept of the tithe—it was not about making money but about developing trust. God still takes care of those who love Him. "'They will be mine,' says the Lord Almighty, 'in the day when I make up My treasured possession. I will spare them, just as in compassion a man spares his son who serves him'" (Malachi 3:17).

Some spoke harshly of the Lord's challenge, trying to drown out Malachi's message. The Lord responded, "You have said harsh things against Me, yet you ask, 'What have we said against You?' You have said, 'It is futile to serve God. What did we gain by carrying out His requirements and going about like mourners before the Lord Almighty?'" (13).

A Final Accounting

God, through Malachi, reminded them that one day the accounts will be settled and all will see who is wicked and who is righteous—those who serve God and those who do not (18). But Malachi could not end his message on such a dire warning. He needed to show that something wonderful was coming to those who trusted and obeyed. And, just as true, that something terrifying awaited the unrighteous and disobedient. Malachi indicates that history and prophecy are not just marking time but are advancing to two events—to the coming of Jesus Christ and the ultimate final judgment of the world. One would come in a measurable period of time—four hundred years—the other to be accomplished in God's time alone.

"'Surely the day is coming; it will burn like a furnace. All the arrogant and every evildoer will be stubble, and that day that is coming will set them on fire,' says the Lord Almighty. 'Not a root or a branch will be left to them. But for you who revere My name, the sun of righteousness will rise with healing in its wings. And you will go out and leap like calves released from the stall'" (Malachi 4:1–2).

The coming of Jesus, who will bring healing and restoration, will establish a new order based on grace, where ordinary people can live free from the penalty and power of sin and have Him recreate in their hearts who God is—holy. And with holiness comes adoration, worship, changed hearts, restored relationships and a deep sense of joy.

Malachi says that the righteous will be "like calves released from the stalls." I can imagine that—leaping, running, bouncing across a meadow—much like a six-year-old child, without a care in the world. But to the unrighteous who will reject Jesus when He comes to bring healing, there will be a spiritual audit in God's time. On that great "day of the Lord" all of mankind's cheapness, rebellion and disobedience will not stand up against the Lord's scrutiny as the rationalizations and excuses fall like dry grass before a wildfire.

Malachi ends with a promise and a warning. Things are desperate but not hopeless. Through the darkness God's dawn is coming. Malachi's listeners had four hundred years to think this over.

During that time there were many who gave up, many who could care less but also many who were ready and eager.

When Jesus was presented in the Temple as a baby, as recorded in Luke 2:21–32, Simeon, an old man by then, said that he could die happy since he had seen the completion of Malachi's promise. I can well imagine this stately gentleman with gray hair and beard, bearing many a care line on his weathered face, leaping and bouncing and rejoicing—just like a new calf.

"So what does this have to do with me?" you may ask. You can choose to be arrogant and rob God, or you can trust Him—with your life, your soul, your family, and even your money.

> *But we never can prove*
> *The delights of His love,*
> *Until all on the altar we lay;*
> *For the favor He shows,*
> *And the joy He bestows,*
> *Are for those who will trust and obey.*
> *Trust and obey,*
> *For there's no other way*
> *To be happy in Jesus*
> *But to trust and obey.*
>
> John Henry Sammis

Thanks, Malachi—we needed the reminder.

SOMETHING TO THINK ABOUT

1. Have we robbed God? How?

2. Why is stewardship a matter of the heart and not of finance?

3. How do we "bring the whole tithe into the storehouse?"

4. Of all the things you have accomplished, which ones will last for years to come?

A PORTRAIT OF PROVISION

The God who provides is revealed in the lives of Naomi who "found a way when there was no way," and Ruth, who dared to embrace the people and God of the Hebrews. The loving shepherd is painted throughout Psalm 23 and in the epistles of Peter, written to encourage a persecuted people. Isaac, the child of promise, reveals God's providential care for the nation of Israel and for the world that would inherit the promise with them.

FIVE

RUTH: GOD WILL MAKE A WAY

MARLENE CHASE

Lt. Colonel Marlene Chase is editor in chief and literary secretary for the Army's USA National Publications, where she oversees the production of *The War Cry, Young Salvationist,* the biannual journal *Word and Deed,* the Women's Ministries Resources, and Crest Books. She conducts communication and publication workshops and seminars, contributing poetry and other creative works to various Christian publications.

The book of Ruth is an exquisitely wrought jewel of Hebrew narrative art. Compact, vivid, and dramatic, its unknown author was a master unparalleled by such literary greats as Chaucer or O. Henry. A love story, the book reveals God's tender care through those who reflect His goodness in their lives.

1: A Way Where There Is No Way

RUTH IS A BOOK RICH IN THEOLOGICAL THEMES, PARTICULARLY redemption. The word redemption itself, in its various forms, occurs twenty-three times. As an episode in the ancestry of David, the book of Ruth sheds light on his role in the history of redemption. While Jewish tradition points to Samuel as the storyteller, it is unlikely that he is the author of Ruth because of the mention of David (Ruth 4:17,21). Such mention implies a date later than the literary style reminiscent of Samuel's era, possibly written within the wide span of time ranging from the monarchy to the post–exilic community.

For some, the book of Ruth is problematic. It has been pointed out that the book illustrates long-term economic security of women as dependent upon marriage to a wealthy man (Ruth's security through Boaz). Such an approach, it is rightly argued, is not structurally adequate to the full humanity of women, at least as we understand it in most western cultures. Some point to the celebration of a boy child (4:13) as indicative that girls are devalued in the narrative. But embodied in the book are the more enduring and underlying principles of inclusion of the stranger and sustenance and respect for all ages and both genders.

"In the context of real life, the Bible seems refreshingly whole, an honest reflection on humanity in relation to the sacred and the profane," writes Kathleen Norris in *Amazing Grace*. The lively and candid book of Ruth, like all of Scripture, is "God-breathed and is useful for teaching, rebuking, correcting and training in righteousness" (2 Timothy 3:16). This exciting narrative invites the reader to sincere exploration of God's purposes through human instrumentation.

God's Faithfulness

The central story is Naomi's passage from emptiness to fullness through the selfless acts of Ruth and Boaz, whom God has chosen to bless Naomi. Unlike the only other book of the Bible that bears the name of a woman (Esther), in the book of Ruth God is not only mentioned but repeatedly referenced by the various characters, most often in their prayers, sometimes in other contexts. Throughout the book, His hand is visible in the movements of people who will honor Him and bring restoration to a grieving woman and a hurting nation.

The story of Ruth reflects the remnant of true faith and piety. It reveals the faithfulness of God through surprising people and means. God chooses to show His love through a Moabitess who proves to be a true daughter of Israel and a worthy ancestress of David. She exemplifies the truth that participation in the kingdom of God is decided not by blood and birth, but by obedience to God and faith in His promises. Ruth's place in the ancestry of David signifies that all nations will be represented in the kingdom of David's greater Son, Jesus Christ (Matthew 1:1).

God's Inclusive Love

In the opening genealogy of the Gospel according to Matthew, Ruth is one of four women included in a list of forty-two generations of male ancestors of "Joseph the husband of Mary, of whom was born Jesus" (Matthew 1:16). The other three women are Tamar (mother of Perez), Rahab, and the "wife of Uriah." None seem to fit a conventional or expected mode. Ruth, Rahab, and the wife of Uriah (Bathsheba) are viewed as Gentiles according to Old Testament tradition, and Tamar is regarded as non-Israelite in later Jewish tradition. This points to the universality of God's love and obedience to Him as qualification for entering the kingdom of God.

God's Peaceable Kingdom

The "once upon a time" of Ruth was "in the days when the judges ruled." It was a time of warfare, violence and continual disobedience on the part of Israel. By contrast, Ruth features a peaceful village, orderly public process and a move by faithful persons toward justice and generosity. The story begins with famine and death as Naomi journeys back to Bethlehem (ironically "house of bread"). It ends with community harvest and rejoicing over the birth of a baby. The portrait of the community may be regarded as a microcosm of the peaceable kingdom envisioned by the prophetic tradition. It is a community where the marginalized are included, children and the elderly are cared for and all persons are nourished.

God's Individual Love

The book opens as Naomi, Ruth's mother-in-law, begins her journey back to God from a position of emptiness. It is not hard to imagine why she said, "call me Mara [bitter]" (Ruth 1:20). Naomi means "pleasant," but there was nothing pleasant about her life as she set off from Moab to her hometown in Judah. She had been emptied of all that gave her life meaning. She was bereaved of both husband and sons. She had no hope for the future because in that culture a woman had no means of support outside of male provision. She had no home, no money and two daughters-in-law for whom she was expected to provide.

She decided to do the only thing she could do—return to her country. Return, perhaps to die. "The Lord's hand has gone out against me!" Naomi says as she urges Orpah and Ruth to go back to Moab, back to their people, back to their gods (1:13). At this point in the narrative she is a desolate woman. If she has any hope at all, it is only that perhaps starvation might be held at bay a little longer.

The account of Ruth shows that God never leaves us, even when we have given up hope. Three generations after Naomi was restored to joy and wholeness, Ruth's great grandson David would testify to the faithfulness of the God who makes a way where there is no way. "Where can I flee from Your presence? . . . If I rise on the wings of the dawn, if I settle on the far side of the sea, even there Your hand will guide me, Your right hand will hold me fast" (Psalm 139:7,9).

In succeeding articles in this series, we will explore how God leads Naomi and Ruth from Moab to Bethlehem, from emptiness to fullness, from despair to hope, from destitution to security. God made a way for Naomi when there was no way. And He makes a way for us who find ourselves without the means to achieve the meaning and joy we crave in our lives. God's plan for our eternal redemption would ultimately bring us to Jesus, the Author and Finisher of our faith, who testified of Himself, "I am the Way, the Truth and the Life."

SOMETHING TO THINK ABOUT

1. Ruth is an example of Hebrew narrative art that is rich in theological themes, particularly redemption. What other themes or topics describing how God works with people can you glean from this introduction to the book?

2. How does God's interaction with Ruth symbolize His inclusive love for people?

3. There are forty-two generations of male ancestors included in the gospel of Matthew. Who are the four women named? What does their inclusion say about the gospel?

4. Have you ever been in a situation where there seemed no way out, like Naomi was? God showed His faithfulness to her and provided a means to hope. How has God revealed a way out of your situation?

2: At the Crossroads

THE MOST MEMORABLE, BEST-LOVED PASSAGE IN THE BOOK OF RUTH PROVIDES A primary redemption motif: "Don't urge me to leave you or to turn back from you. Where you go I will go, and where you stay I will stay. Your people will be my people and your God my God. Where you die I will die, and there I will be buried. May the Lord deal with me, be it ever so severely, if anything but death separates you and me" (Ruth 1:16-17). This passage prompts a question in the reader's mind. What might have led up to that moment when Ruth sealed her intention to accompany her mother-in-law Naomi back to Judah? What persuaded her to make her astonishing fourfold promise?

Ruth was a woman of Moab, born and raised in that country. It was home, familiar, comfortable. She was young and, as implied in the biblical account, beautiful. Surely there were many young men who might have wanted her. Even Naomi was surprised by Ruth's decision. "Return home, my daughters. Why would you come with me? Am I going to have any more sons, who could become your husbands?" (1:11). Why would Ruth decide to go off with an old woman who had no sons, no money, no hope, to a land unknown to her? And why pledge allegiance to a God who was another nation's God?

A Contagious Faith

Ruth's final declaration—to embrace Naomi's God—is most surprising of all. Or is it? Here we must wonder with admiration about the spiritual lives of Elimelech, Ruth's deceased husband, their sons Mahlon and Kilion, and about Naomi herself. Their lifestyle must have been such that Ruth was impressed, compelled even, to hold onto the truth she had been exposed to in her adopted Hebrew family. Had Naomi and her sons spoken of God and His laws regularly at home and lived out their lives in accordance with their faith? Had they lived the commandments as God had instructed?

The commandments were to be engraved in their hearts and passed along to their families. In very graphic terms, the Lord affirmed the singular influence of the home upon growing children and other family members. Faith was to define every action in life. "Impress them on your children. Talk about them when you sit at home and when you walk along the road, when you lie down and when you get up. Tie them as symbols on your hands and bind them on your foreheads. Write them on the doorframes of your houses and on your gates" (Deuteronomy 6:7-9).

It is likely that devotion to God as exemplified in the life of Naomi compelled Ruth to embrace Him too. It should be noted that Naomi was by no means a perfect woman. As the story opens we see a woman who has grown bitter and disillusioned through the pain she has experienced. "The Almighty has made my life very bitter . . . brought misfortune upon me," she laments, Job-like (Ruth 1:20–21). "Don't call me Naomi [pleasant]. Call me Mara [bitter]" (1:20). Yet, in spite of her sadness, she holds onto her hope in God. She does not abandon her faith.

We sometimes think we can have little effect on the salvation of others because we are less than perfect. Maturity in the faith takes a lifetime, but we share the light we have, knowing to whom to go for answers beyond ourselves. C. S. Lewis wrote that "Faith is the art of holding on to things your reason has once accepted, in spite of your changing moods."

Ruth came to a moment of decision to embrace God. But that decision was born of earlier influences building over time as she was immersed in the liberating truths of a God who loves His people with an everlasting love. Nor can we discount the fact that God Himself drew Ruth. Jesus said, "No one can come to Me unless the Father who sent Me draws him" (John 6:44). God can reach even the most unlikely person and turn him or her into a warrior of faith and prayer.

It may be hard for modern persons to fully appreciate the magnitude of Ruth's decision. Commitment to a different religious faith implied an abandoning of the former faith. She was not committing to worship Yahweh as an addition to some polytheistic pantheon of her own, but would entrust herself completely to this God whom Naomi and her dead husband served.

A Universal Opportunity

Scripture reminds us throughout its pages that God woos us to Himself out of love and compassion. Did He draw only Ruth and not Orpah, who turned back to her own country? She was subjected to the same family influences, yet she did not make a commitment to embrace Naomi's people and her God. Orpah should not be faulted for her choice, since she returned to Moab in obedience to her mother-in-law. But, viewing these events as pictures of redemption, we can deduce with confidence the fact that while God's love is universal, His will is that all would come to know Him. But the choice to follow is ours.

Some might suggest that Ruth was simply being kind by not abandoning Naomi, who had lost so much. But her final declaration to embrace Naomi's God goes well beyond kindness, even beyond admiration. Some might argue that Ruth was really acting in her own best interest, that she might have been afraid to live on her own. Even life with an old Jewish woman was better than isolation and loneliness. But Ruth's later actions show that she was hardly a weak woman, afraid to risk, to dare. She proved to be daring indeed, even placing her own reputation at risk by obeying her mother-in-law's instructions.

Ruth has made her choice. She "clings" to Naomi. Her life is no longer her own. She is tied up in the life of Naomi and her God. She will not simply follow but cling—as Adam clung to his wife Eve: "Bone of my bones and flesh of my flesh" (Genesis 2:23). God calls those who would be His children to this kind of proximity. We will have to cling only to Him and His cross.

A footprint, even clearly marked,
Is a cold and distant thing.
I must not simply follow
But dependent, desperate, cling
To wounded hands and bleeding feet,
His throbbing heart my sole retreat.

SOMETHING TO THINK ABOUT

1. Imagine that you were about to embark on a journey into a foreign country where everything would be new and strange. What thoughts would go through your mind? How would you feel?

2. Ruth's memorable declaration to her mother-in-law is a classic of love and devotion often incorporated in wedding ceremonies. What do you think brought about this kind of response by a young bereaved widow for her mother-in-law?

3. Unlike Ruth, Orpah did not go with her mother-in-law. Considering Ruth as a story about redemption, what does Orpah's choice to return to Moab tell us?

4. People rarely make a choice to become Christians based on one encounter, or by reading one chapter of Scripture. Often it comes about after many experiences that influence our lives. Which persons or events in your life affected your decision to become a disciple of Christ?

3: Handfuls on Purpose

THIS SPRINGTIME STORY OF A RELATIONSHIP BEGAN FIRST AS ADMIRATION, THEN developed into friendship, and finally deepened into love. From the union of two faithful but ethnically and economically divergent persons, Boaz of Judah and Ruth of Moab, issued a lifeline of divine proportion.

Naomi and her daughter-in-law Ruth arrived destitute in Bethlehem following the deaths of their spouses "as the barley harvest was beginning" (Ruth 1:22). Harvesting of grain in ancient Canaan took place in April or May—first barley, then a few weeks later, wheat. A series of time-consuming, laborious steps were involved. First the ripened grain was cut with hand sickles (usually by the men). Then the sheaves were bound by the women. Then came gleaning, or gathering of stalks of grain left behind. After the sheaves were taken to the threshing floor by donkey or cart, the grain was threshed (loosened from the straw) either by the treading of cattle or by toothed threshing sledges. The grain was then tossed into the air with winnowing forks so that the wind would blow away the straw and chaff, leaving the grain at the winnower's feet. The grain then had to be sifted to remove any foreign particles and bagged for storage.

Israelite law provided that the edges of the grain fields were not to be harvested. The gleanings (what was not picked up in the first pass-through of those who bundled the grain stalks) were to be left behind for the alien, the poor, the orphan and the widow. Ruth sought out this means of survival for herself and Naomi.

The God Who Is There

The biblical narrator allows us to imagine that Ruth arrived by chance in the portion of the field belonging to the wealthy Boaz. But God was at work behind the scenes. Then, as now, God "moves in mysterious ways His wonders to perform" (Cowper). What appears often to human eyes and minds as happenstance or coincidence is really God working to bring about a good result for the benefit of His people. God redeems His people whom He loves with an everlasting love, but He does not manipulate us in a series of puppet-like maneuvers. He works, rather, in tandem with people, so that a remarkable partnership develops between God and His creatures to bring about His grand design.

So it was that Ruth "found herself gleaning in a field belonging to Boaz, who was from the clan of Elimelech" (2:3). While the narrator tells us in the early verses of chapter 2 that Naomi had a relative of high standing whose name was Boaz, Naomi had not mentioned him to Ruth nor instructed her daughter-in-law to go to his field. It was the providence of God that led her to Boaz (and Naomi would later acknowledge this). "The Lord bless him!" Naomi said. He "has not stopped showing His kindness to the living and the dead" (2:20).

God promised that He would dwell in the midst of His people. It is a central theme through Scripture. From Exodus to Revelation we find the imagery: a holy God "pitching His tent" among His people. He is the God who is there, and He demands that we respond. He demands a response first of all because He loves us and knows that unless we interact with Him we will not survive the journey of life. He also knows that only His life in us can bring purpose, peace, and fullness to our days. God reveals this fact in the beautiful unfolding of the story of Ruth, Naomi, and Boaz.

When God's People Respond

That spring morning, Boaz greeted the workers in his field with the words "The Lord be with you!" They called back, "The Lord bless you!" (2:4). On many occasions characters in this narrative invoke divine blessing upon one another (1:8; 2:12; 2:19,20; 3:10; 4:11). We are reminded of the Christian liturgical greeting "The Lord be with you . . . and also with you." Such greetings have gradually disappeared, unhappily, with the increasing secularization of society. Here, Boaz, the third principal character in the narrative, acknowledges God and goes on to demonstrate a kind and godly spirit.

Boaz learns the identity of the young woman and is quickly impressed with her unselfish nature. He invites her to glean only in his field, promising to protect her and provide for her. Further, he gives instructions to his men to leave extra grain just for her: "Even if she gathers among the sheaves, don't embarrass her. Rather, pull out some stalks for her from the bundles and leave them for her to pick up, and don't rebuke her" (2:15–16).

When God's people respond to others with kindness and goodness, the result can have overarching, even divine consequences. God was able to bless Ruth and Naomi and Boaz himself because of this godly response to another's need, and generations later we are touched by the providence of God because of it.

We see in the attitude of Boaz a picture of God's grace. God not only provides for our needs but leaves handfuls on purpose for us to gather simply because He loves us. "I have come that they may have life," said Jesus, "and have it to the full" (John 10:10). God wants not only to satisfy us but to provide, in the paraphrase by Eugene Peterson, "a better life than they ever dreamed of."

The story might have had quite another ending if Boaz had not responded with kindness to the needs of a foreign young woman. Like God, Boaz could look beyond Ruth's status of "nonbelonging" to include her and make her part of the family. God wants to include you in His family, to provide handfuls on purpose for you, and to give you a better life than you ever dreamed.

SOMETHING TO THINK ABOUT

1. One of the themes illustrated in the book of Ruth is care for the alien and stranger in the land. How is this theme represented in the story of Ruth?

2. We know that "God moves in mysterious ways," but most often He seems to choose to work through people. How is His providence revealed in the lives of Ruth and Naomi?

3. What qualities do you see in Boaz that reveal his godly character?

4. What qualities do you admire most in Boaz? In Ruth? In Naomi?

4: Healing Wings

A VERY DIFFERENT NAOMI FROM THE ONE WE HAVE SEEN UP TO NOW IS EMERGING, and a plan is taking place that will change all the lives of the characters in this splendid narrative. Earlier in this study, we noted Naomi's sense of despair, having lost both husband and sons. Devoid of hope, she will return to Bethlehem, her homeland, to die. "It is more bitter for me than for you, because the Lord's hand has gone out against me" (Ruth 1:13), she tells her daughters-in-law. Orpah is convinced to go back to Moab, but Ruth clings to Naomi. And so it is decided. We can almost see the shrug of resignation as Naomi sets off passively with Ruth tagging along behind her.

Their mutual loss might have embittered Naomi and Ruth toward each other. But in the days that follow, Ruth becomes proactive in providing for her mother-in-law. God's intervention through Boaz—who allows Ruth to glean exclusively in his field—begins to build confidence in Ruth that her mother-in-law will be cared for. But in chapter three, the tables are delightfully turned, and we find Naomi expressing concern for Ruth. "My daughter," she says, "should I not try to find a home for you, where you will be well provided for?" (3:1).

No longer passive or negative, Naomi is moved to make provision for Ruth's future. Gleaning was a stopgap measure. Something more permanent must be devised. Mutual love and concern set in motion a redemptive work that ensures a future of happiness and security for them both.

Redemption and love are inextricably tied. Isaiah writes of God and His people, "In His love and mercy He redeemed them; He lifted them up and carried them all the days of old" (Isaiah 63:9). Though we are His creation, we had to be redeemed from the corruption of sin, and at great cost—the life of the Son of God, who, "having loved His own who were in the world, He now showed them the full extent of His love" (John 13:1).

The Challenge of Obedience

Given the culture of the times, it is no surprise that Naomi looks to marriage for Ruth to solve their need for security. But the manner in which such an end would be achieved is nothing short of daring, and beyond the bounds of accepted convention. Readers of the book of Ruth cannot miss the narrator's frequent reference to euphemisms that spark the imagination and evoke questions. Ruth was to wash and perfume herself, put on her best clothes, then "go down to the threshing floor. . . . When [Boaz] lies down, note the place. . . . Then go and uncover his feet and lie down" (Ruth 3:3-4). What is Naomi suggesting?

Nowhere is there any indication of the consummation of sexual relations, yet the choice of words keeps that possibility before the reader. A conservative publishing house would no doubt have stricken such a reference with all its implications if the story were to be printed today. But Naomi's advice to Ruth is clearly for the purpose of appealing to Boaz's kinsman obligation. Surprisingly, Ruth responds to Naomi's bizarre proposal with full compliance and cooperation: "I will do whatever you say" (3:5).

Her response is reminiscent of our Lord's willing obedience to the most unfair, quixotic proposal of all time—God must die. Thus Jesus prayed on the eve of His crucifixion, "not My will, but Yours be done" (Luke 22:42). Jesus had full trust in His Father, as did Isaac in his father Abraham, and Ruth in her mother-in-law. Her obedience would make all the difference in the outcome of her life and those of generations to follow. Our obedience to God will determine the direction of our lives for all eternity.

The Blessing of the Redeemed

Imagine Boaz's shock to wake at night and find himself partially uncovered with a woman at his feet! A prominent citizen of good reputation, Boaz was surely shocked, uneasy, perhaps even angry. "Who are you?" he demands (Ruth 3:9). Ruth's response, perhaps tremulous, was nonetheless humble and forthright. "I am your servant Ruth." Then she proceeds with her clear request for marriage. Ruth appeals to Boaz's kinsman obligation, though she may not have understood all the legal steps involved in levirate marriage (a law that provided for marriage to a close relative to secure an heir to the dead husband's name). Actually, Boaz was one of a group of kinsmen who had responsibility for the well-being of Naomi and by extension for her daughter-in-law.

Ruth's request of Boaz to "spread the corner [literally 'wing'] of your garment over me" may have been a reference to Boaz's earlier prayer that Ruth would find refuge under God's wings (2:12). The spreading of the corner of the garment was a common practice and is still used in some parts of the Middle East today. It is clearly a reference to the establishment of a marriage bond. Christians quickly recall Jesus' beautiful analogy of His intimate love for Jerusalem: "How often I have longed to gather your children together, as a hen gathers her chicks under her wings, but you were not willing" (Matthew 23:37). Frequent references to wings as sheltering and protecting can be found in Scripture.

Here, the wing of the garment implied redemption as well as intimate relationship. Old Testament references to God's redemption heighten the significance of Ruth's description of Boaz as next-of-kin/redeemer. God is the Redeemer of individuals, the One who is in relationship with them, supports them and rescues them from desperate circumstances. Among Isaiah's many references is this affirmation: "You, O Lord, are our Father, our Redeemer from of old is Your name" (Isaiah 63:16).

God longs for just such an intimate relationship with us. Jesus is our Kinsman/Redeemer, the only one who can restore us to the relationship for which we were born. While such a relationship is ours, sealed by Jesus' death and resurrection for the whole world, we are the ones who must ask for forgiveness and acceptance into His intimate fellowship. His response to our penitence is always gentle and positive, as is Boaz's response to Ruth.

Boaz recognizes the true meaning behind Ruth's proposal and the unselfish reasons behind her act. "The Lord bless you, my daughter," he replies (Ruth 3:10). So it is that when we come to God with honest, repentant heart and seek relationship with Him, He welcomes us as sons and daughters and proceeds to bless us with uncountable riches in Christ who comes "with healing in [His] wings" (Malachi 4:2).

SOMETHING TO THINK ABOUT

1. Naomi began her trek to Bethlehem in a disheartened state, full of bitter thoughts about all she had lost. But something begins to happen. What changes do you see in Ruth at this point in the story?

2. Naomi devises a daring plan. What does Ruth's agreement to follow through with the plan say about her character? About Naomi's character?

3. Has God ever asked you to do something daring, out of your comfort zone? Did you do it? What were the results?

4. How is Boaz and his relationship with Ruth like Christ and His relationship with us?

5. Boaz spreading his garment over Ruth like wings reminds us of God's protection. Consider a time in your life when you felt the healing touch of God.

5: The Confrontation

AFTER FOLLOWING NAOMI'S INSTRUCTION TO APPROACH THEIR KINSMAN BOAZ FOR refuge, Ruth returns to her mother-in-law to report what has happened. She tells of the kindness of Boaz, the six measures of barley with which he sent her away and the unsettling news: A nearer kinsman than Boaz might choose to act as the kinsman-redeemer, according to the custom of providing for those who like Ruth have suffered loss (Ruth 3:16–17).

We wonder about the feelings of both Boaz and Ruth as they part, each aware of a growing bond between them and of the possible barrier that might separate them. From the narrative to this point it is obvious that kindness and mutual respect have blossomed further between these two unlikely characters—the wealthy landowner of Judah and the gentle, impoverished Ruth.

It is just like God to carry out His purposes in ways that bring delight and joy to the hearts of those who choose to follow Him in obedience. His design also proves that what might seem improbable or even impossible to man, He can accomplish—with amazing flair and abundance.

Paul's doxology in the book of Romans testifies to this grandeur of God's ways: "Oh, the depth of the riches of the wisdom and knowledge of God! How unsearchable His judgments, and His paths beyond tracing out! Who has known the mind of the Lord? Or who has been His counselor? Who has ever given to God, that God should repay Him? For from Him and through Him and to Him are all things. To Him be the glory forever! Amen" (Romans 11:33–36).

Confrontation at the Gate

Ruth's symbolic bid for relationship on the threshing floor is given. She has "uncovered his feet" and lain down beside Boaz. How easily he might have taken advantage of her, but he is an upright man who saw the bravery, the loyalty in Ruth, qualities even more attractive than her physical beauty. He urges her not to be afraid and promises to solve the problem.

The role of the redeemer would be fulfilled, Boaz assures Ruth. "If [your closer kinsman] is not willing, as surely as the Lord lives, I will do it" (Ruth 3:13). Boaz grounds his promise in an oath by the name of God who is Redeemer par excellence of the widow and the poor.

Gathering ten elders at the town gate, Boaz confronts the unnamed kinsman who stood to inherit Naomi's property (4:2). It was the duty of the kinsman/ redeemer to buy any land in danger of being sold outside the family. It is possible that Elimelech, Naomi's husband, sold the land in question before departing for Moab. Naomi now has the right to buy the land back but cannot afford to do so.

The narrator does not outline Hebrew law in this case but simply implies that Elimelech's property included not only land but a wife. The kinsman who accepted the obligation must accept the legal right of redemption (an economic advantage) and the moral obligation of marriage to the widow, which could be to his disadvantage.

Apparently, the role of the ten elders was as official witnesses, rather than to take any part in the action itself. We see that others were present too—"the elders of [Boaz's] people" (4:4) and all the people who were at the gate along with the elders (4:11). Apparently, the decision was important to the whole community. Could they have had any idea as they watched and listened that the ancestry of King David would be at stake? What an important moment for every Bethlehemite, representing in microcosm the whole people of God.

The kinsman, who is not named in the narrative, declines the responsibility toward Naomi's family, perhaps fearing that if he had a son by Ruth, and if that son were the only surviving heir, his own property would transfer to the family of Elimelech. It was a risk—but the same risk that Boaz was willing to assume. The agreement between the next-of-kin and Boaz is formalized by the ritual in which the next-of-kin removes his sandal and gives it to Boaz (v. 8). It was an apparently ancient symbol which had to be explained to the audience, but which effectively meant that one was renouncing property rights and passing them to another.

Confrontation at the Cross

Like Naomi, we had an inheritance we were unable to claim. The incursion of sin into the world had left us under the control of the Prince of the Power of the Air. Though created by God for God, we were severed from the One God and Father of us all. The devil boasts a natural claim upon our souls, keeping us from inheriting the supernatural blessing God planned for us in the beginning.

The Apostle Paul attests that "sin entered the world through one man, and death through sin, and in this way death came to all men" (Romans 5:12). Our birthright was stolen by a false kinsman—an imposter, and no real kinsman at all. "Worship the Lord your God, and serve Him only," Jesus warned the devil in the wilderness (Matthew 4:10). All the earth was His by right of creation. But there would be no honorable transfer, as in the removal of the sandal from the hand of the dissenting kinsman to Boaz. God had to redeem us at tremendous cost. In crude sandals and bleeding feet, the Son of God walked the treacherous terrain of this earth all the way to Calvary to purchase our salvation. What a Redeemer! "For if the many died by the trespass of the one man, how much more did God's grace and the gift that came by the grace of the one man, Jesus Christ, overflow to the many!" (Romans 5:15).

Boaz confronted the Bethlehemite kinsman at the gate (where all legal and social affairs were conducted). Scripture tells us that "Jesus also suffered outside the city gate to make the people holy through His own blood" (Hebrews 13:12). Christ's death outside Jerusalem represented the removal of sin, as had the removal of the bodies of sacrificial animals outside the camp to Israel. On the lonely hill of Golgotha, Christ confronted Satan and for all time destroyed the works of darkness and secured our inheritance, eternal life. What a Redeemer!

1. God can do what man often finds improbable or impossible. How does the story of Ruth illustrate this truth?

2. What improbable or impossible thing has God done in your life?

3. Naomi had lost her property, and though she wanted it and had a right to it, she could not afford to buy it back. She had to rely on someone else to redeem what she had lost. Is there a spiritual lesson here about our own redemption?

4. It cost Boaz something to take Ruth as his wife. Ruth must have spent the rest of her life showing her gratitude and respect for her generous husband. It cost Jesus His life to purchase our salvation. How can we best express our gratitude for such a great gift as salvation?

6: The Promised Inheritance

THE LONGER I WALK WITH GOD, THE MORE SURE I AM THAT HE LOVES TO DELIGHT HIS children. It is a truth that Naomi discovers, too. Like an indulgent father with infinite resources to match infinite wisdom, God lavishes good gifts upon us, often without any hint of recognition on our part for the favor He has shown.

To simply sustain the universe He created for our enjoyment would be gift enough, but God chooses to round out the sun's daily course with a technicolor display that defies adequate description. Rather than fold away the growing cycle with solemn silence, God dances in verdant fields and vibrant leaves of crimson, emerald and gold that provide a rich harvest.

When sin destroyed God's perfect creation, He recreated us in the glory of His own Son and marked us forever as eternal sons and daughters of God, immensely rich, favored, and chosen to live in paradise with Him.

"How great is the love the Father has lavished on us, that we should be called children of God!" (1 John 3:1). John's amazement matches that of Paul as the apostle contemplated God's eternal plan: "No eye has seen, no ear has heard, no mind has conceived what God has prepared for those who love Him" (1 Corinthians 2:9). Naomi experiences the lavish love of God who leads her from bitterness to blessing, from unrest to rest.

From Bitterness to Blessing

When Naomi left behind all that she had loved and known in the land of Moab, could she have seen ahead to the glory that awaited her? Like you and I might have reacted, Naomi was focused on what she had lost—her husband, her sons, her livelihood. She very nearly forgot that she still had the best gift of all. God had not deserted her.

When the story began, Naomi walked with Ruth into the town of Bethlehem where "the whole town was stirred because of them. The women, watching them warily from the town gate, exclaimed, 'Can this be Naomi?'

'Don't call me Naomi,' she told them. 'Call me Mara, because the Almighty has made my life very bitter . . . the Lord has brought me back empty . . . the Almighty has brought misfortune upon me'" (Ruth 1:19–21).

Now at the end of this short but exhilarating narrative, the women are once again among the witnesses at the town gate where the redemption of Naomi's property and Boaz' proposal to marry Ruth takes place. They turn to Naomi and declare, "We are witnesses. May the Lord make the woman [Ruth] who is coming into your home like Rachel and Leah, who together built up the house of Israel. May you have standing in Ephrathah [the area around Bethlehem] and be famous in Bethlehem" (Ruth 4:11).

They compared Naomi's coming family to that of Perez, ancestor of Boaz, "whom Tamar bore to Judah" (4:12) through a union based on the levirate practice. Perez raised the tribe of Judah to a prominent place in Israel, even as Ruth's offspring would issue in King David and his dynasty.

The narrator comes to the conclusion of the story: "So Boaz took Ruth and she became his wife. And the Lord enabled her to conceive, and she gave birth to a son. The women said to Naomi: 'Praise be to the Lord, who this day has not left you without a kinsman-redeemer. May he become famous throughout Israel! He will renew your life and sustain you in your old age. For your daughter-in-law, who loves you and who is better to you than seven sons, has given him birth'" (Ruth 4:13–15).

From Unrest to Rest

"Then Naomi took the child, laid him in her lap and cared for him" (4:16). Aged Naomi, who can no longer bear children, obtains an heir in place of Mahlon. What a picture she must have made, cuddling her grandchild with all the women of the city surrounding her and blessing her, wishing her joy. Ruth appears glad to remain in the background as Naomi is lauded by the women of Bethlehem—women who no doubt had once gossiped about Naomi's barren state. Widows were viewed with pity at best, with scorn at worst, for the stigma against childlessness was strong in the ancient cultures. To have seven sons was the epitome of all family blessings in Israel. Ruth's self-less devotion to Naomi receives its climactic acknowledgment in the words of the women: "Your daughter-in-law . . . is better to you than seven sons" (4:15).

It is unusual that the women give Obed his name. In the Old Testament, parents usually named a child. Sometimes God gave instruction concerning the name, but the community did not have this naming role anywhere else than in the book of Ruth. Nor do the words of the women, "Naomi has a son," reveal any kind of word play. Perhaps this unusual circumstance adds to the theme of the story itself, for it is a story of women making a way out of no way, enabled by God behind the scenes and by other faithful people epitomized by Boaz.

Naomi was brought from emptiness to fullness through the selfless love of Ruth and Boaz. The Lord brought Israel from unrest to rest through their descendant David, who selflessly gave himself to fight Israel's battles. The ultimate end of the genealogy in chapter four is Jesus Christ, the great "son of David" (Matthew 1:1) who fulfills prophecy and will bring us into final rest. His tender care, like Ruth's care for Naomi, ensures an inheritance eternal in the heavens (Hebrews 9:15).

SOMETHING TO THINK ABOUT

1. The story of Ruth illustrates how God often provides more than we need, often bringing an extra measure of delight into our lives. What are some of the ways God shows His delight in you?

2. It's easy for us to focus on what we have lost, as Naomi did at the beginning. We forget that if we have indeed lost a lot, we must have had a lot to start with. Perhaps we were seldom grateful for it until we lost it. What can you give thanks to God for today as you focus not on what is lost but on what God has given?

3. Imagine you were among the women from Bethlehem who watched Naomi returning after a long time away. Naomi appeared beaten and alone and sad. What would you say about her to a friend? Now at the end of the story you are again talking with friends from the village. What are you saying to them now?

4. What is important about the final outcome of the story that concerns the lineage of Christ himself?

SIX

ISAAC: THE SCARLET THREAD

DAVID LAEGER

Major David Laeger retired in 2003
from his position as senior instructor
at The Salvation Army's College for
Officer Training in Atlanta, Georgia.
Throughout his service in the Army,
Laeger, with his wife Anna, has
pursued a lifetime of biblical study
with an emphasis on holiness.

*Oh for simpler days! Front porch neighborliness. Casual country walks.
But "the Preacher" of Ecclesiastes warns, "Do not say, 'Why were the
former days better than these?' For you do not inquire wisely concerning
this" (6:10 NKJV). Meditation upon the past brings repose until human
faces appear. Unpleasant memories affect us all in some measure. We
would rather bury them in unmarked graves. Bible characters have not
that option. For our sakes their lives are presented in living color. While
we identify with them, they vicariously take all the blame for our errors.*

1: Like Father, Like Son

ABRAHAM SEEMED TO HAVE LIVED IN SIMPLER TIMES. THE ACCOUNT
of his 175 years leaves us with that impression. In fact, he encountered
moments as intense as any in modern drama. The world affected him then as
it affects godly persons now. Polytheism prevailed. Sexual promiscuity was
advertised freely. Tyranny and terrorism struck the land. Abraham lived with
our same ambience, just in a different guise. He moved through his world

following a nobler standard. He made some errors, but these were obscured by honor he received several millennia later from three great religions and offspring which form a myriad of nations.

Abraham was a friend of God. When they spoke, mutual respect filtered the conversation. So it was while he rested one day beneath the trees of Mamré that the quiet thoughts of yesteryear and future years formed his meditations.

As if his hazy imagination had stepped into living dimensions, three human-like forms appeared to Abraham. He recognized them and ran to worship the One whom he readily identified as *Adonai*. The others were angels accompanying their Lord on a mission of eternal importance.

How must it be to recognize God? Is it absurd to think He would, or even could, so appear today? The idea of God is so nebulous now. The human spirit is a vacuum from which has been pressed out all divine influence, and in its place has flowed poisons from a godless world.

Abraham, we need you for answers to our needy spirits. Your riches were not your reason for living. Your friendships were few, your pleasures different, your conscience more sensitive. Men distanced themselves from you. Your intimates were not even as dear to you as your longing to please God. We remember Isaac, the eternal reason the three mysterious guests came to you. You and Sarah had passed the years of sexual possibility and pleasure. Sarah laughed when God promised a son from your own union.

But God has a plan borne from the beginning of our race, a genealogical cord reaching from Adam to Christ. Some call it a "scarlet thread" woven through the fabric of a race of people. The great progenitor Abraham had to prove his faith before the weave continued. The Lord said to Abraham, "At the appointed time I will return to you, according to the time of life, and Sarah shall have a son" (Genesis 18:14 NKJV).

"And not being weak in faith, . . . he did not waver at the promise of God . . . being fully convinced that what He had promised He was able also to perform" (Romans 4:19–21 NKJV). And so was born to him Isaac *Abrahamson!* A cherished son who would prove to be like his father, a man of miracle, faith, submission, peace, sorrow, prayer. The biography of one bleeds into the other.

Often the divine name conjoins with these men. He is the God of Abraham, Isaac and Jacob. But we may also call Him our God if we walk with Him. The traffic of their day did not crowd Him out. They waited patiently, focused intently on Him—and so should we. The Lord God of Abraham, Isaac and Jacob longs to visit the soul of man. In that, the complex becomes simpler— if not to understand, at least to bear.

SOMETHING TO THINK ABOUT

1. How was Abraham's life as complicated then as ours is today?

2. How was Abraham "a friend of God?" How can we be His friend, too?

3. How did Abraham recognize God and then obey when everything sounded impossible?

4. Is spite of our complex society, how can we be attentive to God's leading in our lives?

2: Son of Laughter

ABRAHAM'S WORLD WAS BUSY. NONETHELESS, THE VOICE OF THE LORD REGISTERED in his mind—for when God speaks, the righteous remember. "Sarah conceived and bore Abraham a son in his old age, at the set time of which God had spoken to him" (Genesis 21:2 NKJV).

"The time of life" (18:10) for Sarah included every moment of embryonic and fetal development. If it grows, it lives. That physical mass of cells has a human psyche. They develop together, one intricately intertwined with the other. "I am fearfully and wonderfully made and skillfully wrought" (Psalm 139:14,15 NKJV).

Isaac resembled the family in looks and temperament. But before any human consideration, there was divine involvement. Isaac was not born from a mere act of passion or parental planning. His pedigree is from the Lord. Jehovah was first to name him *Yitshaq,* meaning "laughter" (Genesis 17:21). A beautiful name, with a hint of divine humor.

Abraham and Sarah laughed at the very idea of such a child. Then they laughed with Isaac. They would later become angry at laughter against him. The antagonism of half-brother Ishmael would later be used providentially in the course of Isaac's life.

The precious son of the camp is named for the emotion of the moment, as well as from a prophetic command. The Spanish customarily say of birth that a baby is "brought to light" or *dara luz.* From the darkness of the womb, a child enters into earth's bright environment. Maternal pain subsides. Paternal worry disappears. Loving touches seem to melt its tender flesh. The most helpless of creatures captivates the strongest among us.

Isaac's parents laughed. The miracle baby was born! From his loins a miracle race would spring forth. That prospect proves yet to be an indomitable plan, which neither genocide nor geography can alter. It is divinely set and attested to in both testaments. God has a sure covenant with Abraham and Isaac.

Eight days after his birth, Isaac was circumcised. Other cultures observed the rite for sanitary reasons or to appease a god. This time there was a divine and human reason. Circumcision was the removal of a fleshly veil, the cutting of a covenant, the perpetuation of an accord between God and His people. In Abraham's seed, all nations would be blessed—with Isaac as the immediate seed. Circumcision marked identity with that covenant.

It is said that eight days after birth is the safest time in a newborn's life for circumcision. The Christian interpretation describes it as symbolic of the removal of sin from the heart. Although Moses (Deuteronomy 10:16) and Jeremiah (4:4) both direct their people to the spiritual application of circumcision, New Testament theology does not present a new concept, only a new power by which it may be wrought. The ultimate seed of Abraham is Christ. By Him the covenant, continued in Isaac, penetrates the human heart. The cycle of life is completed in Christ, for in Him a spiritual birth is realized. Heaven resounds with laughter from the Father, as the divine touch melts into the newborn spirit. Behold, one more grain of life; one more increase in the covenantal family of God—through Jesus Christ our Lord.

1. Why was Isaac called "son of laughter?"

2. Was it funny, as in strange, or funny, as in humorous, showing the divine humor?

3. What was the covenant made between God and Abraham?

4. How does Christ complete the promise of the covenant made to Abraham and his heirs?

3: Son of Conflict

TROUBLE AROSE IN THE CAMP OF ABRAHAM WHEN, THIRTEEN YEARS BEFORE THE birth of Isaac, Abraham fathered a child by Hagar, his wife's handmaid. Ishmael was born from that parentage before the son God had promised Sarah and Abraham. According to the times and customs of that day, he was not an illegitimate son. Hagar served as a surrogate for Sarah.

Oh, the centuries of conflict that developed thereafter. The descendants of Isaac and Ishmael would know natural hatred forever. History records that truth, even beyond the biblical record.

With Isaac yet to be born, why did God allow the birth of Ishmael? Divine plans, as they often do, supersede the finite plans of men. God saw the end from the beginning.

Scriptures give us both positive and negative lessons from the conflict between these two brothers. God assured Hagar and Abraham that Ishmael would also prosper as a great nation (Genesis 21:13,18). However, an earlier prophecy to Hagar characterized Ishmael's existence as that of "a wild donkey of a man; his hand will be against everyone, and everyone's hand against him. And he will live in hostility toward all his brothers" (Genesis 16:12).

A spiritual truth is found in the relationship of Isaac and Ishmael, through Sarah and Hagar. Paul wrote of their brotherly conflict in Galatians 4:22: "Abraham had two sons, one by the slave woman and the other by the free woman."

In the Christian, a battle often rages between the indwelling Holy Spirit and the flesh, between what we have become in Christ and what we were before Christ came in. The latter resembles Ishmael, the wild man, the bondson. The former resembles Isaac, the freeborn son, the promised seed. If both reside in the camp of the soul, the sin with which we are born mocks the newborn creature into which we have been reborn. One must go.

Victory over sinful passion is possible in this life. But that comes only through yielding to the Holy Spirit. Anglican preacher Phillips Brooks wrote, "The power of the Holy Spirit! An everlasting spiritual presence among men." Brooks then follows with a poetic thought from Jones Very:

> *Wilt thou not visit me?*
> *The plant beside me feels the gentle dew,*
> *And every blade of grass I see*
> *From thy deep earth its quickening moisture drew.*

Yes, Thou wilt visit me:
Nor plant nor tree Thine eye delights so well,
As, when from sin set free,
My spirit lives with Thine in peace to dwell.

We need to undergo the anesthesia of the Holy Spirit for a deep work of spiritual surgery. Ishmael must go! Isaac must grow without inward strife—there is enough strife outside.

But unlike physical anesthetics, the work of the Holy Spirit makes us fully conscious of that which causes our pain. And unlike the surgeon's knife which requires healing, the Spirit of God heals as He operates. The one key to His success is that fine line of decision by the human will. The secret is in the yielding. "Get rid of the slave woman and her son, for the slave woman's son will never share in the inheritance with the free woman's son" (Galatians 4:3).

SOMETHING TO THINK ABOUT

1. Why didn't the Lord fulfill His promise of a son and heir through Ishmael?

2. His did Abraham's impatience complicate the Lord's completion of His promise?

3. How would you feel if you were Ishmael or his mother and were cut out of the Lord's grand inheritance? What provision did God make for Ishmael?

4. How has the prophecy concerning Ishmael—"He will live in hostility toward all his brothers"—played out in the history of the Middle East?

4: Son of Sacrifice

IN A COMMANDING VOICE THE LORD INSTRUCTED ABRAHAM TO OFFER HIS ONLY SON Isaac as a burnt offering. This was no light conversation, nor a long one, but the message was clear and has significance for us as a portrait of love's obedience.

If ever an account so clearly parallels the sacrifice of Jesus Christ, it is this. Significant beyond its time, the record was not kept simply as a trial of faith for one man. The testimony of witnesses affirms the historical and religious importance of that event. And in the midst of a mosque in Jerusalem lies the rock upon which Isaac lay beneath the point of Abraham's dagger.

Human hearts were involved there in that ancient day. Abraham's soul was challenged to the deepest degree. Isaac was Abraham's life, the miracle of the camp, the heir to his father's treasures.

"Take now your son," said the Lord. The only preliminary address was the call of Abraham's name. No comforting preamble—just a succession of statements, ending with one strong command. Isaac must be sacrificed.

"Offer him as a burnt offering," said the unwavering voice. So this man of faith, obedient before, proved his loyalty once again.

What if Sarah or the young servants accompanying them that day had been made aware of the coming deed? Nothing dissuaded Abraham. His heart was fixed on divine things. Such a test became a hallmark for men and women of later generations. But it would find its grandest, most perfect form in the sacrifice of God's beloved Son, Jesus.

The burnt offering of Hebrew animal sacrifices has become known as the "holocaust"—an offering totally consumed and ascending in the smoke of its altar fire. Such an offering connotes complete consecration to God. Steadily up the steeps of Mount Moriah, Abraham climbed toward the rocky summit. Isaac bore the wood; Abraham carried the fire. That moment is similar to Christ's walk toward His crucifixion. Abraham and Isaac repeated the provision for sin God had already supplied in his omniscient eternal state, as Christ is "the Lamb that was slain from the creation of the world" (Revelation 13:8).

The experience of both Isaac and Jesus is filled with holocaustal meaning. Each was a *Via Dolorosa* (Way of Sorrow) that first ran secretly through the passageways of heaven. Each would have its peculiar altar and fire, offerer and victim. Satisfied with Abraham's obedience and Isaac's submission, the angel of the Lord halted the process by saying, "Do not lay a hand on the boy. . . . Now I know that you fear God because you have not withheld from me your son, your only son" (Genesis 22:12). In Jesus' case, God the Father, satisfied with His Son's gracious love, accepted Him, with no one else to stand in His place. Jesus' life was offered with the only words that would finalize the essential act: "It is finished!"

The reason for the crucifixion is stated in the verse "For God so loved the world that He gave His only begotten Son, that whosoever believeth in Him should not perish, but have everlasting life" (John 3:16 KJV). And Abraham "reasoned that God was able to raise the dead, and figuratively speaking, he did receive Isaac back from death" (Hebrews 11:19). Abraham's beloved Isaac was a forerunner of our beloved Jesus.

SOMETHING TO THINK ABOUT

1. Why did the Lord command Abraham to offer Isaac as a sacrifice? Would the Lord demand murder just to make a point? Why such a radical test of faith and trust?

2. Could you offer your child as a sacrifice if the Lord demanded it? Why? Why not? What would be the end limit of your willingness?

3. How does Christ test our obedience today? What offering does He require?

5: The Heavenly Man

"HE WENT OUT TO THE FIELD ONE EVENING TO MEDITATE" (GENESIS 24:63). IN THIS simple verse, Isaac's heart is revealed. Everything in the passage leads to Isaac, but he is hidden in the shadows until the right moment arises.

This segment of his life incorporates many themes: Abraham's vow with his servant, the servant's search for Isaac's bride, Rebekah's character and beauty and the union of Isaac and Rebekah. Abraham grew anxious about a wife for his son. The woman must come from the same racial roots. But more than fifty years and considerable terrain had separated Abraham from his people. Abraham called in his chief administrator, entrusted him with the sacred task and sent him out to search for a bride for Isaac. The servant, coming into the land of Abraham's roots, paused to pray, pleading for the fulfillment of both his duty and Abraham's will. His prayers displayed unselfish devotion to the great cause for which he was sent.

Even as the servant prayed, the answer came. Rebekah came toward the man, water pitcher borne upon her graceful virgin form, ready to serve the servant and his entourage. She personified all that he sought. Rebekah's unconscious response evoked praise from Abraham's messenger. He prayed. God moved. Rebekah came forward to a plan already prepared. Isaac's chosen bride had encountered her fulfillment, through the ministry of a faithful servant.

Passing over the eastern horizon, nearing her new home in the evening hours of the journey, Rebekah caught sight of Isaac. There he was, standing upon a grassy plain, meditating heavenward, while looking earthward. Isaac was a heavenly man with an earthly vision. There they met, and the romance of the scarlet thread continued. The home of the man became the home of the woman ". . . and he loved her." Isaac, God's promised man, wed Rebekah, God's chosen bride. Every movement of the drama has higher and nobler overtones.

Similarly, God has sent forth His Holy Spirit into the world, seeking a bride for His beloved Son. Christ's bride is the Church, comprised of souls responding to the Holy Spirit's searching. He prays. In Him is vested from the Father, in this case, the life of the Son. There is a covenant to complete, a nuptial bond to satisfy.

It is the work of the One sent to bring into the far reaches of the world the merits of Jesus' life and work, then to give the believer the assurance that he or she is called to a divine family. And so His is completed when, in accord with the free choice of the penitent soul, a relationship is begun between God and men. The Son awaits with love for those who believe in the precious ministry of this divine servant, the Spirit of God. It is through that relationship that our earthly existence takes on heavenly dimensions.

Let us look homeward, toward the Savior who stands not far from us, even in earthy fields, interceding with the Father for that which will be His bride forever. Christ's vision is His Church as His wife, "who has herself ready" (Revelation 19:7). That should be our mutual anticipation.

Let us know the comforts of divine love found in a relationship with Him. For He is comforted in our acceptance, and like a betrothed maiden, we become aware of the depth of His devotion.

Something to Think About

1. Read Genesis 24:63. What was the focus of Isaac's meditation? What was his response to meeting Rebekah?

2. Read Genesis 24. How did Abraham's servant know the right choice in a mate for Isaac?

3. What did Isaac think of the arranged marriage and the bride chosen for him?

4. Read Revelation 19. How has Christ found and chosen a "bride" worthy of a special love relationship with Him?

6: Twin Temperaments

AFTER TWENTY YEARS OF CHILDLESSNESS, ISAAC'S PLEAS FOR HIS WIFE'S FERTILITY were answered. But the twins Rebekah carried warred in her womb. A prophecy revealed the reason: "Two nations are in your womb. . . . One people will be stronger than the other" (Genesis 25:23). God's redemptive hand continued to spin the thread, weaving the pure messianic fabric. The character of each twin would differ like seeds sown in different soil.

In Isaac, the traits seemed pure. As Abraham's beloved son and heir, he was well guarded in the camp. There he enjoyed the knowledge of providential promise. But Isaac was also an outdoorsman. Nature's fragrances appealed to him. Grass wet with dew invigorated him. He was a connoisseur of woodland game, grain, and grapes.

Esau ventured far afield in earthy pleasure. Oblivious to God, his blood pumped wild for temporal freedom. Esau even prostituted his divine endowment (Hebrews 12:16–17). Jacob, a homebody, dwelt too much upon his selfish center. Possession pervaded his imagination. Even physical birth portrayed their personal tendencies. Esau was hairy like a furry animal. Jacob was smooth like a snake. Jacob followed Esau in birth, "his hand grasping Esau's heel" (Genesis 25:26), as if to touch a weakness. Eden was repeated! God had said to the serpent in Eden, "I will put enmity between you and the woman, and between your offspring and hers you will strike His heel" (3:15).

Here is re-enacted that satanic attempt to steal the birthright of humanity. At the heel of our weakness, Satan would wrest from us our Christ-bought rights. Isaac is not passive, but peaceful. He grieves for his sons. But not all who are of Isaac are his children, says Paul (Romans 9:6–13). Years of bitterness would pass before Isaac's blessing fell at last upon one of them.

How mysterious the ways of God! He foreknows. He foreordains. Those who are predestined are like highway signposts set by the Authority who knows the traffic flow. Others may join in the predestined pleasures by faith at the preappointed signals. All may be saved, but not all will heed the cautions. The wrong road leads to a bridgeless chasm into which the disobedient plunge, stepping over a precipice into an eternity without God.

Both sons of Isaac ran in the wrong direction. But for the sake of all humanity, God intervened in the life of one. The extorted birthright and blessing would find legitimacy at last.

God ultimately intervened for us all through Jesus Christ. But as sure as God has a plan, Satan has a distraction, an enticement to affect our sin-driven senses. "The heart is deceitful above all things, and desperately wicked; who can know it?" (Jeremiah 17:9). "Just as sin entered the world through one man so also through the obedience of the one man the many will be made righteous" (Romans 5:12,19). Is there war in a person's soul? The answer parallels one's relationship to God. An unsaved person may not be aware of the struggle between sin and righteousness. But one born into God's family will sense the combat between the spirit of God and the spirit of sin.

Don't be like Esau, or like Jacob before he personally knew the God of Abraham and Isaac. Pray for Christ's spirit to be born in you.

SOMETHING TO THINK ABOUT

1. What went wrong in the way the parents loved and cared for Jacob and Esau?

2. What were the boys' positive character traits?

3. What were their negative character traits, and how did these traits shape their lives in response to God and each other?

7: Famine in the Soul

CRUMBLING STUBBLE COVERED THE DUSTY FIELDS. LANGUID AIR HUNG MOISTURELESS above the rocky hills. Vineyard stalks bore shriveled branches. Clanging buckets sank into the deepening space of thirsty wells. Indigents with bone–drawn skin cried out for nourishment.

As a famine enveloped the camp, Isaac moved toward the Mediterranean Sea, settling near Gerar. There he encountered another kind of hunger. Green meadows blanketed the rain–blessed terrain. The fragrance of harvest satisfied the expectations of appetite. The pungence of the sea lightly seasoned the cooling breeze. The laughter of sufficiency brightened fuel–lit table lamps. Whistles rather than groans floated through the streets. All seemed well in the land of plenty, until this stranger camped by the caravan crossroads near the Philistine town.

Isaac's multitude spread large upon the hazy horizon. His father Abraham had been there before. To protect himself in his sojourns, Abraham had called Sarah his sister. And she was his half–sister, having the same father but different mothers. In Egypt, the Pharaoh rebuked Abraham for endangering his people with such a cover–up. But he did it again in Gerar later. Now Isaac was telling the same lie.

Rebekah's beautiful features attracted the men of Gerar. Passes were made, no doubt. Morally famined hearts hungered for sexual satisfaction. It was okay by the mores of the place, Isaac knew. He feared that if the men discovered Rebekah was his wife, they would kill him to get to her. But Isaac and Rebekah, the flame of youthful love burning between them, touched hands within sight of the royal Philistine house. Cautious during the long encampment at Gerar, they at last relaxed their guard with a feeling of security. The affection displayed in that moment was enough to confirm them as married. But to Isaac's surprise, the Philistines demonstrated a sense of morality after all. The famine was in Isaac's heart.

Why did he fear? Was he not God's anointed? Had God not recently appeared to him, assuring blessing, even in Gerar? Yes. But there was a moment of famine, a weakness of the soul revealed. Fear overwhelms the heart, fogs the mind, constricts the voice. The soul becomes as barren as a barn in famine. Strength is like wind-blown chaff on the dusty ridges of thought. The godliest among us, unprepared, may fall into unwarranted, often premeditated fear. Another kind of fear, however, is justifiable. The Lord prophesied through the prophet Amos, "The days are coming . . . when I will send a famine through the land . . . of hearing the words of the Lord" (8:11).

Who can determine the full scope of Isaac's momentary relapse? Although this one instance is sealed in writing, it is repeatable. It behooves us to know the Word of God, its generative power, its reassuring strength, its purifying refreshment. May we know its fertility within, in that day when famine pervades the land and the soul.

SOMETHING TO THINK ABOUT

1. Why did Abraham call his wife his sister? Why did Isaac tell the same lie?

2. How does fear often overwhelm our desire to do the right thing?

3. How can a godly fear be healthy rather than crippling?

4. When our souls become desolate and hungry to the point of spiritual famine, is there a remedy?

8: Life Wells

A ROPE AROUND HIS WAIST AND ANOTHER TIED TO A CANDLE DANGLING DOWNWARD, an explorer carefully descends an old well. As long as the candle burns, he can continue safely. But should he hear the brief sizzle of his extinguished candle, he knows his discovery has reached its limit. It would be dangerous to go further than he can see.

We are like well shafts, with souls deeper than the physical surface of our bodies. Divine light is required to truly understand our nature. God will give revelation as far as it is safe for us to grasp. But the well is deep, the shaft faulty. The water is muddy and filled with debris.

Such were the wells of Abraham. Philistine foolishness filled the shafts. Driven by envy of Isaac's prosperity, they sought to cut off that contributing supply to his camp. The labor of his father to bring precious water out of those subterranean depths was ruined. So peaceful Isaac, sensitive to divine directions, moved away from the contentions, settling in a valley near rediscoverable wells.

When Isaac's servants dug these wells, the Philistines immediately claimed possession. But at last one well, *Rehobeth* (spaciousness), was christened free of interference. It was a bounteous well, an assurance of blessed fruitfulness. Isaac breathed restfully—debris removed, shaft repaired, the water rose within reach. That is an inward assurance of the divine claim. But the well may overflow. It is that well illuminated by prophecy.

Isaac's moves resemble God's work upon human hearts. He, the Divine Explorer, wishes to go deep, to restore the flow of divine influence. Jesus said of the salvation experience, "the water I give . . . will become . . . a spring of water, welling up to eternal life" (John 4:14). "Whoever believes in Me, as the Scripture has said, streams of living water will flow from within him. By this, He meant the Spirit, whom those who believed in Him were later to receive" (John 7:38–39).

But the flow comes not out of mere human endeavor. In true spiritual experience we don't move from well to well. The well moves into us: "Therefore with joy you will draw water from the wells of salvation" (Isaiah 12:3). "In that day a fountain shall be opened for the house of David and for the inhabitants of Jerusalem, for sin and for uncleanness" (Zechariah 13:1).

Its flow began at the cross of Christ in His death outside Jerusalem. "But one of the soldiers pierced His side with a spear, and immediately blood and water came out" (John 19:34). A Roman lance penetrated the Wellspring of Life, out of whom poured the elements of new birth. That was a well without contention, except for those who refuse to drink and to those who falsify claims about it. Never was the Father's well to become one of quarreling or bitterness. The well of Christ evidences an Isaac-like peace.

Isaac's wells were old wells rediscovered. He didn't need to go far to find them. The mound of earth, ringed with moisture seeping through the ground, called attention to the great potential below. So lies the fount of the Church of Jesus Christ—just within reach, but covered with worldly debris. Let us go back to the ancient well. Old, but youthfully fresh. For the sake of Christ and His Church, let us sing with the ancient saints, "Spring up, O well!" (Numbers 21:17).

Isaac "breathed his last and died, and was gathered to his people, being old and full of days" (Genesis 35:29). Into the immortal well he descended, into the light of familiar fellowship, into the bosom of Abraham—to rest unto the coming of Christ.

And when He came, the well burst open. Christ arose, the saints flowed forth like intermittent streams throughout Jerusalem (Matthew 27:52,53) and onward to heaven (Ephesians 4:8)—to the God of Abraham, Isaac, and Jacob.

SOMETHING TO THINK ABOUT

1. Beyond the obvious need for water, why were wells in the Genesis account so treasured?

2. What did Isaac do when the Philistines contested the ownership of the wells? Why not stand and fight?

3. The water was still there, but they had to dig deeper to get it. In what way must we "dig deeper" to discover all that God has planned for us?

4. What kind of water flows through the hearts and lives of believers?

SEVEN

PSALM 23: PROVIDENTIAL PROMISES

MARLENE CHASE

The Army's National Book Publishing Plan, under the direction of Lt. Colonel Marlene Chase, publishes three books each year to fulfill its goal of enabling our contemporary Salvationist voices to endure for future generations as witnesses to the continuing force and mission of The Salvation Army.

Is any passage in Scripture more loved by children of any and every age? The cadences of the 23rd Psalm have soothed our hurts and banished our fears for thousands of years, and its timeless truths remain to speak to our human situation. In times of peace, its poetic lines delight us, giving form to spontaneous praise. In times of sorrow and encroaching death we whisper its words of comfort. The providential promises embodied there shelter and sustain us, drawing God nearer still. This series explores the rich fabric of the best–loved Psalm by examining its promises of possession, provision, privilege, protection, presence, and prospect for eternity.

1: The Lord is my Shepherd, I shall not be in want.

THE 23RD PSALM IS NOT A MAGIC TALISMAN THAT WHEN REPEATED mysteriously removes trouble from our doors and provides us with a scar–free pilgrimage through this world. This well loved Scripture is to be interpreted in the spirit of God's intent and ideal for mankind—that we may love and enjoy God forever. It is a promise of spiritual well–being and perpetuity that is absolutely to be depended upon.

Foundational Truth—"The Lord Is"
Foundational Truth—"The Lord Is"

Great foundational truth and surety are to be found in the first three words of the Psalm: "The Lord is . . ." The fact of God's existence and His interest in mankind is a truth that must be embraced by faith before any of its further promises and provisions apply. God is. The Salvation Army frames this *a priori* doctrine this way: "We believe that there is only one God who is infinitely perfect, the Creator, Preserver and Governor of all things, and who is the only proper object of religious worship."

It is the same foundational truth with which all Scripture begins: "In the beginning God . . . ." This truth must be affirmed for anything that follows in Psalm 23 to make sense. The writer to the Hebrews notes, "Anyone who comes to Him must believe that He exists and that He rewards those who earnestly seek Him" (11:6).

The fact that God *is* provides the basis of all the comfort and promise that is to follow in the words of the Psalmist. "I am the Alpha and the Omega," says the Lord God, "who is, and who was, and who is to come, the Almighty" (Revelation 1:8).

Personal Application—"My Shepherd"

But beyond the fact of His existence is the vital truth that He has given His life to mankind. The great God of the universe, who needs nothing and no one, has chosen to set His love upon us, to be our provider of all that is necessary to life and living. "The Lord is my Shepherd"—not simply a shepherd or the shepherd—but mine! This is the great wonder that sends us to our knees in adoration and worship.

"God is love," John states clearly in his epistle (1 John 4:8). "This is how God showed His love among us," he continues, "He sent His one and only Son into the world that we might live through Him" (1 John 4:9). Centuries earlier, God outlined what our lives are all about: "What does the Lord your God ask of you but to fear the Lord your God, to walk in all His ways, to love Him, to serve the Lord your God with all your heart and with all your soul and to observe the Lord's commands and decrees" (Deuteronomy 10:12–13). We, His crowning creation, are His love interest, and He is to us a personal God whose love for us personally will never end. Spontaneous praise must be our response to such unmerited favor.

Benjamin Franklin wrote, "Let me then not fail to praise my God continually, for it is His due, and it is all I can return for His many favors and great goodness to me; and let me resolve to be virtuous, that I may be happy, that I may please Him, who is delighted to see me happy."

That is the wonder of it. God delights in us. For that reason He has chosen to be the Shepherd who will guide us through the confusing maze of life to the glories of a heaven He has provided for our happiness. But we must make no mistake. The command is clear: "Love the Lord your God with all your heart" (Deuteronomy 6:5). We are His possession and, wonder of wonders, He is ours!

Psalm 23 is a declaration of promise based on God's covenant with mankind whom He has chosen to "love with an everlasting love" (Jeremiah 31:3). The promise is personal; it is spiritual; it concerns the real life of mankind that is immortal, that was made for God. We must not cheapen or confuse the intent of "The Lord is my Shepherd" by missing the truths inherent in all of Scripture.

Spiritual Provision—"I Shall Not Be in Want"

"I shall not be in want" means that our spiritual needs for purpose, immortality, truth, love and faith are available because God has set His love upon us. It does not mean that we'll never experience hunger or desire in a physical sense. It doesn't mean that children will never know cruelty at the hands of the careless or unregenerate. It doesn't mean saints will be miraculously spared the terrors of evil intent.

Philip Yancey has written, "Nothing in Scripture hints that we Christians should expect life to be easier, more antiseptic, or safer. We need . . . the courage to cling to God, Job-like, despite the world of pain and sometimes because of it. Christianity calls us to complete identification with the world—the suffering world."

But in that suffering world, those who depend on God for spiritual sustenance, and the strength to endure whatever pain may be part of our journey, have a Shepherd without peer.

SOMETHING TO THINK ABOUT

1. Does Psalm 23 promise that God will remove all trouble and suffering from our paths once we put faith in Him?

2. What basic truth must be affirmed before we can take hold of the Shepherd's promises?

3. The Bible indicates that God has more than a general interest in mankind as a whole, that every individual who ever draws breath is known and loved personally. How does this psalm underscore that teaching? How does that change the way you read it?

4. When you have experienced a time of deep need (or want), what has it meant to you to read the promise of provision in Psalm 23?

2: He makes me lie down in green pastures, He leads me beside quiet waters, He restores my soul.

R. C. SPROUL SAYS THAT HIS FAVORITE ATTRIBUTE OF GOD IS SOMETHING CALLED, IN theological terms, "aseity." Aseity is the quality of God having life in and from Himself. As self-existent, self-sufficient and self-sustaining, God does not have it in Him, either in purpose or in power, to stop existing; He exists necessarily, with no need of help or support from us.

The Apostle Paul, in his address to the men of Athens, emphasized this doctrine: "The God who made the world and everything in it is the Lord of heaven and earth and does not live in temples built by hands. And He is not served by human hands, as if He needed anything, because He Himself gives all men life and breath and everything else" (Acts 17:24–25).

This quality of God, which can be ascribed to no other being, should bring us to our knees with the recognition that as God, He deserves the worship of His creatures. And it should remind us that we are completely dependent upon Him for life and sustenance. We could not live one day without Him. As human beings we are fragile. Cut off our oxygen for a few minutes and we die; go without water for a few days and we die; without food, a few days more would cause our demise. But God can never die; and this One who is from everlasting to everlasting has "given all people life and breath and everything else."

The Psalmist, with his shepherd imagery, underscored this providence. Without the shepherd's guiding, the sheep would be at a loss to find good pasture and clean water. His providence flows from His character and is the beneficent outworking of His sovereignty whereby all events are directed and disposed to bring about those purposes of glory and good for which the universe was made. Rebellious people, like stubborn sheep, often turn to other means of satisfaction, but the Good Shepherd saves them from themselves. God has sustained dominion over a rebel world, which He governs with both goodness and severity. "He causes His sun to rise on the evil and the good, and sends rain on the righteous and the unrighteous" (Matthew 5:45).

Love flows from His being as well and coincides with His providence that intends good for every person. Green pastures and quiet waters are picturesque of God's rich provision and imply contentment and nourishment. Quiet waters (literally "waters of restfulness") reflect His own peace and integrity, which He wants His creatures to enjoy. They belong to the souls who trust Him regardless of the turbulent storm through which they may be passing. "When you pass through the waters, I will be with you;" He promises, "and when you pass through the rivers, they will not sweep over you" (Isaiah 43:2). The restfulness of God is greater than any threat and often is most clearly understood in the tempest.

In his book *In the Presence of His Majesty,* Oswald Chambers asks, "Why does God bring thunderclouds and disasters when we want green pastures and still waters? Bit by bit we find, behind the clouds, the Father's feet; behind the lightning, an abiding day that has no night; behind the thunder, 'a still, small voice' that comforts with a comfort that is unspeakable. The whole claim of the redemption of Jesus is that He can satisfy the last aching abyss of the human soul, not only hereafter, but here and now."

Spiritual Restoration

God has provided everything we need to bring our lives to the fulfillment for which we were created: to love God and to enjoy Him forever. There is no natural calamity that can withhold us from His promised presence, no terror so engulfing that His providence cannot overcome it and no sin so insidious that He cannot forgive it.

In spite of mankind's sin and fall from his original position of grace, God did not abandon His creation. He has retained dominion over a rebel world and given the ultimate sacrifice in order to restore it to favor. Such is His peerless providence.

King David knew well what he was talking about when he wrote in Psalm 23 that the Lord "restores my soul." He was an adulterer, a murderer, yet God's child because of God's provision. Prophetically pointing to the cross, Isaiah underscored the completeness of God's provision through the blood of Jesus: "Come now, let us reason together, says the Lord. Though your sins are like scarlet, they shall be as white as snow; though they are red as crimson, they shall be like wool" (Isaiah 1:18).

Was any pasture greener or any water more nourishing than the presence of this One who is without beginning or end and whose nature is Love? Paul urged Timothy to "command those who are rich in this present world not to be arrogant nor to put their hope in wealth, which is so uncertain, but to put their hope in God, who richly provides us with everything for our enjoyment" (1 Timothy 6:17). In this way, Paul wrote, they would "take hold of the life that is truly life" (6:19).

SOMETHING TO THINK ABOUT

1. We often think of God providing for special or unusual needs that arise out of life's challenges, but we forget that daily He is meeting our needs. Make a list of those things that you depend upon God for.

2. What images in this part of the Psalm suggest that God often goes beyond simply meeting needs to lavishing good gifts?

3. At times we take God's gifts and squander or destroy them. Indeed, Scripture indicates that all of us have done this. (Romans 3:23 says that "All have sinned and come short of God's glory.") What images in this Psalm point to God's response to our failure?

4. We often put our trust in persons and things that we can easily see and understand—family, friends, money, talents. What quality of God makes putting trust in Him different and superior to any other object of our attention?

3: He guides me in the paths of righteousness for His name's sake.

"THE LORD IS RIGHTEOUS IN ALL HIS WAYS," DAVID AFFIRMED IN HIS PSALM, "AND LOVING toward all He has made" (145:17). And God says of Himself, "There is no God apart from Me, a righteous God and a Savior; there is none but Me" (Isaiah 45:21). This verse outlines God's nature—righteous and loving. On these twin points we see God's singular "otherness." Lesser gods have managed to be righteous, at least to some degree; some have claimed to be loving. None has been revealed to be both righteous in all ways and loving to all.

The Shepherd's Name

"He leads me in the paths of righteousness for His name's sake," writes the Psalmist. What holy privilege to be led in the same path that God Himself walks. If we are to fulfill the purpose for which we were created, it will take the Shepherd to lead the way! Without His guidance we are doomed to follow the broad way that leads to doom. The incursion of sin into the perfect world God made brought about all sorts of delusions and false directions that lure us from our purpose. But God leads us in righteous paths, at immeasurable cost to Himself, because of who He is. Righteous is His name. He can be no other.

We were "created to be like God in true righteousness and holiness" (Ephesians 4:24). Only frustration and destruction can come to the creature that does not fulfill its destiny. A flower that is born to flourish and reproduce but instead is cut off from the source of nourishment withers and dies. It is useless. Men and women, created to love and serve God in righteousness, fall short of their destiny if they pursue a lesser road than that outlined by their Creator.

God demands that we be holy as He is holy. The Psalmist asks, "Who may ascend the hill of the Lord? Who may stand in His holy place?" The answer echoes in his own voice, "He who has clean hands and a pure heart" (Psalm 24:34). But we throw up our hands in despair when we realize how impossible it is to be holy as God is holy. Like the little boy who meant to stay clean until his mother came for him, we find ourselves mussed and misshapen, dirty and walking a very crooked mile. But our Shepherd has made provision for us through the shed blood of Jesus Christ. And He will lead us in righteous paths for His name's sake.

The Shepherd's Intent

"How shall a young man cleanse his way?" the Psalmist asked. The answer is in the pronouncement that followed John the Baptist's challenge to live uprightly: "Look, the Lamb of God, who takes away the sin of the world!" (John 1:29). As Jesus emerged upon the green hills of Galilee, the baptizer pointed to the One who would show us how to walk uprightly in a bent world.

Though surrounded by evil at every turn, Jesus clung solidly to the path of righteousness. In the midst of sin He remained pure and true. And the righteousness of that One, Jesus Christ, has been imputed to us because of His death and resurrection.

"For the grace of God that brings salvation has appeared to all men. It teaches us to say 'no' to ungodly passions, and to live self-controlled, upright and godly lives in this present age, while we wait for the blessed hope; the glorious appearing of our great God and Savior, Jesus Christ, who gave Himself for us to redeem us from all wickedness and to purify for Himself a people that are His very own, eager to do what is good" (Titus 2:11–14).

The Shepherd's Enabling

Is it possible to be upright people in a bent world? What kind of God would demand what we could not accomplish? He proved that we could accomplish it, and continues to empower and enliven the spirits of men and women who choose to follow Him, who choose to walk upright in a bent world. The righteous path is not always the one bordered by green pastures and quiet waters. Jesus allowed His followers no delusion: "Wide is the gate and broad is the road that leads to destruction, and many enter through it. But small is the gate and narrow the road that leads to life, and only a few find it" (Matthew 7:13).

But provision has been made for all, and He is able to keep us in all our ways, the Word says. We are not only called to righteous living but promised the help of the Holy Spirit for every day. "Your strength will equal your days," is His promise (Deuteronomy 33:25). Paul, writing to his spiritual son Timothy, affirmed, "I know whom I have believed, and am convinced that He is able to guard what I have entrusted to Him for that day" (2 Timothy 1:12).

He leads us in the paths of righteousness for His name's sake! What blessing to be there, to remain there, strengthened and renewed every day by His Spirit.

SOMETHING TO THINK ABOUT

1. The Psalmist indicates two qualities of God that are unique in their combination from any other god or person. What are they?

2. Amazingly, He wants to give us His name and to share these qualities with us. How does it make you feel when you compare who you are with who He is?

3. If the way of righteousness is not always bordered by "green pastures" or "quiet waters," what do you make of God's promise to lead us there?

4. Think of a time in your life when everything seemed dark and hopeless (barren pastures, raging waters). How did these times relate to "paths of righteousness"?

4: Even though I walk through the valley of the shadow of death, I will fear no evil, for You are with me; Your rod and Your staff, they comfort me.

EVEN THE PHRASE "THE VALLEY OF THE SHADOW" SENDS A CHILL DOWN OUR SPINES. We have all been there, either in imagination or actual journey. Death is the one certainty that every person must face. In our natural beings we fear even the thought and tend to brush away all reminders of death, even our own aging. But death, the final frontier, the evil one's great threat, need hold no terror for the one who has put his or her hand in the Shepherd's own, for He has conquered it.

Victor Hugo's words inspire those in the valley: "Have courage for the great sorrows of life and patience for the small ones; when you have laboriously accomplished your daily tasks, go to sleep in peace. God is awake."

It would be one thing to be guided through the valleys by a shepherd who was familiar only with the heights, One who could only urge us higher from His exalted throne above us. But we do not have a shepherd "who is unable to sympathize with our weaknesses, but we have One who has been tempted in every way, just as we are—yet was without sin" (Hebrews 4:15). He knows about the valley of the shadow. "But we see Jesus, who was made a little lower than the angels, now crowned with glory and honor because He suffered death, so that by the grace of God He might taste death for everyone" (Hebrews 2:9). Death, the final enemy, has been vanquished.

At the cross, the evil one's fate was sealed, and death's hold was broken. Paul reminds us of the prophecy fulfilled when Christ broke through the prison bars of sin and its penalty. "Death has been swallowed up in victory. Where, O death, is your victory? Where, O death, is your sting?" (1 Corinthians 15:55). Then he affirms this truth with spontaneous praise, "Thanks be to God! He gives us the victory through our Lord Jesus Christ" (57).

But it is part of the enemy's strategy to recall us to an old bondage. Not content with the final outcome of the struggle, he would fool each of us into believing that he is stronger than the Author of Life. Suzanne Massie in her book *Journey* wrote of her experiences during years of treating her son's hemophilia. She acknowledged that

> *Evil is near. Sometimes late at night the air grows strongly clammy and cold around me. I feel it brushing me. All that the devil asks is acquiescence. . . . Not struggle, not conflict. Acquiescence. Accept, accept that I have won, whispers the devil. You can see for yourself that life is unjust, unfair, that suffering is ordinary. Who is stronger? I am, of course. Just despair, my dear, despair. Only tell me that I am strong, that evil rules.*

But the truth is much stronger than the lie, and the evil one's demise will be seen by every eye when Christ returns in His glory. But we need not fear the valley of the shadow now because our Shepherd is awake and His rod and staff comfort us. The shepherd's rod was largely used as a weapon to fend off intruders who would scatter the flock. Perhaps it was used as well to nudge strays back into the fold, to count off each sheep as it was lovingly led into the fold at night.

As people God loves, we need not fear His discipline. "The Lord disciplines those He loves, and He punishes everyone He accepts as a son" (Hebrews 12:6). The writer to the Hebrews continues to encourage us by comparing human discipline to that designed by God. "Our fathers disciplined us for a little while as they thought best; but God disciplines us for our good, that we may share in His holiness." We are led in the paths of righteousness "for His Name's sake" (Psalm 23:3).

Like the rod of discipline, the shepherd's staff was used for the protection of the sheep. Its hooked end could easily slip around the body of a sheep lodged in punishing briars or trapped in the crevice of a dangerous cliff. We who follow Him can be comforted to know that God's protection is promised in times of danger. Often the rod and the staff are used in conjunction but always with the purpose of saving or restoring life. David acknowledged that God "lifted me out of the slimy pit, out of the mud and mire; He set my feet on a rock and gave me a firm place to stand" (Psalm 40:2).

Paul encouraged Timothy by reminding him that the Christian is safe in the protection of the God who loves him and saves him. "The Lord will rescue me from every evil attack and will bring me safely to His heavenly kingdom" (2 Timothy 4:18). Our Shepherd has promised to be with us always, even to the end of the world, guiding, discipling, lifting, chastening in order to present us whole and unblemished before the Father. What holy privilege. What undaunted protection!

1. The "valley of the shadow of death" is a familiar landscape to all of us. We will all one day face death—our own and perhaps that of other persons we love. How is it possible that we can live without fear of it?

2. Even though Jesus conquered death at the cross, the enemy of our souls is not willing to concede defeat and often tempts us to doubt God. How can we triumph over these doubts? What has helped you deal with the death of someone close to you?

3. Consider the uses of the shepherd's rod and staff. What is God's purpose in "comforting" us with the discipline these objects represent?

4. Have you experienced God's discipline? What was the outcome? Did it match God's stated purpose for discipline in Hebrews 12?

5: You prepare a table before me in the presence of my enemies. You anoint my head with oil, my cup overflows.

OF ALL THE PROMISES INCLUDED IN THIS TIMELESS PRAYER, NONE IS SWEETER OR more pivotal than the surety of God's presence with us. Without the Shepherd, we are a harassed and helpless flock at the mercy of every greedy influence and careless whim.

Such was the condition of the people whom Jesus encountered. They were oppressed by political overseers who abused them, by religious leaders who manipulated them for personal gain. There was little hope of rising out of the poverty and bondage in which they found themselves. "When He saw the crowds, He had compassion on them, because they were harassed and helpless, like sheep without a shepherd" (Matthew 9:23).

The table is a figure for that place where Jesus dines in intimacy with His own. On the table are many good things—protection, nourishment, comfort, rest, encouragement—but the compassionate, irreplaceable Shepherd Himself is central. It is important to honor God and not the gifts He has given because Satan is well able to counterfeit most of the things we are prone to treasure. Shakespeare's Hamlet says of the ghost that stalked his grief:

> *The spirit that I have seen may be the devil: and the devil hath power to assume a pleasing shape; yea, and perhaps out of my weakness and my melancholy, as he is very potent with such spirits, abuses me to damn me.*

Ponder God's Promises

Tucked away in the fast-moving Acts of the Apostles is a brief reference that purports an astounding truth. "Last night an angel of the God whose I am and whom I serve stood beside me and said, 'Do not be afraid, Paul'" (27:23). It happened as Paul was traveling to Rome, surrounded by his enemies, to answer charges of sedition and treason. But Paul, God's obedient servant, had the attention of the most powerful protector of all, God Himself. Isn't it the province of every Christian to have this assurance? Did not Jesus say to all of us, "Surely I am with you always, even to the very end of the age" (Matthew 28:20)?

Have you ever been preoccupied and failed to notice when someone came into the room or stepped beside you? I have been at times so deeply engrossed in thought that a person's presence went unmarked at first. Then suddenly I became aware and even jumped with fright. Can that happen to us, spiritually speaking? If so, how can we remain aware, ready to be touched by Him?

God told Joshua, "Do not be afraid or terrified because . . . the Lord your God goes with you; He will never leave you nor forsake you" (Deuteronomy 31:6). The writer to the Hebrews reminded us that His promise is for all believers. "God has said, 'Never will I leave you; never will I forsake you'" (Hebrews 13:5). Salvation Army officer Brigadier Joseph Korbel, arrested in Czechoslovakia for his faith, was condemned to live in a prison camp for ten years. Only the promises of God sustained him and others in the midst of their enemies. Korbel was forced on one occasion to stand outside in the dead of winter. With his hands tied over his head to menacing barbed wire, he whispered the promises of his God. The sky darkened and his heart grew faint; he felt he could not endure more. Suddenly, Korbel felt a strange warmth. He looked up and saw "a pair of beautiful white hands covering [his] own." God gifted this suffering servant the reality of His powerful presence in his darkest hour.

Promote God's Plan

We can find a fresh awareness of God's presence if we steadfastly promote God's plan. "Trust in the Lord with all your heart and lean not on your own understanding; in all your ways, acknowledge Him, and He will make your paths straight" (Proverbs 3:5–6). If we are truly His sheep, listening for our Master's voice instead of going ahead on our own, we have His promised presence. He is always with us. It is we who stray.

Often we ignore God until the moment of danger. Then, having not learned to look for Him, or to listen for His voice, we do not recognize Him. By seeking the guidance of the Spirit and living in obedience to God, we can experience His presence in real and loving ways.

Practice God's Presence

"Be still and know that I am God" (Psalm 46:10). This implies an action of our will. It's important to acknowledge God's presence, to turn to Him in prayer and thank Him for being there, even when we don't feel Him near. Knowing that the Lord stood beside him made Paul able to endure what lay ahead, even the possibility of torture and death. Pondering the promises of God, promoting His plan, and practicing His presence were sound measures the early Christians employed. Now, as then, He is beside us in the battle. That's the overarching message of Psalm 23. It is the tender reality for all of us who follow the Shepherd. It is the Lord's presence that makes our hearts overflow with joy.

1. What does the table in the wilderness represent?

2. It is important to note the location of the table. The enemies that surrounded the table in the psalm might have been bears or lions. What are some of the enemies that work to keep us from intimacy with Christ?

3. Like Paul, we can be more aware of God's presence if we look for Him—practice His presence with us. How can we do this in our modern situations?

4. Can you think of examples from the lives of other Christians or your own when God provided His intimate self at the very moment of greatest danger from an enemy?

6: Surely goodness and love will follow me all the days of my life, and I will dwell in the house of the Lord forever.

DAVID NOW COMES TO THE FINAL AFFIRMATION OF HIS SONG OF THE SHEPHERD. HE has outlined all the possessions, provisions and privileges of those who follow the Lord. Now comes the crowning gift—enjoying God's covenant gifts on earth and living forever with this One who loves us with an everlasting love. One comes to the end of Psalm 23 and wants to shout "hallelujah" and at the same time is awed into silence at such grace.

Goodness and love were covenant benefits well known to the Israelites to whom God had said, "Know that the Lord your God is . . . a faithful God, keeping His covenant of love to a thousand generations of those who love Him" (Deuteronomy 7:9). The benefits depended upon the Israelites keeping the terms of the covenant between themselves and God. They well knew that obedience to Him was the key. God said, "If you pay attention to these laws and are careful to follow them, then the Lord your God will keep His covenant of love with you, as He swore to your forefathers" (Deuteronomy 7:12).

We are of the thousand generations later who still inherit the promise. Some would like to read Psalm 23 as a kind of mantra in which our repetitions magically bring good fortune and blessing. But such a careless interpretation would be to misunderstand the person of God. It would as well take the very heart out of life and in the end lead the unwary to certain destruction.

Goodness and love follow those who obey God's laws. But it is important to understand that we are not promised a life of ease and continual pleasure. The Bible does not promise that our journey through life will be trouble-free. "In the world you will have tribulation, but be of good cheer. I have overcome the world," Jesus said in John 16:33. He overcame it with His sacrificial love revealed on Calvary. It is the goodness and love of Jesus Christ which are given to us as eternal possessions. We receive them by faith, and as we follow Christ these gifts follow (literally pursue) us through life and beyond.

The idea of pursuit is a wonderful insight because it accords with the truth that God from the very beginning has pursued mankind with His love. Not content to remain in the vaulted regions of heaven, He descended to earth in order to reclaim His lost children so dearly loved. And at what price His pursuit! Francis Thompson vividly describes the pursuit of the "Hound of Heaven" in his poem by that title:

> *I fled Him, down the nights and down the days;*
> *I fled Him, down the arches of the years;*
> *I fled Him, down the labyrinthine ways*
> *Of my own mind; and in the mist of tears*
> *I hid from Him.*

In more than seventy lines of poetic verse Thompson chronicles his flight from the "Hound," and at the climax God "Halts by me that footfall;/Is my gloom, after all,/Shade of His hand, outstretched caressingly?/'Ah, fondest, blindest, weakest,/I am He Whom thou seekest! Thou dravest love from thee, who dravest Me.'"

How lovingly and persistently He pursues us, not forcing His laws upon us but giving His love to us. And when we recognize who He is and how dearly He has sought our company, we obey His laws out of love. He pursues us not only to secure our redemption, but He stays with us for the long haul—through the trials that will come, through the sorrows that assail us, through the temptations that are the portion of every Christian.

His love follows us, assuring us that we are His. He does this through His Holy Spirit, our Comforter given when Jesus returned to heaven. "I will not leave you as orphans; I will come to you. . . . On that day you will realize that I am in My Father, and you are in Me, and I am in you" (John 14:18, 20). What assurance this must have given to those despondent disciples who stood gazing up into heaven, longing for sight of the One whom they loved, the One in whom all their longings were engaged. And what confidence it gives us now to know that we will not be left in this world as orphans, but our Father will be our Father always in this world and the next.

There is a wonderful parallel passage to Psalm 23 in John's Revelation. Imagine John on the lonely Isle of Patmos where he had been exiled. Perhaps as he waited and prayed and even as God gave Him the astounding visions contained in the book of Revelation, John remembered something! Surely John had learned the psalm of David. His friend Jesus may have even quoted it as He quoted so many Psalms during His thirty-three years on earth. Maybe John was thinking of Psalm 23 when he wrote this verse of the Revelation: "For the Lamb at the center of the throne will be their shepherd; He will lead them to springs of living water. And God will wipe away every tear from their eyes" (Revelation 7:17).

John is writing what God reveals about the end times and about heaven. Among the great passages about the Lamb that fill Revelation is this one about the Lamb being the shepherd and leading His own to springs of living water. From these springs they will never have to leave but will be forever nourished and refreshed because of the Eternal Lamb, now at the center of the throne of God. And all their sorrows will be at an end for He will "wipe every tear from their eyes."

The Lord is my shepherd when first He created me and loved me, when He purchased my salvation and followed me with His love, and all the way to Heaven where our union will be hallowed forevermore. That's the great prospect—love for eternity with the Shepherd and Lamb of God!

SOMETHING TO THINK ABOUT

1. What are the covenant blessings assured in the final passage of Psalm 23?

2. We sometimes hear Christians teach that God promises the Christian prosperity in this world and that when we don't experience it, something is lacking in our faith. Contrast this idea with God's ultimate purpose for mankind.

3. "Goodness and love shall follow me," writes the Psalmist. What do the words "follow me" indicate? What does this concept say about the nature of God?

4. Contrast John's Revelation (chapter 7) with Psalm 23. What do we learn about God's ultimate aim for those who love Him?

EIGHT

PETER AND THE PEOPLE OF GOD

BRAMWELL H. TILLSLEY

General Bramwell H. Tillsley (Retd.) served as The Salvation Army's international leader from 1993 to 1994. From his home in Canada he continues to write for Salvation Army publications and is featured at Bible conferences and seminars. He is the author of several books including *Life in the Spirit* and *This Mind in You.*

Those who were once "pilgrims and strangers" are addressed as God's chosen and promised His special care during times that would try their faith and allegiance. Throughout Peter's letters, God's people learn both what is promised and what is expected, echoing the closing benediction of Jesus' promise of peace—to those who trust and obey.

1: Joy in Suffering

IN HIS FIRST EPISTLE, PETER WROTE TO CHRISTIANS EXPERIENCING difficult times. They were "harassed by all kinds of trials" (1 Peter 1:6, Phillips). In the letter, Peter reminds them that what life does *to* us depends on what life finds *in* us. On more than fifteen occasions, Peter refers to the suffering that Christians will experience because of their faith (2:19–23; 3:14–18; 4:1–4,15–19; 5:10). He reminds them that they should expect suffering because their way of life is in sharp contrast to the ways of the world (4:12). Jesus had previously indicated that this would be the case: "In the world you will have many trials and sorrows" (John 16:33).

The purpose of Peter's letters was to bring encouragement to a discouraged people. "I have written to you briefly . . . encouraging you" (1 Peter 5:12). To accomplish this, Peter reminds them that this life is not the last act in the drama, referring to them as "strangers and pilgrims" (2:11). This phrase described a person resident in a country not his own. In one sense we are all pilgrims, for our true citizenship is in heaven (Philippians 3:20). When the New Testament writers refer to us as "strangers and pilgrims" (Hebrews 11:13), they are not urging withdrawal from the world, but are rather helping us see things in the light of eternity. "For here we have no continuing city, but we seek one to come" (Hebrews 13:14).

At the moment, we are living in an alien world where Satan is the god and prince (John 14:30; 2 Corinthians 4:3–4). This being true, the absence of Satanic opposition would indeed be strange. God declared war on Satan after the fall of man (Genesis 3:15), and Satan has been attacking God through His people ever since. Our trials are varied. Peter described them as "many colored" or *poikilos* (1 Peter 1:6). The only other time he employs this word is in 4:10 to describe the grace of God. The inference is that God's grace, which is also "many colored," exactly matches our need.

A Life Full of Hope

Peter moves quickly from speaking of our present condition, which is transitory, to the permanent hope we have in Christ. He describes this as a "life full of hope" (1:3 Phillips), which lies in sharp contrast to our condition outside of Christ. "You were excluded from God's people, Israel, and you did not know the promises God has made to them. You lived in a world without God and without hope" (Ephesians 2:12). Peter then amplifies what he means: "Thank God, the God and Father of our Lord Jesus Christ, that in His great mercy we have been born again into a life full of hope, through Christ's rising from the dead. You can now hope for a perfect inheritance, beyond the reach of change and decay, reserved in heaven for you" (1:3–4 Phillips).

The Christian's rebirth happens by the will and act of God. "Born, not of blood, nor of the will of the flesh, nor of the will of man, but of God" (John 1:13). This rebirth ushers in a stability of life which is unknown outside of Christ. Our inheritance is described as imperishable, undefiled and unfading (1:4). The inheritance of the Christian is God Himself. "The Lord is the portion of mine inheritance" (Psalm 16:5 KJV). Perhaps this is why Peter constantly links glory with suffering. Through suffering, we are being prepared for glory. "Though now for a little while you may have suffered grief in all kinds of trials. These have come so that your faith . . . may be proved genuine and may result in praise, glory and honor when Jesus Christ is revealed" (1:6–7). When we are born again, we exchange the passing glory of man for the eternal glory of God. Suffering today means glory tomorrow. "If so be that we suffer with Him, that we may be also glorified together" (Romans 8:17 KJV).

Helen Keller provides us with a beautiful example of how we can turn our suffering into glory. Speaking at a college where she was receiving a special honor, she responded with these words:

> *Once I knew the depth where no hope was and darkness lay on the face of all things. Then love came and set my soul free. Once I fretted and beat myself against a wall that shut me in.*

My life was without a past or future, and death a "consummation devoutly to be wished."
But a little word from the fingers of another fell into my hands that clutched at emptiness,
and my heart leapt up with the rapture of living. I do not know the meaning of darkness, but
I have learned the overcoming of it.

We in the western world seem to experience little suffering because of our Christian faith. Could this be due to a lack of nerve on the part of the church to challenge a contemporary world with the message of the cross? Are we willing to live according to the teachings of Jesus with uncompromising zeal? Of course there is a price to be paid. "Everyone who wants to live a godly life in Christ Jesus will be persecuted" (2 Timothy 3:12). This challenge, however, is matched with a beautiful promise from 2 Timothy 2:12: "If we endure, we will also reign with Him."

To the old rugged cross I will ever be true,
Its shame and reproach gladly bear;
Then He'll call me someday to my home far away
Where His glory forever I'll share.

(George Bennard, The Salvation Army *Song Book* #124)

SOMETHING TO THINK ABOUT

1. Why should Christians expect suffering in this world?

2. Can you recall an experience when God's "many-colored" grace met one of your "many- colored" trials?

3. Helen Keller turned her suffering into glory, saying, "love came and set my soul free." The suffering you are passing through may become glory, too. How does this happen?

4. What is God's promise to those who are suffering for Christ (2 Timothy 2:12)?

2: God's Provision

IN HIS LETTER TO NEW CHRISTIANS AROUND THE WORLD, PETER MAKES REFERENCE to the contrast of their old life with their new. "Once you were not a people, but now you are the people of God" (1 Peter 2:10). This change occurred as a result of their new relationship to God, made possible through Christ. Peter goes on to describe this process.

He begins by indicating that all three persons in the Godhead were involved. In 1:2 he speaks of them as being "elect." This title had previously belonged to Israel alone (Deuteronomy 7:6; Isaiah 45:4). To be "elect" means to receive God's grace. This privilege is the result of God's initiative, not ours. Salvation is not the upward reach of man but the downward reach of God. "We love Him, because He first loved us" (1 John 4:19). Extreme positions have been taken in the matter of election and free will, but it should be clear that anything that denies God's right to take the initiative or denies man's responsibility to respond is an unbalanced position. Richard Halverson wrote, "Nothing God planned interferes with human freedom. Nothing humans do frustrates God's sovereign plan." Someone has said that the doctrine of election is easy to understand: God has one vote and that is always for you. Satan has one vote and that is always against you. You have the other vote, and that decides the election. We have been "chosen according to the foreknowledge of God the Father, by the sanctifying work of the Spirit, for obedience to Jesus Christ and sprinkling by His Blood" (1 Peter 1:2). We have been chosen by the Father; purchased by the Son; set apart by the Spirit.

The Suffering Lamb

Peter then writes of the cost of our redemption. "For you know that it was not with perishable things such as silver and gold that you were redeemed . . . but with the precious Blood of Christ, a lamb without blemish or defect" (1:18–19). To "redeem" means to set free by paying a price. For example, a slave could be freed with money, but no amount can set a lost sinner free. Only the Blood can redeem us.

When Peter spoke of Jesus as the lamb without blemish, his mind was going back to some Old Testament pictures. The doctrine of sacrifice is first recorded in Genesis 3, when God killed animals that He might clothe Adam and Eve. Then the Passover lamb was slain for each household (Exodus 12). The prophet Isaiah described the Messiah as a lamb. "He was led like a lamb to the slaughter" (Isaiah 53:7). John the Baptist pointed to Jesus and said, "Look, the Lamb of God who takes away the sins of the world" (John 1:29). In heaven, the song of the redeemed is "Worthy is the Lamb" (Revelation 5:11–14).

Peter clarifies that Christ's death was by divine appointment, not by accident. "He was chosen before the creation of the world, but was revealed in these last times for your sake" (1 Peter 1:20). Here we have a vision of God who was Redeemer before He was Creator. His redeeming work was not an emergency measure to salvage something that had gone wrong, for Jesus was "the Lamb that was slain from the foundation of the world" (Revelation 13:8).

The Triumphant Christ

Peter then reminds his readers that Jesus is not only the Lamb who was slain; He is also the resurrected and triumphant Christ to whom God the Father gave glory. The New Testament writers seldom separate the cross from the resurrection. "Through Him you believe in God, who raised Him from the dead, and glorified Him, and so your faith and hope are in God" (1 Peter 1:21). In 3:18 Peter returns to the theme of the sacrificial death of Christ. "For Christ died for sins once for all, the righteous for the unrighteous, to bring you to God." The work of Christ was unique, never to be repeated. "He died to sin once" (Romans 6:10). To "bring [us] to God" is a technical term meaning "to gain an audience at court." Because of the cross we have open access to God and may come boldly to the throne of grace. "Let us then approach the throne of grace with confidence, so that we may receive mercy, and find grace to help us in our time of need" (Hebrews 4:16). Sin interrupts the relationship which exists between God and man. The object of sacrifice is to restore that relationship.

Peter sees the work of Christ as a triumph. "It saves you by the resurrection of Jesus Christ, who has gone into heaven and is at God's right hand—with angels, authorities, and powers in submission to Him" (1 Peter 3:21–22). His position is one of supreme authority. He is the ruler of the universe. "And God placed all things under His feet and appointed Him to be head over everything" (Ephesians 1:22). When we read the paper or watch the news, we are tempted to ask: What is it all coming to? Is God really in control? The answer is found in the Word. "God purposed long ago in His sovereign will that all human history should be consummated in Christ, that everything that exists in heaven or earth should find its perfection and fulfillment in Him" (Ephesians 1:10, Phillips). God is still on the throne.

SOMETHING TO THINK ABOUT

1. All three Persons of the Trinity were involved in our redemption according to 1 Peter 1:2. What role did each take?

2. Our salvation was not an afterthought. What verse of Scripture proves this?

3. The object of the sacrifice of the Lamb was to restore the relationship between God and man. Because of Christ we can "gain an audience at the court of God"!

4. We can remind ourselves in time of terror and the seeming rise of evil that "all human history (will be) consummated in Christ . . . [and will] find its perfection and fulfillment in Him" (Ephesians 1:10).

3: The Call to Holiness

THE PEOPLE TO WHOM PETER WROTE WERE DESCRIBED AS "STRANGERS AND PILGRIMS" (1 Peter 2:11). Prior to establishing a new relationship with God through Jesus Christ, their lives left much to be desired. "For you have spent enough time in the past doing what pagans choose to do—living in debauchery, lust, drunkenness, orgies, carousing and detestable idolatry" (4:3). All this has changed, thus Peter adds: "Once you were not a people, but now you are the people of God; once you had not received mercy, but now you have received mercy" (2:10).

Peter describes their new status: "But you are a chosen people, a royal priesthood, a holy nation, a people belonging to God, that you may declare the praises of Him who called you out of darkness into His wonderful light" (2:9). The picture of the church in these verses parallels God's description of Israel in Exodus 19:5–6 and Deuteronomy 7:6. The church is to God and the world what Israel was meant to be. We are:

- A chosen people, which of course speaks to the grace of God. Jesus said, "You did not choose Me, but I chose you" (John 15:16).

- A royal priesthood, the priest being the one who had access to God and whose task it was to open the way for others. The word for priest (*pontifex*) means "bridge-builder."

- A holy nation, or *hagios,* meaning "different." We are thus dedicated to God's will and God's service.

- A people belonging to God. Very often the value of something is determined by who has owned it. An ordinary thing acquires new value if it has been in the possession of a famous person. The Christian takes on new value as one who belongs to God.

A young prince was playing with some commoners when suddenly his true identity was discovered. The children were amazed, and commented, "But I thought you said you were a nobody." The prince replied, "I am nobody, but my father is the king."

> *I'm the child of a King;*
> *With Jesus my Savior,*
> *I'm the child of a King!*
>
> (Harriet Buell, The Salvation Army *Song Book* #354)

In light of who we are, the challenge comes in 1 Peter 1:15,16: "But just as He who called you is holy, so be holy in all you do; for it is written: Be holy, because I am holy." This had been God's message to Israel in Leviticus 11:44,45, 19:2 and 20:7.

The exhortation to holiness begins with a negative statement. "As obedient children, do not conform to the evil desires you had when you lived in ignorance" (1 Peter 1:14). Paul urged the Church in Rome not to be conformed to this world (Romans 12:2). So Peter urged his readers not to be conformed to their former passions which had dominated their lives prior to their entrance into God's family (Leviticus 20:26). Children inherit the nature of their parents. Since God is holy, His children are exhorted to be holy. We are to be "partakers of the divine nature" (2 Peter 1:4). "God is light and in Him is no darkness at all" (1 John 1:5). Any holiness we have in character and conduct is derived from Him. Having said this, there are a number of misconceptions many have regarding the life of holiness.

A Holy, Joyful People

Holiness does not make a man or woman any less a man or woman. Holy means "different" or "separate," thus the Temple and the Sabbath were considered holy. However, because the Temple was considered holy, it did not cease to be a building. Likewise, we do not cease to be human. Our "humanness" and our "holiness" are not opposites of which we cannot have both. General Frederick Coutts reminded us that "we should not make the mistake of supposing that holiness means the eradication of our normal, human appetites. The redirection and control of all to the divine glory, yes, but the eradication of none."

The experience of holiness is not the enemy of life's joys. Samuel Logan Brengle wrote: "Next to virtue, the fun in the world is what we can least spare." Holiness is an experience to be enjoyed, not endured. C. S. Lewis was right when he stated: "How little people know who think that holiness is dull." How beautifully Mother Teresa embodied her own teaching that "true holiness consists in doing God's will with a smile." It was because they were a joyful people that Christians were able to conquer the world.

Holiness involves being separated from sin, but also being separated unto the gospel. To be set apart for God does not mean we are set apart from men. William Penn stated that "true godliness does not turn men out of the world but enables them to live better in it, and excites their endeavor to mend it." A genuine experience of holiness can be developed only in the field of personal relationships. It undoubtedly has an other-worldly inspiration but a this-worldly application.

Simply put, holiness is Christlikeness. It is the revealing of Christ's own character in the life of the believer. It is conforming to the image of God's Son, for Jesus is our standard. There is no such thing as holiness apart from Christ in you. No wonder Peter would write, "Once you were not a people but now you are the people of God" (2:10).

He wills that I should holy be
That holiness I long to feel,
That full divine conformity
To all my Saviour's righteous will.

(Charles Wesley, The Salvation Army *Song Book* #419)

SOMETHING TO THINK ABOUT

1. A young boy playing with friends was discovered to be a prince. "I am nobody, but my father is the king," he said. How could we apply this statement spiritually?

2. Conforming to the world's standard is easy, but children of God are called to be different. We are called to be holy, a concept that seems unattainable, but would God call us to something we could not do?

3. What are some common misconceptions about the life of holiness?

4. To be holy means to be separate or different. The Temple was considered holy, but it did not cease to be a building. How can this metaphor be applied spiritually?

THROUGHOUT HIS EPISTLE, IT IS OBVIOUS THAT PETER WAS AWARE OF THE CONCERNS of the people to whom he was writing. He begins by referring to them as "strangers in the world, scattered throughout Pontus, Galatia, Cappadocia, Asia, and Bithynia" (1 Peter 1:1). They were away from home, with no permanent residence. Peter describes them as "aliens and strangers in the world" (2:11). This situation created an unstable environment in which to live.

Although they rejoiced in the promise of future hope, the present was difficult. "Though now for a little while you may have had to suffer grief in all kinds of trials" (1:6). They were totally misunderstood by the people among whom they lived. "Live such good lives among the pagans that, though they accuse you of doing wrong, they may see your good deeds and glorify God in the day He visits us" (2:12).

They were exposed to physical persecution. "Dear friends, don't be surprised at the painful trial you are suffering. . . . Rejoice that you participate in the sufferings of Christ" (4:12,13). The Apostle Paul prayed for this experience. "I want to know Christ and the power of His resurrection and the fellowship of sharing in His sufferings, becoming like Him in His death, and so, somehow, to attain to the resurrection from the dead" (Philippians 3:10,11). This may be easy to pray, but not easy to experience.

A Formidable Foe

Peter was very much aware of the power of Satan. "Your enemy the devil prowls around like a roaring lion, looking for someone to devour" (1 Peter 5:8). Of course, very often, Satan himself masquerades as "an angel of light" (2 Corinthians 11:14). The word Satan means "adversary," while the Devil (*diabolos*) literally means a slanderer. In His High Priestly prayer, Jesus portrays Satan as a person. With reference to the disciples, He prays, "protect them from the evil one" (John 17:15). In the disciples' prayer, we read: "And lead us not into temptation, but deliver us from the evil one" (Matthew 6:13). In the preface to *The Screwtape Letters,* C. S. Lewis warned of "two equal and opposite errors" concerning Satan. The errors, according to Lewis, are either in taking the devil altogether too seriously or in not taking him seriously enough. Satan should be taken seriously because of his immense power, but not too seriously, because he has been defeated. According to Peter, he is to be "resisted" (see 1 Peter 5:9).

Peter reminds his friends that they will be "insulted because of the name of Christ" (4:14). They will also "suffer according to God's will" (4:19). To these people Peter longs to bring a message of encouragement. He does in 5:7—"Cast all your anxiety on [God] because He cares for you." J. B. Phillips translates this verse as "You can throw the whole weight of your anxieties upon Him, for you are His personal concern."

A Faithful Friend

Do we really believe that God cares for the individual? Many, it would seem, do not. This is the case with thousands of young people, as evidenced by the rash of teen suicides. Every year in the United States approximately 400,000 young people attempt suicide. The prevailing attitude is one of despair, indicating the need for an anchor to provide a sense of hope. Perhaps our knowledge of the universe militates against a belief in God's concern for the individual. Scientists tells us there are stars so far away that light traveling at 186,000 miles per second will take fifty million years to reach us. In such a world, can God be aware of my personal needs?

Listen to the message of the Psalmist. "He heals the brokenhearted and binds up their wounds. He determines the number of the stars and calls them each by name. Great is our Lord and mighty in power; His understanding has no limit" (Psalm 147:3–5). The prophet Isaiah added: "For this is what the high and lofty One says . . . 'I live in a high and holy place, but also with him who is contrite and lowly in spirit'" (Isaiah 57:15). God has two thrones: one in heaven and the other in a humble, human heart. To such a God Peter says, "You can throw the whole weight of your anxieties on Him, for you are His personal concern."

Jesus put the matter in simpler terms when He spoke of the sparrow. We read in Matthew 10:29: "Are not two sparrows sold for a penny? Yet not one of them will fall to the ground apart from the will of your Father." Luke, giving the same illustration, wrote, "Are not five sparrows sold for two pennies? Yet not one of them is forgotten by God" (Luke 12:6). You don't need to be an Einstein to note the discrepancy in these two accounts. In Palestine, a purchaser could buy two sparrows for one penny. If he was prepared to spend two pennies, he received not four sparrows but five. But Jesus said that even the one that was "thrown in" mattered to God. "Don't be afraid; you are worth more than many sparrows" (Luke 12:7).

A feature of the Bible is its chapters of names and genealogies. Paul Tournier says, "There was a time when I thought these chapters could well have been omitted from the Bible. Then I came to see they are but symbols of the infinite number of people God knows by name." Peter's message of encouragement does not answer all of our questions. It does, however, help us center our thoughts not on the changing circumstances of life, but on the unchanging character of God.

SOMETHING TO THINK ABOUT

1. Imagine that Peter is writing to you while living in the twenty–first century. How would his instruction and encouragement apply?

2. Do you rejoice when called upon to participate in Christ's suffering? In what ways do some Christians today fit this description?

3. What are some of the devil's masquerades?

4. Reading the genealogies of the Bible are symbolic of the infinite number of people God knows by name. Thank Him at this moment that He knows your name, too.

THE RECURRING THEME THROUGHOUT PETER'S EPISTLE IS THAT OF GRACE. "GRACE and peace be yours in abundance" (1 Peter 1:2). "Set your hope fully on the grace to be given you" (1:13). "As heirs with you of the gracious gift of life" (3:7). "This is the true grace of God. Stand fast in it" (5:12). In 5:10 Peter reminds his readers that this grace will:

- **Restore**—a word commonly used for setting a fracture or, as in Mark 1:19, mending nets. This epistle was written to those who had endured much suffering. Suffering can, of course, drive a person to bitterness and despair. It may take away any faith we may have. But if accepted in the trusting certainty that a father's hand will never cause his child a needless tear, suffering can provide an experience that the easy way of life could never bring.

- **Make you strong**—or fill you with strength. This phrase literally means to make as solid as granite. To change the image, it means that if, through suffering, we continue to trust Christ, we will emerge like steel that has been tempered in the fire. Of course, a life without effort becomes weak or flabby. Our faith only emerges with true strength when tested in the furnace of affliction. The wind will extinguish a weak flame, but it will fan a strong flame unto a greater blaze.

- **Settle**—or lay a strong foundation. Suffering drives us to the very bedrock of our faith. Jesus spoke of the house founded on the rock that was able to withstand the storm (Matthew 7:24–27). A believer, equipped by God, will "continue in [the] faith, established and firm" (Colossians 1:23).

David Seamands, a Christian counselor, summed up his career with these words: "Many years ago, I was driven to the conclusion that the two major causes of most emotional problems among evangelical Christians are these: the failure to understand, receive, and live out God's unconditional grace and forgiveness; and the failure to give out that unconditional love, forgiveness, and grace to other people."

Rejoice in Suffering

A major theme of the New Testament is that suffering for the Christian is inevitable. "For it has been granted to you on behalf of Christ not only to believe on Him, but also to suffer for Him" (Philippians 1:29). When Paul and Barnabas visited churches, they warned the people that "we must go through many hardships to enter the kingdom of God" (Acts 14:22). The encouraging feature was that they were serving "the God of all grace" (1 Peter 5:10). This was the God who gave the assurance: "My grace is sufficient for you" (2 Corinthians 12:9), and this enabled the Apostle Paul to respond, "Our competence comes from God" (2 Corinthians 3:5).

A major obstacle to faith in the lives of many people is the whole question of suffering. There is no slick or easy answer to this vast and complex challenge. It was not a part of God's original creation. "God saw all that He had made, and it was very good" (Genesis 1:31). Sometimes, however,

God uses suffering to speak to us. This does not imply that He causes the suffering. Leslie Weatherhead suggested that sometimes God uses lamps he has neither made nor lit to bring glory to Himself. It is sometimes during illness that we catch a vision of what is really important and of value. It is not so much our situation but our reaction to the situation that really matters. If I become bitter and resentful, I still have the problem and also the bitterness as well. On the other hand, suffering can produce depths of character, sensitivity, understanding and spiritual reality, and thus it is anything but a disaster. The Apostle Paul wrote of this in Romans 5:3–4: "We also rejoice in our sufferings, because we know that suffering produces perseverance; perseverance, character; and character, hope."

After writing on the inevitability of suffering, Peter gives his readers his final benediction. "Peace to all of you who are in Christ" (1 Peter 5:14). This was an echo of the words of Jesus Himself. "I have told you these things, so that in Me you may have peace" (John 16:33). "Peace I leave with you; My peace I give you. I do not give to you as the world gives. Do not let your hearts be troubled and do not be afraid" (John 14:27).

There are few things for which men so wistfully long as peace. In the New Testament, peace is not simply a negative concept. It does not merely describe the absence of trouble and hardship and distress. It is not the chief end or goal of life but rather the consequences of something else. The verb form means to "bind together." It thus speaks of right relationships. Righteousness and peace go together (see Psalm 85:10). In the New Testament, God is called the "God of peace" no fewer than six times. We can experience the peace of God only when we have made our peace with God. A Chinese proverb reads:

> *If there is righteousness in the heart, there will be beauty in the character. If there is beauty in the character, there will be harmony in the home. If there is harmony in the home, there will be peace in the nation. If there is peace in the nation, there will be peace in the world.*

SOMETHING TO THINK ABOUT

1. What can grace accomplish in the Christian life?

2. What can grace accomplish in your life today?

3. Recall a time when you found God's grace sufficient for you in a very real way.

4. "Righteousness and peace go together," we read in Psalm 85:10. Should we be surprised then at the absence of peace in the world?

A Portrait of Perfection

Luke set out to write a gospel of Jesus Christ for the whole world. Indeed the footprints of the Master mark ordinary lives with splendor. The writer to the Hebrews pictures One who is the express image of God, yet One who came to live among us, to be one of us, to never leave us. In unexpected ways He revolutionizes the lives of saints past and present.

NINE

LUKE: A SYMPHONY OF HOPE

JAMES FARRELL

Major James Farrell served in the Army with his wife Barbara for more than twenty–seven years. He held various appointments throughout the Southern territory including the College for Officer Training in Atlanta. Major Farrell retired in 1999. He continues his teaching career in Ocala, Florida.

With Luke as our guide and the Holy Spirit as our inspiration, we enter into his joyful gospel, a song of salvation, put together as tightly as a Beethoven symphony and as beautifully and poignantly as Brahms' "Requiem." We will discover the wonders that thrilled and agonized his soul and, in so doing, recognize the clear measure of our own hope.

1: Luke's Symphony in Themes and Words

LUKE'S SONG IS BOTH INTRICATE AND PROFOUND. THE PRELUDE IN the first four verses describes how the Gospel came to be written: "Many have undertaken to draw up an account of the things that have been fulfilled among us" (1). We discover that it seemed good to Luke also, "since I myself have carefully investigated everything from the beginning . . . to write an orderly account for you." The content is a clarion call sounding the great declaration of all "the things that have been fulfilled among us."

It was written to Theophilus (translated "God-lover"), a man of possibly equestrian rank who converted to Christianity. Luke addresses him as "most excellent." Coincidence? Or is it only those who have the "shout of a King among them" who can sing this great declaration?

"God is not a man, that He should lie, nor a son of man, that He should change His mind. Does He speak and then not act? Does He promise and not fulfill? . . . The Lord their God is with them; the shout of the King is among them" (Numbers 23:19–21). Like snatches of notes in the overtures of Broadway musicals, Luke has included hints of his gospel's themes in the prologue (5–25).

We will see how our Lord touched the poor, the disenfranchised, the diseased, the lepers, the blind, the bereaved, and even the dead. We'll catch a glimpse of the Lord's anger smoldering against the hypocrisy, conceit, and indifference of those who prided themselves on knowing His Father and boasted of their connection to Him. We will see His care for women and their little ones. And we will witness this same Jesus urging them to "watch" for Him to come again, and how He clarified the signs so that we, too, can watch and understand the times in which we live.

And in a dark place between Zion and Golgotha we will see Him pray and teach His disciples to pray. Luke reports from that prayer vigil on Jerusalem's Mount of Olives that the Master had to admonish His disciples for lapsing from prayer into sleep (Luke 22:46). "Up!" He says even now. "To prayer—or to temptation."

The prologue presents these themes which we meet again and again in the gospel, bringing us the joy of recognition when we do, like meeting old and beloved friends. These truths will bury themselves deep within us if we so allow.

How Luke's Gospel Came to Be

The Gospel of Luke is a monument to Christ. It reads with a naturalness and reasonableness that attests to its authenticity. Yet Luke, so far as anyone knows, never met Christ. Whence then his "intelligence"? How and where did he come upon this treasure? Paul the apostle is the key. He is the link here between heaven's voice and earth's ear.

Some traditions have Luke meeting Paul on the apostle's second missionary journey at Troas in what is now Turkey (Acts 16:10). It is after this meeting that the third person pronouns "they and them" in Acts are replaced by the first person pronouns "we and us."

Luke was a brilliant scholar, obviously. And brilliant people, once they suspect truth, begin to crave it. Paul opened a crack in Luke's dark soul, and a shaft of heaven's light, like an arrow, found his own heart. The Holy Spirit and Paul's words drove his spirit. The Bible speaks of friendship such as theirs: "as iron sharpeneth iron, so a man his friend" (Proverbs 27:17 KJV). Approximately twenty years after Paul's glorious conversion, their intellects met, the sparks flew and Luke became a new creation in Christ.

They walked dusty roads, climbed rugged hills, sailed wild seas, with hardly a break in conversation. The eyes of the teacher full of awe for the thing he was teaching; the eyes of the student sparkling with the radiance of discovery. The Holy Spirit filled both giver and receiver. "Wait!" Luke may have shouted, "I have to write this down."

Luke watched as Paul became more and more pressed by enemies growing ever bolder. The Romans imprisoned Paul, the Jews scourged him, the pagans stoned him, the waters of the sea rushed to engulf him. Yet he kept balanced, kept bright with heaven's light, rejoicing and singing, helping and giving. And Luke recorded it, marveled at it, was gladdened by it. It confirmed and authenticated everything that was ringing and singing inside him.

Then there was that final Passover when Paul went up to Jerusalem bearing funds for the church there. The Jewish leaders were watching for him, waiting for him. They plotted to kill him but were prevented, and Paul was locked away in a dungeon in Caesarea.

"Go, dear Luke," he may have whispered through the iron bars, "go and find the facts. Record everything in a book. Look for eyewitnesses; many still live who were touched by Him. Go; see His mother Mary, who lives with John in Ephesus. She can tell you of the circumstances of His birth and life and death. There are others. Lepers and blind, rich and poor. All have stories. All love Him dearly. Go, gather these fragments and build them into a monument of testimony to Him. He is worthy, dear friend, . . . He is worthy!"

And Luke rushed, pen in hand, back to the land that Jesus trod to gather and to sort facts, which he compiled and tested against each other. The history must be accurate. Luke would be accurate. The Holy Spirit would see to that. The conclusion became clearer, the light grew brighter. Luke affirmed Jesus as the Messiah. He met all the criteria, from His conception to His ascension.

Suddenly, the Time Is at Hand

Prayer is the first theme we meet. It resounds in a priest named Zechariah as he goes about his duties in the Temple on a spring morning about the year 4 B.C. He's been a "pray-er" of many years, as has been his wife Elizabeth, then beautiful with age.

Both had observed the Lord's commandments "blamelessly" for years (1:6). But they couldn't conceive children. No doubt they brought this problem to God in prayer. Then one day, their prayers were answered from heaven through the archangel Gabriel: "Do not be afraid, Zechariah; your prayer has been heard. Your wife Elizabeth will bear you a son, and you are to give him the name John" (13). Zechariah has a hard time believing it, but not his wife. This is the first hint of the preciousness of women in this gospel.

Just as suddenly, we are swept into the presence of the young virgin at her prayers at the moment when the same angel salutes her and gives her the wondrous news. Mary is to give birth to the world's mighty Savior. "You will be with child and give birth to a son, and you are to give Him the name Jesus. He will be great and will be called the Son of the Most High" (31–32). She believes. Note the contrast: an old man who is a priest with great doubt, his wife with no doubts, and a young virgin through whom the genesis of this history will take place. All are believers. All are simple and good people. All are among the blessed poor, who wait on God for deliverance.

A second theme arises, the *Holy Spirit*. The angel informs Zechariah that Elizabeth will give birth to a child who will be great in the sight of the Lord and will be filled with the Spirit even from birth (15). Not only is the child with the Holy Spirit but so is his mother, in whose womb he will leap for joy at the sound of Mary's voice six months later. Zechariah, who finally comes around, is also filled with the Spirit and gives a prophecy concerning the Messiah who will be born. "The rising sun will come to us from heaven to shine on those living in darkness and in the shadow of death, to guide our feet into the path of peace" (78–79).

Then we meet the theme of *Joy*. Joy is everywhere in this gospel. Mary rushes off to see the only one who could understand her great news. When they meet, Elizabeth shouts for joy and embraces the young virgin. Both have that rich deep laughter that wells up mysteriously from secret wells within. Who can doubt that she and Mary talked all day and into the night? Who can doubt that they embraced Zechariah and laughed their joy into him, and that his faith grew stronger until it gushed forth at the dedication of his son John (68)?

We must ask ourselves and answer as honestly as we can: When the Truth presents itself to me, what will I do with it? The Divine hunger is a wonderful, mysterious thing. The more this hunger is fed, the more it grows and the more delightful and adventurous it becomes.

"The Spirit of the Lord is on Me," Luke reports Jesus announcing, "because He has anointed Me to preach good news to the poor. He has sent Me to proclaim freedom for the prisoners and recovery of sight for the blind, to release the oppressed, to proclaim the year of the Lord's favor" (4:18–19). Freedom from guilt, anger, resentment. Freedom from this wild and seemingly out-of-control world.

SOMETHING TO THINK ABOUT

1. How did the Gospel of Luke come to be? Who is Theophilus—a real person or a composite audience?

2. If Luke had never met Jesus, where did he get his information? Who is he?

3. Why would the Gospel of Luke be considered "a monument to Christ"?

4. Describe how Luke portrays the person and mission of Jesus Christ. Is his presentation different from the other gospel writers? How?

2: Through the Eyes of Women

LUKE'S EMPHASIS ON WOMEN IS DELIBERATE. CONSIDER THE FIRST REAL BELIEVERS in Jesus as God's Son were women—His mother Mary and Elizabeth, the mother of John the Baptist. The first to believe in Him resurrected were women—Mary Magdalene, Joanna, as well as others who had followed Him from Galilee and witnessed His crucifixion (Luke 23:55). We meet women at strategic places throughout Luke's narrative. They represent turning points that keep his majestic gospel song flowing.

In Luke's day (and still today in many nations) women were treated little better than domestic animals. Divorce was just a matter of course. A man could put away his wife "for bringing shame to him," and that "shame," according to their law, could include as tiny an offense as burning his supper. Jesus turned Jewish law upside-down by showing them how foolish and blasphemous their interpretations were. He cut through convoluted laws and customs to bring them back to God's original intent—an intent that can be described as unconditional love for the person, regardless of gender, race, or other criteria. While man looks at the outward appearance, God looks at the heart.

One of the most precious stories in the Gospel of Luke deals with a woman of "ill repute" (6:36–50), a prostitute who, according to the synagogue and its traditions, was hopeless and only-worthy of scorn. But not to Jesus. Simon the Pharisee, a religious expert, had invited Jesus to dine not out of respect, but because He had become a renowned Rabbi and it was prestigious to have such a dinner guest—especially this supposed wonder worker. That the host's attitude bordered on contempt is indicated by even the simplest courtesies being withheld from Jesus that day (water for His feet, a kiss of welcome to this home).

Meanwhile, this woman of questionable past is readying herself for the mission of her life. She had stood at the edge of one of the crowds that constantly flocked to hear Jesus. She discovered her mission when she listened to the One who "spoke with authority." She must have found Him approachable, unlike the judgmental religious leaders quick to condemn.

His words attacked and then melted her heart—words like "come unto Me all ye that labor and are heavy laden, I will give you rest. My burden is easy, My yoke light" (Matthew 11:28,30 KJV). Those words embraced her and filled her with hope. And she whispered the prayer which has saved millions and millions of others before and since; "O God, have mercy on me, a sinner!" Standing there, on the edge of that crowd, she became a child of Heaven, a daughter of the King.

When she heard that Jesus was at Simon's house, she resolved to go and see Him. She took up the most precious thing she had, an alabaster bottle of ointment, and made her way. How like her we are when moved deeply by the Lord. We give. We visit. We serve. As it was with this woman, so it always is in this kingdom of Divine compulsion.

The dinner guests, reclined around the supper table, talked quietly. Imagine the mixed emotions of that dinner party. Some curious, some resentful, some threatened, some scornful. Suddenly, at the door, appears the whore of Capernaum! Her eyes are fixed only on Jesus. Eternal issues have for her been raised. Nothing else matters. She stops behind Him, weeping. Her tears fall on His feet. She kneels, unbraids her hair and tries wiping His feet, as if to wipe away the remnants of her own sin forever. The more she tries, the more her tears fall. The guests watch in silence broken only by her weeping.

She kisses Jesus' tear-stained feet over and over, her wounded soul pouring itself onto Him. She knows He takes her sin and sorrow into Himself and returns to her joy and wonderful release.

Simon dismisses the Nazarene. "If this man were a prophet, he would know who is touching him and what kind of woman she is—that she is a sinner" (Luke 7:39).

Jesus rebukes the lovelessness of the Pharisee with a simple question about forgiveness. "You invited Me, Simon, to your house, and gave Me no water for My feet, but look, she washes them in tears and dries them with her beautiful hair. You gave Me no welcoming kiss, but look Simon, she kisses My feet! My head received no anointing from you Simon, but see, this woman anoints My feet. And why is she doing this Simon? Because her sins, all of them, are forgiven; therefore, she loves much; but those who love little show they feel little need to repent" (see Luke 7:44–47).

"Go," He tells the seeking woman, "your faith has saved you." As Alfred Edersheim explains, "Heaven's own light had fallen upon her, heaven's own voice had come to her. She believed it all, and it had saved her."

Anna

Anna was old, a nobody, going about her duties in the Temple in Jerusalem in a routine so familiar as to make her all but invisible. No doubt some regarded her as a pathetic figure, like one who, in T. S. Eliot's poem "Preludes," goes about "gathering fuel in vacant lots." But she was one of the faithful ones who looked to the heavens for the redemption of Israel as promised in the Scriptures. Her years of fasting, praying, and watching were about to be rewarded (see Luke 2:36).

Despite the Temple peddlers, the arrogance of the priesthood, the strutting Pharisees, the call for political solutions, and Roman oppression, the Temple was her home, her heart, and still the breath of Israel's soul. In spending her life in quiet adoration, she discovered the great secret: the Law was not meant to be a litany of rules floating like a sword over one's head but permission to enter the King's realm. Two millennia later she lives in heaven with Jesus, serving in the great Temple with unimaginable joy! Instead of shrinking in fear, Anna asked, "May I enter in?" to which Jesus by His nature responded, "Of course, little one, come abide with Me."

When we change from the "must I?" of stubborn rebelliousness to the "may I?" we, too, begin to live in the true freedom of God's love.

Mary and Martha

Neither had known Him before that day. Doubtless they had learned of Him and His message from one of the pairs of disciples He had sent out to prepare His way (10:1). Both were impressed, and Martha, the mistress of the home, extended the invitation for Jesus to dine with them.

It was a festive time, the Feast of Sukkot (Tabernacles), a time of ingathering and remembrance. The Lord had instructed, through Moses, that Israel should celebrate by putting up booths (Sukkots) as a reminder of how their forefathers had fared during those times in the wilderness when Moses led the Hebrews out of Egypt. There was an almost frantic busyness in the house, for not only was the Stranger of Galilee about to arrive, but brother Lazarus might at any time return from the ongoing feast with guests of his own!

When Jesus arrived, they realized how different He was for His loveliness. Both resolved to honor Him with their best. Martha prepared the meal, rushing to and fro, distracted before the Sukkot in which He sat teaching. Mary, struck by Him who spoke as no one ever had, became so inspired that nothing else mattered. Martha became angry. "Lord," she said, sidling up to Him, "don't You care that my sister has left me to do all the work by myself?" (11:48). A gentle reproof, a loving look, a tender touch on her hand, and all is peace. Henceforth, "Jesus loved Martha and her sister" (John 11:5).

He wants us. Simply us. We get caught up in pressure and lose Him in the externals. Small wonder He had pleaded with us in the Psalms: "Be still and know that I am God" (Psalm 46:10).

The Bondage and the Rescuer

When Jesus entered a rustic, remote synagogue in northern Galilee, it was an ordinary Sabbath. The people and their synagogue ruler didn't seem very impressed by His presence (Luke 13).

A woman, sick and bent, prepared herself for worship as she had done for the past eighteen years. She hobbled on her crutch, seeking her usual seat, her spirit and eyes riveted only to the dust under her feet. Just one more of those throwaways, those nobodies hardly worth attention.

But not to Jesus. Jesus was there that day. "Woman," He said smiling, "you are set free from your infirmity." She stopped, stunned by the voice and the power it poured on her. Jesus embraced her, and immediately she was made straight. She lifted herself slowly and without pain. She looked into His eyes and knew whence came her healing, "and praised God" (13:13).

So it is for those of us who have been bound in some routine of sin and its consequent crippling guilt. She was freed by His touch, and that miracle is standing just outside the door of any of our hearts waiting also to heal, restore, save, and make straight (see Revelation 3:20).

"Where Were the Men?"

We find Luke's focus at the end of his gospel to be the same as the beginning—on women. The horrible day of Jesus' crucifixion had passed, leaving gloom. Judas had betrayed Him. Peter had denied Him. The disciples had fled from Him in His hour of trial. But some did not betray or deny or flee, and Luke gives their names: "It was Mary Magdalene, Joanna, and Mary the mother of James" who were early at the tomb that morning bringing spices and ointment they had prepared (see Luke 24:10).

It was to them that the angels appeared! It was they who rushed to the disciples to give them the news. But Luke tells us that "they did not believe the women because their words seemed to them like nonsense" (24:11). Nonsense? Child's talk? Women's speech? Once again they saw only through sin's eyes, even though Jesus had showed so much of God's wisdom to them.

The godly among women have been teaching this truth ever since. Despite the lack of respect they may have endured, they keep pointing to the light. The wise among us listen and follow this same Master, walking with joy to glory. Generations in that great day yet to come when God holds His great banquet will rise up and call them blessed. Be among them.

1. Why did Luke place such emphasis on the role of women in his gospel? How is this reflected in his writing?

2. How and why does Luke recount the story of a woman of questionable past without condemning her?

3. Which type do you more closely identify with—Mary or Martha?

4. Where were the men, especially Jesus' disciples at the cross?

3: Lepers, Outcasts, and the Dead

HOW PITIABLE IT MUST HAVE BEEN FOR A JEW AFFLICTED WITH DISEASE IN THE DAYS Jesus walked the earth. The Rabbis attributed the condition to sin. In his Bible commentaries, Alfred Edersheim describes their attitude: "'No disease without fault,' they said, and 'no death without sin,' and 'no pain without transgression,' and 'the sin is not healed, 'til all your sins are forgiven you.'"

How sad! God looked upon this in sorrow and anger. His Word in Leviticus 13:45 ("The person with such an infectious disease must wear torn clothes, let his hair be unkempt, cover the lower part of the face and cry out 'Unclean! Unclean!'") was taken to horrible extreme, yet rationalized as the means of upholding God's law. Luke makes it clear in his gospel that what was foremost in Jesus' mind was the crushed hope of His sorrow-filled, disease-ridden little ones.

Lepers

How did that leper dare come, stumbling, crying, gasping for help from the Savior? "While Jesus was in one of the towns, a man came along who was covered with leprosy. When he saw Jesus, he fell with his face to the ground" (Luke 5:12). He knew the rules! Keep no company except with those like afflicted. No touching. No being touched. Wear a sign around your neck clearly reading "Unclean! Unclean!" But he came anyway—face riddled with running sores, caked with dirt, lower lip and chin covered with a filthy rag, clothes rent, hair stiff and disheveled. Yet he dared approach. He sensed in Jesus an acceptance, an attitude of permission he hadn't found elsewhere.

There is in us all an awareness that there is something more. This isn't all. That conviction must have welled up in this poor man when he saw Jesus that day . . . the day everything changed.

"Jesus," he sobbed, pleading, "Lord, if You are willing, You can make me clean." There. It was out. The poor wretch crumbled prostrate at Jesus' feet, the bystanders shocked by the spectacle.

Jesus looked at the man, knelt beside him, touched tenderly the pockmarked face, looked deeply into the man's very soul and said, "I am willing. Be clean." And he was! Immediately! Instantly! He knew it! He felt life itself with its wondrous strength surge all through his being. He would speak! He would shout! He would dance and sing!

Jesus said, "Don't tell anyone, but go show yourself to the priest and offer sacrifices that Moses commanded for your cleansing, as a testimony to them" (14). It was to be a witness to those who were, even then, plotting His death. A witness that He was no lawbreaker, rather, that He was the One—the Promised One prophesied to both obey and fulfill the Law.

Outcasts

Demons—malevolent beings who control their targets, relentless and never satisfied. Disembodied and dark spirits that hunger for human habitation. Demonic activity was intense when the Messiah walked the earth. They knew Him, raved against Him, engaged in mortal combat with Him. After Jesus' ascension into heaven, their intensity slacked somewhat, taking more to the background in those "high places"—"For our struggle is not against flesh and blood, but against the rulers, against the authorities, against the powers of this dark world and against the spiritual forces of evil in the heavenly realms" (Ephesians 6:12). But, sure as day follows night, as the time of Jesus' return nears, they will resurface, and again, woe to the world. "Then I saw three evil spirits . . . of demons performing miraculous signs, and they go out to the kings of the whole world, to gather them for the battle on the great day of God Almighty" (Revelation 16:13).

A desperate father brought his only child to the Savior. Jesus was not there. He appealed to the nine disciples who were. "My son is possessed," he pleaded. "He will surely die, and that violently, unless he is delivered" (see Luke 9:38). They try. They call on God, attempting to replicate the prayers of Jesus. Nothing. They challenge the demon. Still nothing. The Scribes and Pharisees scoff and scorn their effort, pointing, laughing, shaking their heads, belittling the faith of the people.

Suddenly Jesus is there! His face is alight with the vestiges of the glory He had passed through on the Mount of Transfiguration, where he had taken Peter, James, and John with Him to pray. "As He was praying, the appearance of His face changed, and His clothes became as bright as a flash of lightning. . . . A voice came from the cloud, saying, 'This is My Son, whom I have chosen; listen to Him'" (29,35). The disciples' failure to help the desperate father followed this stunning transfiguration.

"Unbelieving and perverse generation," Jesus growls, "how long shall I stay with you and put up with you? Bring your son here" (41). The demon, knowing now who confronted him, tore at the boy, throwing him into wild paroxysms of screaming and flailing. Any parent who has ever tried to soothe and comfort a screaming child out of control can understand this desperate father. Unless God intercedes there is only hopelessness and despair. God did! God does! "Jesus replied, 'What is impossible with men is possible with God'" (18:27). Jesus touches the outcast, and the demon departs.

136

When a loved one dies, a great chasm yawns. Death mocks our inability to prevent it, our hopelessness in the face of it. Nothing left but aching void. So goes the world, until Jesus forever changes it. So it was for a poor widow in a city called Nain. But not before she trudged behind the open coffin bearing the corpse of her beloved son to the open grave (7:12). Coming in the opposite direction, up that narrow path toward the gate of her city, walked Jesus. Death was about to be swallowed up in life! Everything as she understood it, was about to change for her—for all those present that day, and for any of us who believe this day. She learned that death is not the last word. It is, in fact, God's appointed steward to usher us into His presence, the friend that brings us "home." Every home alight with love and joy is but a shadow of our real home, where everything is complete, alive with love.

"Don't cry," He says to her. "I have overcome death for you. I am the way home." The sad procession slows. He edges by the women to the funeral of the bier. "Young man, I say to you, get up!"

The flutter of an eyelid, a movement of a finger, an intake of breath, and the dead lives! Our own dead souls, once awakened in the same way, are called out by this same voice, "into His marvelous light" (1 Peter 2:9). Let your mind return to the moment when you said "yes" to this light. Let your heart throb to its mystery, and you will live in holy joy and gratitude.

Something to Think About

1. Why did Jesus perform miracles of healing?

2. The disciples were unable to drive the demon out of the young boy. What went wrong?

3. Why did Jesus tell the leper not to speak of his healing?

4: Luke and the Last Times

OLD TESTAMENT PROPHETS INCLUDING JOEL, ZECHARIAH, ISAIAH, AND EZEKIEL SPOKE of it. Eschatology! The "end" things or last days. The Greek word *Eschata* refers not to the latter days but to the very last days; that is, not a general but a very specific time. There is an end. We are in danger of not seeing it rush toward us, but it is coming—and swiftly.

While scholars rejoice in the grand hope Paul refers to in his letter to Titus: "We wait for the blessed hope—the glorious appearing of our great God and Savior Jesus Christ" (Titus 2:13), how sad that the vile sin of the world is about to bring down the house in judgment:

> *Take heed, you senseless ones among the people; you fools, when will you become wise? Does He who implanted the ear not hear? Does He who formed the eye not see? Does He who disciplines nations not punish? Does He who teaches man lack knowledge?* (Psalm 94:8–10)

For the upright will live in the land, and the blameless will remain in it; but the wicked will be cut off from the land, and the unfaithful will be torn from it. (Proverbs 2:21–22)

A great judgment and tribulation is coming. Jesus and all His prophets gave us evidences to look for when that time is to draw near. Those signs are becoming more and more obvious in these days. One of Jesus' very last words to us was "Be always on the watch, and pray that you may be able to escape all that is about to happen, and that you may be able to stand before the Son of Man" (Luke 21:36).

Floating in Indifference?

As the *Eschata* approaches we find ourselves either mired in heated controversy or floating in serene indifference! Many dismiss the whole thing with a shrug, saying, "Who can know these things?" But that gives little help to others looking for hope. What did Luke say? He said Jesus was close to despair over what little heed would be paid to His Kingdom in the last days: "When the Son of Man comes, will He find faith on the earth?" (18:8). Jesus also despaired over the ever-burgeoning sin that would infect and inflame people of the earth.

Jesus' Predictions in Context

When in Luke's Gospel we read Jesus' pronouncements about the last days and His return, what was the context? Was He speaking to and for the Church yet to be born, or was He speaking to and for Israel, standing before Him in the persons of those first Jewish followers?

Israel was and is the hub, the centerpiece, around which all Bible prophecy orbits. From Genesis throughout the Scriptures, Israel is the main character among nations in God's grand drama. She was then, she is now. Jesus was speaking to Jews, some believers (Luke 21) and many not (Luke 12, 13 and 17). He knew the Jews would be thinking and hearing and understanding from their own mindset concerning the *Eschata*.

The Church's understanding of itself would have to wait until Pentecost, and ultimately for Paul and John to come along and unveil and explain the mystery which was hidden all those centuries in the Old Testament, but now revealed in the New. Then the Church could understand what its mission would be and what glorious destiny was reserved for it. The original Greek word for "Church" is *ecclesia*, meaning "the called-out ones"—from unbelief into His glorious light.

Jesus connected true faith with the knowledge and happy anticipation of His return. Isn't it a bit ironic that as the end draws near, indifference and interference grow also? People who take these things seriously are more and more dismissed as extremists. These brave hearts point out the obvious—that the world is sinking deeper and deeper into the confusion of rebellion.

"First of all, you must understand that in the last days scoffers will come, following their own evil desires," writes fisherman-turned-disciple Peter. "They will say, 'Where is this coming He promised?' Ever since our fathers died, everything goes on as it has since the beginning of creation" (2 Peter 3:3–4). That's a lie, friend; don't be taken in by it.

138

Bleakness at the Edge of Dawn

Jesus said to His disciples, "go out into the whole world, tell them, show them, demonstrate the truth, die for it if necessary" (see Mark 15:16). They did. They went out preaching and healing everywhere. They were loved. They were hated, lauded, killed. The gospel spread slowly over the centuries, all over this world of His, the creeping dawn chasing the darkness.

You would think that after all this time the Light would shine everywhere. It doesn't. Look out on the world. What do you see? You see what He said you would see . . . desolation. A careful, inductive, reasonable, and objective reading of the text concerning the last days, the *Eschata*, reveals this. No wonder such proclaimers of God's Word are called doomsayers. Creatures of the night dominate, it seems. As John writes, "The light shines in the darkness, but the darkness has not understood it" (John 1:5). Jesus said that as the end drew nearer and nearer the darkness would thicken and cloak everything: "The fifth angel poured out his bowl on the throne of the beast, and his kingdom was plunged into darkness" (Revelation 16:10).

America's citizens once held high principle. We held a faith that braced, gave authority to, and undergirded our policies and politics. We were once a people that held high vision. No more. These things are openly scorned and laughed at. We have forfeited the high ground. Is there another who is able to step in our vacated place? No. Scan, if you will, east, west, north, south. You will find nothing, no safe haven for Christ's Word, for His wisdom, or even for what used to be common decency! As it says in Isaiah, "All have gone astray," all greedily looking out for themselves while betraying their highest values. There is a madness abroad. It is a bleak thing, this.

Signs of Deceit

Jesus pointed out specifics. He directed our eyes to the natural world, to the spirit world and political world, and what would happen there. The swarming Pharisees demanded that Jesus tell them when the kingdom of God should come. He replied that the kingdom of Heaven was already in their midst. He said that anyone who accepts Him into their heart as Lord and Savior, in them will be the "kingdom" also. Of course, the Pharisees sneered and dismissed Him. So He turned to His disciples with a warning: "The time is coming when you will long to see one of the days of the Son of Man, but you will not see it. Men will tell you, 'There He is!' or 'Here He is!' Do not go running off after them. For the Son of Man in His day will be like the lightning, which flashes and lights up the sky from one end to the other" (Luke 17:22–24).

It is a warning to them and us about many coming and clothing themselves in His very name in order to deceive and lead astray. It always has to do with deceit. Satan and his smoke screens continuously confuse, substitute, dodge, infiltrate our churches, our hearts and minds in order to frustrate and negate the truth, especially the truth of Jesus' near return.

Jesus said that nations or "race" (in Greek, *ethos* means "races") "would rise up against race and kingdoms against kingdoms." Look around. The delicate balance of power among nations is erupting into open hostility, conflict, and death, and racial polarization is now evident among numerous ethnic groups around the world.

Jesus also said natural calamities would increase (21:11). There have been more terrible earthquakes, hurricanes, and tornadoes in the past few years than ever before. Jesus said that disasters (plagues) would ravage our lands (17:28). Sexually transmitted diseases range the world over, "as it was in the days of Lot." HIV/AIDS has claimed more than one third of Africa's population, and starvation haunts millions. Spiritual and psychic plagues, such as loneliness and depression, stalk millions more here at home.

So, my dear Salvationist and anyone who tries to hear what the Spirit is saying: Prophecy needs to be learned. God will give understanding. He gave us "marching orders," among which is "Blessed are all those I find watching!" (12:37). "Look up, beloved, your redemption draws near. Even so, come Lord Jesus" (Luke 21:28, Revelation 22:20).

SOMETHING TO THINK ABOUT

1. Luke tells us to "be always on the watch" (21:36). Why? What are we watching for?

2. How would you live differently if you knew Jesus would be returning next week?

3. Is the world and society moving toward a conclusion, or is it just moving? Is it getting better, worse, or just different?

TEN

THE UNEXPECTED JESUS

ROBERT E. THOMSON

Recorded throughout the four gospels are incidents in which Jesus was asked an honest question to which He gave a forthright, logical answer. There were other times, however, when Jesus responded to queries with answers that appeared to skirt the issue raised and sometimes seemed absolutely rude. A closer look reveals unexpected insights into Jesus.

1: Making Water into Wine

ONE SUCH OCCASION WAS THE WEDDING FEAST IN CANA, TO WHICH Jesus, His mother and His disciples had been invited. The celebration, as was the custom, probably lasted for several days. It was the responsibility of the groom and/or his parents to see that there was an abundance of food and wine for the guests. To be caught short of either would be an embarrassment to the parents as well as to the bridal couple.

Now their worst fears were realized. The festival was in full swing, and the supply of wine had been completely depleted. Mary, realizing the gravity of the situation and hoping to avoid the public humiliation of her friends, searched out her Son. Quietly she made known the dilemma: "They have no more wine."

Commissioner Robert E. Thomson retired from active service in 1993 after his last appointment as Eastern territorial commander. Commissioner Thomson served in the Central and Eastern territories and was national editor in chief from 1970 to 1972. He continues to write for *The War Cry* as well as other Army publications.

What was it that Mary expected Jesus to do? If more wine was to be purchased, that would be the responsibility of the groom and his family. If a public announcement needed to be made, that would fall to the master of the feast. Did Mary know in her heart that Jesus, her child but also the only begotten Son of the Father, had the ability to perform miracles? Up to this time, which was very early in His public ministry, Jesus had not performed any miracles. Mary had no experience that would make her aware of Jesus' power to change water into wine. Did she have an inner assurance that He would be able to avert a potentially devastating experience? We don't know.

What we do know is that she made Jesus aware of the problem. We know, also, that this gentle God–man, who on other occasions was kindness itself to His mother, responded in what appears to be a most uncharacteristic way. "Dear woman," He answered, "why do you involve Me? My time has not yet come" (John 2:4). The rebuke as translated in the King James version is even more severe: "Woman, what have I to do with thee? Mine hour is not yet come."

There is no doubt that Jesus' statement to His mother was a rebuke. She seemed to be running ahead of His schedule. She was "forcing His hand," so to speak, making it necessary for Him to reveal Himself earlier than He had planned. The situation was not unlike others that occurred later, when Jesus performed miracles and then commanded the recipient of divine grace to "tell no man." It never worked. Those who had been healed just could not refrain from making their good fortune known.

It's possible also that God the Father was using Mary to bring about a revelation to the world which Christ, for whatever reason, was reluctant to make. Jesus' statement to His mother was a rebuke. But it was not given in an unkindly manner, nor was it intended to be a put down. It merely was a reminder to Mary—and to us—that our timetable may not necessarily coincide with the divine schedule. God's timing is always perfect. Paul, when writing to the Galatians, reminded them that "when the time had fully come, God sent His Son" into the world. There was a time for Him to live under the care and supervision of Mary and Joseph. There was a time for Him to begin His ministry. There was a time for Him to perform His first miracle. There was a time for Him to reveal Himself as the true Son of God.

Although on this occasion Jesus rebuked his mother, the outcome was happy. Water was changed to wine. The master of the feast was pleased. The bridegroom was commended. Jesus was glorified. And "His disciples put their faith in Him" (John 2:11).

2: Seeing the Kingdom of God

NICODEMUS IS PERHAPS ONE OF THE BEST KNOWN OF THE "LESSER PERSONALITIES" in the New Testament, for it was to him that Jesus made the surprising statement, "No one can see the kingdom of God unless he is born again." It was an unexpected statement for two reasons:

· It enunciated a concept that was radical and never before had been expressed; and

· It came as a response to a question that Nicodemus had not asked.

143

Nicodemus was a Pharisee and a member of the Sanhedrin, the Jewish ruling council. He was intelligent and well educated. Nicodemus was very much aware of the stir caused by the carpenter of Nazareth. Perhaps he had heard Jesus preach and perform miracles or heard eyewitness accounts. In any event, Nicodemus was convinced that Jesus was a representative of the one true God, to whom he and his fellow council members gave allegiance. But not all of Nicodemus' colleagues shared his view. Some saw Jesus as an impostor, others as a rabble rouser or nonconformist.

Not many days earlier Jesus had stormed into the Temple, overturned the tables of the money changers, drove from the sacred precincts those who sold animals for sacrifice, and turned loose the animals themselves. He had shouted. "How dare you turn My Father's house into a market!"

"What miraculous sign can you show us to prove your authority to do all this?" they had demanded. Jesus had replied, "Destroy this temple, and I will raise it again in three days."

Jesus had been referring to the temple of His body, but the religious leaders understood Him to be saying that in three days He could rebuild Herod's temple, which had taken forty-six years to construct.

In order to keep his reputation unsullied and to avoid criticism, Nicodemus later sought out Jesus under the cover of darkness. His approach to Jesus was: "Rabbi, we know You are a teacher who has come from God. For no one could perform the miraculous signs You are doing if God were not with him" (John 3:2).

Could not Jesus have given a straight, simple response? Could He not have said, "Nicodemus, you are a very perceptive man. Yes, I have come from God on a most important mission"? But Jesus seemed to ignore the statement, saying, "I tell you the truth—no one can see the Kingdom of God unless he is born again" (3). Was Jesus answering a question unspoken by Nicodemus but burning in his heart? Was he saying in effect, "Let's skip what is not essential and get right to the heart of the matter"? Undoubtedly, Nicodemus went through a series of mental gymnastics trying to understand. "How can a man be born when he is old?" Nicodemus finally asked, "Surely he cannot enter a second time into his mother's womb to be born?" (4).

Then Jesus took the opportunity to explain the possibility and necessity of spiritual birth, of being born again of the Spirit of God. And it was on this occasion that Jesus uttered what has been described as "the gospel in a nutshell," a verse of Scripture more widely known and more often quoted than any other: "For God so loved the world that He gave His one and only Son, that whoever believes in Him shall not perish but have eternal life" (16).

Nicodemus understood what Jesus was saying, and so do we.

3: Taking Up the Cross

DURING HIS EARTHLY MINISTRY, JESUS CALLED MANY PEOPLE TO FOLLOW HIM. SOME, like the apostles, responded gladly and affirmatively. Others, like the rich young ruler, were unwilling to accept the invitation. Only rarely did someone volunteer for discipleship. But there was one who did. He was a scribe, a teacher of the law, and well versed in the Scriptures.

Jesus had been involved in a healing ministry, ridding Peter's mother-in-law of a fever and driving unclean spirits from those who were possessed by demons. So large a crowd gathered around Him that Jesus made plans to cross to the other side of the Sea of Galilee. It was then that the unnamed scribe approached Jesus and said, "Teacher, I will follow You wherever You go" (Matthew 8:19).

It was a bold declaration to make. Surely the scribe would have known that even though the common people were flocking to Jesus, religious leaders were less than happy with what He was doing. In fact, a decision to become a follower of Jesus would have put the scribe's very life at risk.

Jesus had told enough parables, healed enough people, and acted counter to the tradition of the elders enough times to make Him an enemy of the religionists of the day. Being a scribe, the volunteer would have been more aware than most of the extent to which Jesus' teachings contradicted the traditions taught by the scribes and Pharisees. But he saw something in Jesus that was attractive and compelling. Perhaps it was a hasty decision, an emotional response to the charisma of the man of whom the temple guards said, "No one ever spoke the way this man does." Or it may have been the culmination of much thought and prayer.

Would we not expect Jesus to respond by throwing His arms open and extending a hearty welcome to the rich young ruler, who was willing to make such an unqualified commitment to Him and His cause? It would seem the logical and natural thing for the Master to do. Instead, Jesus made a statement which certainly was not calculated to encourage the man in his decision: "Foxes have holes and birds of the air have nests, but the Son of Man has no place to lay His head" (8:20).

Perhaps the disciples were less surprised by Jesus' statement than we are. They knew the cost of following Jesus. They would soon hear Jesus say to another large crowd, "If anyone comes to Me and does not hate his father and mother, his wife and children, his brothers and sisters—yes, even his own life—he cannot be My disciple" (10:37). The comment, rather, had more to say about the scribe than about Jesus. Tradition tells us that Peter was crucified upside-down; that Thomas, pierced by a lance, died a martyr's death; that Andrew, like his Lord, died on a cross. Would the scribe have been able to remain faithful to the end? The Lord never suggested to His followers that the path would be easy. On the contrary, He declared: "If anyone would come after Me, he must deny himself and take up his cross and follow Me."

Whether or not that particular scribe did decide to follow Jesus, we do not know. But we praise God for countless Christians of ages past and present who, having heard the unexpected response, nevertheless have chosen the "narrow road that leads to life" and become a part of the great host who march in His train!

4: Reaching the Gentiles

FROM TIME TO TIME DURING HIS MINISTRY, JESUS FELT THE NEED TO REMOVE HIMSELF from the crowds, to seek strength and renewal in solitude. On one occasion He made His way to Tyre, a Gentile community near Galilee. There He found lodging in a home, hoping to keep His presence in the area a secret. But His fame as a preacher and healer made anonymity impossible. Word spread that the Teacher from Nazareth was in the vicinity.

As soon as she heard about Jesus, a woman of Greek origin who had been born in Syrian Phoenicia made it her business to find Him. She had a deep concern for her daughter, who was possessed by an evil spirit. Finding Jesus, the woman fell at His feet, begging Him to drive the demon out of her daughter.

"First, let the children [meaning the Hebrews] eat all they want," He said. "It is not right to take the children's bread and toss it to their dogs" (Mark 7:27).

In our time and culture, such a response would be considered rude and harsh at best. At worst, it would be cause for a lawsuit on the basis of racial discrimination. Jesus was not suggesting that non-Jews were not worthy of respect. Rather, He was indicating that His primary target for ministry was the chosen people. In effect, He was saying, "It is My intent to make the Jews the first recipients of My miracles. I want them to be persuaded to follow Me and My heavenly Father." Earlier, in sending out the twelve disciples, He had said to them: "Do not go among the Gentiles or enter into any town of the Samaritan. Go rather to the lost sheep of Israel" (Matthew 10:5–6).

The woman did not take offense at the response. Apparently she knew enough about Jesus and His ministry—and about the God worshipped by the Jews—that she was not put off. She agreed that the Jewish people were entitled to be the primary recipients of the gospel. However, she grasped the significance of the word "first."

Having no quarrel with Jesus giving precedence to the Jewish people, she reasoned that after that, was there not room for consideration of the Gentiles? The woman replied, "Yes, Lord, but even the dogs under the table eat the children's crumbs" (Mark 7:28). Jesus could not deny this logic. And He knew the truth of John's statement, as yet unwritten, "He came to that which was His own, but His own did not receive Him" (John 1:11). Jesus granted the woman's wish. "For such a reply," He told her, "you may go; the demon has left your daughter" (Mark 7:29).

Jesus' initial response was unexpected, but the final outcome was all the desperate woman could have hoped for. In a broader sense, it opened the way for both Peter and Paul to take the good news of the gospel to the Gentile world. It was a harbinger of the spread of Christianity to Europe and, ultimately, to the outermost parts of the world. Like the daughter of that woman, we who are not Jews also have the privilege of experiencing spiritual healing through faith in Jesus Christ because of divine love plentiful enough to reach everyone.

5: Counting the Cost of Salvation

EVERY MAN, WOMAN, AND CHILD WHO EVER ATTENDED SUNDAY SCHOOL IS PROBABLY familiar with the story of Zacchaeus. He was a wealthy Jew, who lived in Jericho and made a handsome living as a tax collector for the Romans. Because of his occupation, he was viewed by his contemporaries as a sinner before God and a traitor to his country. He was in the employ of the oppressor and considered to be no better—perhaps worse—than the heathen.

Though ostracized by fellow Jews, Zacchaeus was not void of spiritual sensitivity. When he learned that Jesus was coming to the area, he determined that he must see the much-heralded Teacher whose preaching, teaching, and miracle working were having such a profound effect on people. The Bible indicates that because he was short, he climbed a sycamore-fig tree in order to get a good view of Jesus. It must have taken a good deal of fortitude for this rich, sophisticated businessman to throw caution to the wind, run ahead of Jesus and His entourage, and scamper up a tree as he probably had not done since boyhood.

When Jesus reached the spot, He noticed the figure hidden among the branches, and He spoke to Zacchaeus. The crowd was amazed. They might have expected Jesus to rebuke Zacchaeus for his traitorous ways, for serving as an agent of the Roman government, for seeking personal gain by charging more than the assessed tax. There is no way they could have been prepared to hear Jesus say, "Zacchaeus, come down immediately. I must stay at your house today." It was an invitation Zacchaeus could not refuse. He had climbed the tree expecting only to catch a glimpse of the Prophet. Now he was to be rewarded far beyond anything he could have dreamed or desired.

The immediate reaction of the crowd was to mutter, "He has gone to be the guest of a 'sinner.'" but neither Jesus nor Zacchaeus was intimidated. They had things to discuss.

Unfortunately, Luke does not give an account of what transpired as Jesus and Zacchaeus broke bread together. We can assume that the Holy Guest spoke lovingly and directly to the chief tax collector of the district. We can also assume that Jesus explained to His astute, businesswise host the necessity of counting the cost of any venture. And we can assume that the Divine Visitor outlined the plan of salvation. These assumptions are based on the results of their meeting. We know, first of all, that Zacchaeus found salvation, for Jesus declared, "Today salvation has come to this house." What a surprise this must have been to the disciples who, just shortly before, had heard Jesus say, "I tell you the truth, it is hard for a rich man to enter the kingdom of heaven!" (Matthew 19:23). Jesus had intimated that it was nearly impossible for a rich man to be saved, but now He was declaring in no uncertain terms that the wealthy Zacchaeus had found salvation!

We also know that a great transformation had taken place in Zacchaeus. This man, who had accumulated a fortune through dishonest means, now stated freely, "Look, Lord! Here and now I give half of my possessions to the poor, and if I have cheated anybody out of anything, I will pay back four times the amount." What a marvelous change came to the life of one who had an unexpected encounter with Jesus Christ.

6: Life Coming from Death

JESUS WAS NEARING THE END OF HIS EARTHLY MINISTRY. DURING THE PRECEDING three years He had met and welcomed hundreds of people, including those who sought His advice, those who needed physical healing, and mothers who wanted Him to bless their children. Now the Lord and His disciples were among the many thousands who had traveled to Jerusalem for the Passover celebration.

Also in the city were a group of Greeks who likewise had come to worship at the feast. They had one request: to see Jesus. They made their desire known to Philip, an apostle who had a Greek name but who was Jewish. Philip shared the request with Andrew, and the two of them together went to tell Jesus.

It is possible that these visitors had heard Jesus and witnessed some of His miracles. Based on experience, the disciples had reason to believe that Jesus would welcome the visitors who had traveled so far. "Bring them to Me," is what Andrew and Philip expected to hear. Instead, Jesus said, "The hour has come for the Son of Man to be glorified. I tell you the truth, unless a kernel of wheat falls to the ground and dies, it remains only a single seed. But if it dies, it produces many seeds" (John 12:23-24).

In making this unexpected reply, Jesus was foretelling His own death. Within a few days He would give His life on the cross and be buried in the tomb of Joseph of Arimathea. He was also enunciating a principle of the spiritual life—a principle which remains unchanged and immutable. Perhaps the key to Jesus' assertion is that He was willing, even eager, to meet with men and women of any race or color, any social or economic class, any age or background. But Jesus was and is to be met on His own terms.

All too often Jesus has been pictured as a weak, effeminate person who was not prepared to face the realities of life. True, He was the Man of Sorrows. True, He was the Good Shepherd who was willing to give His life for the sheep. True, He was the gentle Jesus, meek and mild. However, He chose to face up to life as it really is, and He urged His followers to do the same. Jesus was ever the realist—no namby-pamby coddler of the weak. Neither was He a hand-shaking, back-slapping salesman looking at the world through rose-tinted glasses.

On the contrary. When curiosity seekers came looking for Him, eager to meet the Miracle Worker from Galilee, He challenged them with the hard facts of reality. How many people in succeeding centuries have said to themselves and others, "We would like to see Jesus"? But when they have discovered that Christianity involves a cross and a challenge and a checkbook, they have moved away quickly, unwilling to meet the demands of discipleship with Jesus.

Having pointed out the principle of life coming from death, of multiplying by dividing, Jesus made another statement that no doubt was unexpected by His hearers. It brought the general principle down to the level of personal practicality that everyone can understand.

"The man who loves his life will lose it, while the man who hates his life in this world will keep it for eternal life" (John 12:25). It was the statement of a paradox that is absolutely true, a statement that saint and sinner should consider well.

SOMETHING TO THINK ABOUT

1. What is the most significant outcome of the entire water to wine episode?

2. What does being "born again" mean to you? Has the overuse of the term weakened the spiritual impact of Jesus' revolutionary teaching?

3. Why does "discipleship" in the best sense of the word, come at so high a price? What is required?

4. Why were the Jews to have precedence in receiving the gospel? Why did "His own" not receive Jesus? What would have happened had the gospel been reserved for the Jews only?

5. Why did Jesus single out Zacchaeus for special attention rather than criticize him for collaborating with the Roman government?

6. How can you lose what you save and save what you lose?

ELEVEN

FOOTPRINTS OF JESUS

Arthur R. Pitcher

Trained as an Army officer in Newfoundland, Commissioner Arthur R. Pitcher held appointments in that country as well as in Canada, the Caribbean, and South Africa. Commissioner Pitcher retired from the position of territorial commander of the USA Southern territory in 1984.

1: Footprints in the Morning

That evening after sunset the people brought to Jesus all the sick and demon–possessed. The whole town gathered at the door, and Jesus healed many who had various diseases. He also drove out many demons, but He would not let the demons speak because they knew who He was. Very early in the morning, while it was still dark, Jesus got up, left the house and went off to a solitary place, where He prayed (Mark 1:32–35).

IT WAS EARLY MORNING IN CAPERNAUM. THE EARTH AROUND PETER the fisherman's cottage was marked by many sandals, and last night's events could be read in the footprints. The trail of a single shoe dragged along. The distinct imprint of a stick accompanying another footstep. The uneven steps of a blind person, groping forward. Hundreds of sandal marks, some in patterns of four where men had carried a stretcher. Some bare footprints. Some ragged markings made by sandals that had outlived their usefulness. All were the prints of those searching hard for a miracle, for deliverance. Last night in this very spot, they found what they were looking for.

It was that morning when Peter gazed at one distinctive pair of footprints cutting across the patterned terrain. A long time before daybreak Jesus had made these footprints as He moved toward some chosen spot of quiet rendezvous with His Father. Perhaps He was now in the crevice of a rock on the seashore, the constant rhythm of the sea accentuating His communal words.

It was to be this way for the next three eventful years. People would follow Him with such an anxious yearning, such intense needs, that He would have few undisturbed hours of meditation or reflection. The footprints of Jesus were those of a man who had much to do, and not much time in which to do it, as He criss-crossed the crowded ways of life.

And deliberately He still walks across our crowded ways. If only we knew of His availability out of the busy corridors of life would emerge a shared companionship. One dominant relationship would be there—not always to silence the turmoil of our despair but to breathe tranquility into our noisy Gehennas.

Peter found Jesus later that morning and said, "Everyone is looking for You." Jesus knew then, and knows now, that the strength He had already gathered before sunrise would be shared with the waiting world, and would never be exhausted, forever available to those who need Him.

2: Footprints Through Nazareth

He went to Nazareth, where He had been brought up, and on the Sabbath day He went into the synagogue, as was His custom. And He stood up to read (Luke 4:16).

THE ROUTES OF THE ROMAN EMPIRE PASSED THROUGH GALILEE AND THE LITTLE village called Nazareth, whose name means "Guardian." Located about halfway between the Sea of Galilee and the Mediterranean Sea, it was almost unknown until the sandals of the Son of God came to tread its unspectacular streets.

Today, as then on market days, the produce of the land and the imports from the world are sold in its busy market booths. The boyish feet of Jesus had, no doubt, darted in and out among the busy shoppers as, in curiosity, He listened to the vendors magnifying the splendor of their wares, in the process learning much about the work which was to be the scene of His redemptive mission and sacrificial love. But when the barefoot experience of His boyhood had passed, after His sandaled feet had trodden the rough and barren wilderness of temptation and His footprints been left on the threshold of many a troubled home, the marketplace had become much more than the venue of boyish exploration. It had assumed the honor of the place where a Galilean preacher brought His eternal message to His fellow Galileans.

Now He is home! The carpenter turned preacher has come back to Nazareth. Strange how, when crowded hours, the demands of people, and the impossible load of human need become unbearable, your heart and then your footsteps turn toward home.

Mary, who had kept so many things and pondered them in her heart, would most certainly have been a loving confidante; His Nazareth home a "port in a storm" for His weary body and pressured mind. It is too bad that we have no record of those walks in the garden, those intimate moments of sharing when the other members of the family were in bed, or those breakfast conversations. But we do have the picture of the Sabbath morning when, as always, His sandaled feet trod the familiar way to the synagogue. There He made His challenging claim to be the fulfillment of the sacred promise of Isaiah 61: anointed preacher to the poor, proclaimer of liberty to captives, light-bringer to the blind, reliever of the oppressed, and herald of the Lord's favor.

The trouble was that the residents of Nazareth had bought their ox yokes from Him too often, or brought them to Him for repair. They could not connect carpenter with prophet, nor village lad with Messiah. When He rebuked their narrowness of vision and racial intolerance, it was too much. Their law knew how to deal with false prophets and blasphemous pseudo-Messiahs. They repudiated the claims of their "homegrown Deliverer." The whole episode would have ended in ritual murder, except that His sandaled feet still had a divine errand to fulfill and they carried Him through the lynch mob to waiting tasks and redemptive destiny.

3: Unerased Footprints

IT WAS ON A SATURDAY LONG AGO THAT, FOR THE FIRST TIME IN YEARS, NOWHERE ON earth was heard the sound of the footsteps of the Son of Man. They lay silent in death. But, as Phillips Brooks wrote:

> *And when sunrise smites the mountains,*
> *Pour light from heavenly fountains,*
> *Then the earth blooms out to greet*
> *Once again the blessed feet;*
> *And her countless voices say,*
> *"Christ has risen on Easter Day."*

His feet trod our earthly pathways for another forty days, and then out of His dusty sandals He rose to walk the pathways of glory, which He had abandoned for our redemption. And yet, in the heart of those who love Him, those who need Him, those who yearn for Him, there is not a road of experience on which we cannot, by faith, lovingly behold His footprints. Albert Orsborn wrote so beautifully:

> *For when my fainting heart,*
> *The burden nigh o'ercame,*
> *I saw Thy footprints on my road,*
> *Where lately passed the Son of God.*

Oh, the blessed discovery, in life's burdened and confused day, that He has already passed that way. And, like Robinson Crusoe on his lonely island discovering a footprint, we exclaim, "I am not alone. There is another, for I have seen His footprints in the sand." So we rejoice that the Eternal Other is here, where we struggle and press forward, and that He not only shares our existence but defeats forever our sense of loneliness.

> *And never more alone, since Thou*
> *Art on the road beside me now.*
>
> (Albert Orsborn, The Salvation Army *Song Book* #59)

And He walks the triumphant way of our ultimate victory. May our own sense of expectation be reflective of these words of Lyman Whitney Allen:

> *He is coming, O my spirit, with His everlasting peace,*
> *With His blessedness, immortal and complete.*
> *He is coming, O my spirit, and His coming brings release.*
> *I listen for the coming of His feet.*

SOMETHING TO THINK ABOUT

1. What kind of footprints would Jesus leave if He visited your neighborhood?

2. What kind of footprints would you leave showing your need for healing?

3. Why did the hometown people treat Jesus with such disrespect? Didn't they understand the many prophecies, or did they think they understood them too well?

4. Looking back at how God worked things out, have there been occasions when you could imagine the footprints of Jesus on the road of your life?

TWELVE

HEBREWS: ALL IS BETTER IN JESUS

EVELYN MERRIAM

Major Evelyn Merriam is administrative assistant to the president of women's ministries for the Eastern territory. She has served with her husband Paul in corps and divisional appointments and at Japan's territorial headquarters in Tokyo. Major Merriam is a frequent contributor to *The War Cry*.

We do not know who wrote the New Testament's book of Hebrews, but we are certain that it was written before 90 A.D. when Clement of Rome quoted from it. The two most likely authors are Apollos and Paul, though Barnabas, Silas, Jude, Luke, Priscilla, and Aquila could also have penned its thirteen chapters on the place of Jesus in Jewish tradition. Early Christian scholars did not let this uncertainty lead them to exclude this unique, authoritative, inspired work from the canon of Scripture.

1: The Perfect Copy

THIS DEEP DISSERTATION ON THE RADICAL IDENTITY OF JESUS THE Christ is preceded by the Book of Philemon, a short (one chapter) letter by the Apostle Paul on pressing personnel matters for the advancement of the gospel in Asia Minor. Hebrews is followed by the five chapters of the Book of James, in which the relationship between faith and works is discussed at length.

Hebrews was likely written for Jews in many congregations, not for a particular gathering. It probably addresses those Jews—even priests—who began turning back from their new faith to the familiar traditions of Judaism. This was one of the predominant obstacles early Christianity had to overcome—namely, how to maintain its roots in Jewish tradition while establishing its own identity. The Book of Hebrews encourages Jews to see patterns in the Mosaic tradition that lead to Jesus as the Messiah:

> *Therefore, holy brothers, who share in the heavenly calling, fix your thoughts on Jesus, the Apostle and High Priest whom we confess. He was faithful to the One who appointed Him, just as Moses was faithful in all God's house* (Hebrews 3:1-2).

There is nothing wrong with honoring the living faith of dead people, but perpetuating the dead faith of living people is another matter. The author of Hebrews details how Jesus complements and completes the Jewish understanding of God's revelation of Himself. By doing so, the author encourages Jews to resist falling back into the security of tradition. As the occupying force in the Middle East, the Romans had provided the Jews some measure of protection. However tenuous the terms, it must have been tempting to seek security rather than face persecution from both sides for professing faith in Christ.

Judaism is not belittled in this book but honored and transfigured. The word the author uses to claim that Jesus is the supreme crowning of Judaism is "better." This word occurs thirteen times in Hebrews, and the theme of Jesus as the better choice and God's only way of salvation threads throughout, as does the emphasis on the finality of the redemptive work of Christ.

Who Jesus Is

The author leads us through many principal truths, and begins by urging readers to "fix your thoughts on Jesus, the Apostle and High Priest whom we confess" (3:1). Although God revealed portions of His truth in myriad ways through the generations, Hebrews makes clear that God has spoken definitively "in these last days . . . by His Son" (1:2). As Commissioner Harry Read expresses it: "Although other revelations will come, none will supersede the revelation given already through Jesus. All that was revealed through the prophets was preparatory to the incarnation of the Son, and all that is said after the exaltation of Christ derives from and looks back to His life, death and resurrection. Under the Father, there is no greater authority than the Son."

He is the sole expression of the glory of God. One commentator paraphrases a portion of the book's preamble thus: "As the rays of the sun reveal the glory of that celestial body and are identified with it, so Christ radiates the glory of God and is identified with Him." The preamble moves to a second metaphor, that of a seal impressed upon soft wax and leaving an exact imprint—symbolizing the Son as the "exact representation of [God's] being" (1:3). As General Frederick Coutts says, Hebrews reveals Jesus as the "very nature of God perfectly imprinted on the plastic material of human life." This same preamble uncompromisingly says that Jesus is far superior to angels.

His name, position and relationship with God is above any other being. Yet for our sakes, He chose the limitations of entering into a sub-angelic role, becoming human, suffering and dying so we could be free from sin's power and the fear of death.

The writer goes on to say that we are not left in doubt as to the fullness and completeness of salvation through the sacrifice of this perfect High Priest: "This salvation, which was first announced by the Lord, was confirmed to us by those who heard Him. God also testified to it by signs, wonders and various miracles, and gifts of the Holy Spirit distributed according to His will" (2:3-4). God has shown His endorsement of the gospel through His Word, witnesses, wonders, and distribution of gifts to believers, including the coming of the Holy Spirit on the day of Pentecost in the same era as the crafting of the Book of Hebrews. And God still bears witness to so great a salvation through bestowals, baptisms of the Holy Spirit, and the witness to glory of His own people.

"This glory we share," Colonel Milton Agnew clarifies, "will be His glory shining out of our lives. Being sanctified brings His glory into our lives in a never-ending cadence." Something of what the poet Shelley called the "white radiance of eternity" will be evident in the followers of the Light of the world. "Both the One who makes men holy and those who are made holy are of the same family. So Jesus is not ashamed to call them brothers" (2:11).

The first chapters of Hebrews identify Jesus as the Author of creation, outlasting the habitable world as the timeless One, the perfect image of divinity, the outpouring of the divine, a faithful High Priest, the pioneer of our salvation. Richard Jukes helps round out the list:

My heart is fixed, eternal God,
Fixed on Thee;
And my unchanging choice is made,
Christ for me.
He is my prophet, priest and King.
Who did for me salvation bring.
And while I've breath I mean to sing:
Christ for me.

(The Salvation Army *Song Book* #356)

SOMETHING TO THINK ABOUT

1. A key theme of Hebrews is that Jesus is "better." Better than what? Better how?

2. Who was the target audience of Hebrews?

3. How do we honor the faith of our spiritual ancestors? Is our faith alive or dead?

4. What does Hebrews say about the fullness and completion of salvation through Jesus Christ? (See 2:3-4.)

WE LOOK TOWARD SUMMER VACATION FOR A REST. BUT OFTEN WE PACK THE DAYS with travel, activity, visiting, projects. We may tell ourselves this is a healthy change from routine, but it is not rest. Lack of sleep is a modern epidemic. Without rest our outlook, coordination, productivity and clarity of thought suffer.

In the rhythm of days, rest is essential for all living things. Adults need to sleep about one third of each day. W. Philip Keller reminds us of the value of restful physical and spiritual interstices in his book *As a Tree Grows*. Frequently when thinking about growth we forget the condition of rest. In the design of living things, bodily structure and strength need to be rested and restored. Dormant periods for trees precede the demanding surges of growth.

We can fail to enter the rest that God has designed in and for the world. Hebrews 3:7–4:11 conveys how early Christians were warned that their unbelief and disobedience would lead them from true restoration. What exactly is the rest to which God invites us?

The well known words of Jesus, "Come to Me, all you who are weary and burdened, and I will give you rest" (Matthew 11:28), constituted the key life verse for Augustine in the fifth century and for Andrew Fuller, the home partner of missionary William Carey. Christians across the ages have responded to Christ's refreshing invitation. In Jesus' day it would have heralded a great relief from the imposed burdens the teachers of the law laid on the average man (reminding us of a rest from salvation by works). Earlier, Isaiah averred that in heeding the Word of the Lord, rest would result, but in refusing to listen, the Scripture would become merely monotonous rules.

In a way, this "rest" is a rest from sin. Hearing the message of salvation, repenting of sin and having faith in Christ—these things mark the beginning of a heart at rest. Augustine noted, "Thou hast made us, O Lord, for Thyself and our heart shall find no rest till it rest in Thee." The rest from worry, fear, and uncertainty is another aspect of the "rest" the writer to the Hebrews may have had in mind. The anthropologist Margaret Mead claimed that "the greatest gift we can give our children is to teach them to rest in the gale." A rest from life's burdens is offered to the believer. In the words of General Frederick Coutts: "As one psychologist said, 'Rest is found in what is, never in what ought to be.' As Paul, Martin Luther and countless others have discovered, peace comes by resting in God's unconditional love for us. That is where we start—we go on from there to grow in grace. But we must experience God's infinite succor before we can face, in His strength, His infinite demand. Restless souls frequently know a great deal about God's demand but little of His succor." Henri Nouwen describes this rest as being at home: "Worrying causes us to be all over the place, but seldom at home. One way to express the spiritual crisis of our time is to say that most of us have an address, but cannot be found there. We know where we belong, but we keep being pulled away in many directions, as if we were still homeless."

The readers of this first century epistle would immediately think of the Sabbath rest which had been part of the Jewish culture for many generations. After the Exodus, being able to keep a Sabbath day would have been a new experience for the recently released slaves of Egypt. Only free people can take a day off. From its inception, the Sabbath concept was a reminder of the divine pattern of creation which included rest: "And God blessed the seventh day and made it holy, because on it He rested from all the work of creating that He had done" (Genesis 2:2–3).

We still need to avoid work and worry on a day meant for worshipping God with other believers and appreciating the beauty of His creation. John Greenleaf Whittier's verse comes to mind:

> *O Sabbath rest by Galilee!*
> *O calm of hills above,*
> *Where Jesus knelt to share with Thee*
> *The silence of eternity,*
> *Interpreted by love!*
>
> (The Salvation Army *Song Book* #567)

Is there a greater promise implied when the author of Hebrews refers to entering into this rest? Though under Joshua the Jews who had escaped from slavery in Egypt did attain an end to their wanderings by entering Canaan, the Israelites did not enter God's rest. Centuries later the Psalmist was still offering the promised rest to Israel (Psalm 95), and centuries after that the New Testament writer mentions it again in Hebrews 3–4.

If Joshua had led the people of Israel into true rest, God would not have spoken of "another day" (Hebrews 4:8). A life of purity, holy living, and perfect love was offered to the Hebrew Christians and is offered to us today. By His death, resurrection, and ascension, Jesus opens the way into the "rest" of holiness, a better rest, a complete rest. Songwriter William Henry Windybank phrased it this way:

> *Though you know your sins forgiven,*
> *Greater things await you still;*
> *Freedom here from sin's dominion,*
> *Power to do the Master's will.*
> *Fear no danger, He is with you,*
> *Let no foe your steps arrest;*
> *Seek today the Father's blessing,*
> *Enter now the land of rest.*
>
> (The Salvation Army *Song Book* #433)

From the biblical text we infer that final and supreme rest, heaven, of which all spiritual "rest" on earth is a type. Later in the book of Hebrews, Abraham and others are shown as models of people of faith who were looking expectantly toward and living for heaven (see 11:10,15,16).

Whatever the interpretation of the "rest" which remains for the people of God, we find that it may be forfeited, missed, or rejected (4:9–11). The warning to the first readers remains a warning to us. Other problems we may encounter shrink in comparison with the results caused by unbelief. Hebrews 3:19 is plain: "They were not able to enter [God's rest] because of their unbelief."

Commissioner Harry Read explains, "If, as the Bible reveals, all the blessings of God are for those who believe in Him and His Son, Jesus, it must follow that unbelief precludes us from those blessings, exposing us to this world's disadvantages, and to the next world's judgment. We are free to choose . . . but great consequences hang upon our choice." Entering into the promised rest takes vigilance and diligence. We are urged to exert ourselves to enter that rest (4:11).

Divine resources for keeping an active, living faith fresh are available to us through the Spirit of Christ. Our chief resources are the Word of God and prayer. Chapter four closes with reference to both. "For the Word of God is full of living power. It is sharper than the sharpest knife, cutting deep into our innermost thoughts and desires. It exposes us for what we really are" (4:12 NLT). And regarding prayer, because of Jesus' ministry on our behalf, we are urged to come freely to the throne of grace to receive God's timely mercy and help (4:16).

As we decide to obey God and respond to His stimuli, He does His part to work in us to make us more like Christ. What do we do when He whispers to our hearts, "Come you apart and rest awhile"? (See Mark 6:31.) Philip Keller says that it is easier to make typical excuses than to obey. "Even a few minutes of deliberate quiet and solitude to focus on Christ each day can rest our spirits and fit us for days of growth in God."

The cheering sight of fresh flowers delights us each spring. But long before petaled cups catch early spring rains, the gardener plants the bulbs out of sight in the fall. The quiet, dormant time of the year allows for the development of roots that will support growth and beauty later. For a flourishing Christian life, return to the place of rest in Christ in all seasons, where you will be cultivated for growth in the love of God.

SOMETHING TO THINK ABOUT

1. What needs to change in your life to achieve what the rest of Hebrews suggests?

2. How can we be "at rest" while still being active and energetic?

3. How does faith and belief make rest possible?

4. Western Christians pride themselves on being "on the go." How can we balance what is often frenetic activity with rest and reflection?

3: Growing in Faith

WHEN THE MUSIC CAMP BEGINNERS' BAND PLAYED A SHORT PIECE, WE WERE PLEASED at the progress many had made. Some had never held a horn before joining the band, and could now play a recognizable tune. Among them, playing more crisply than the others, was an experienced band member who had played in the beginners' band for five years. If she stayed at this rudimentary level, she would coast along without a challenge and always think herself "best" among her peers. Each year those around her would be younger. Since she was capable of more, it seemed a childish ploy for attention. Someone needed to convince her to move to the next level.

The writer to the Hebrews cajoled some for seeming to be constantly rebuilding foundations when they should have been adding to the structure. Their themes of repentance, abandonment of dead formalism, along with issues of resurrection and eternal judgment had become repetitive. "Therefore let us leave the elementary teachings . . . and go on to maturity, not laying again the foundation of repentance from acts that lead to death, and of faith in God" (6:1). Evidently some had not grown up and moved ahead in their faith. The writer expected the Hebrew Christians to exhibit some trademarks of Christian maturity such as moral discrimination (5:14), love, helpful deeds, noble activities, fellowship, encouragement (10:24,25) and contentment (13:5).

Colonel Milton Agnew points out that when the writer says, "Let us . . . go on to maturity" (6:1), the verb "go on" in Greek signifies being carried, as if by a divine hand, if we allow it. God is at work in the Christian's progress. We do our part by choosing righteousness and by exercising mental discipline rather than sloth. When we come to know what is godly and then act on what we know, we move forward in our faith. And what about our view of God's discipline in our lives? Hebrews 12:10 reminds us that He "disciplines us for our good, that we may share in His holiness." To maintain this discipline we should:

· recall the greater sacrifice of others before us and thereby see our own discomforts in perspective;

· remember Jesus' example in making the suffering of the cross a confirmation of His loyalty; and

· accept adversity, though not sent by God, as an instrument of His loving discipline to train our souls.

Living victoriously through suffering brings glory to God and peace to our hearts. Former international leader of The Salvation Army, General Frederick Coutts, explains that aiming to live at peace while pursuing holiness will not make Christians merely peaceable, but rather peacemakers—active fighters against evil and its disruptive nature.

The first century writer is well aware of what the Hebrew Christians have already endured. They have suffered alongside others and because of their beliefs have borne the loss of possessions with only eternal gain as consolation. So the writer encourages them to continue fully and patiently to accomplish the will of God and enjoy what is promised. Jesus is coming again. Trust in God through Jesus. Live by faith. (10:32–39.) Take the risk that faith implies. Embrace God's promise as Abraham did. Develop a strong hope, as if hope were an anchor thrown into God's very presence where Jesus has gone ahead of us. Know that by faith and patience, you will inherit the promise (6:10–19). Perhaps if he lived today, the writer would design a bumper sticker stating, "Anchor your heart in God." The same message is found in Priscilla Owens' familiar song, "Will Your Anchor Hold?" that follows.

We have an anchor that keeps the soul
Steadfast and sure while the billows roll;
Fastened to the rock which cannot move,
Grounded firm and deep in the Savior's love.

(The Salvation Army *Song Book* #280)

"Growing up is a journey into integration," asserts Madeleine L'Engle in *The Summer of the Great-Grandmother*. It is a sense of living in two worlds simultaneously. It is like the extra-territoriality we observe in someone who has lived for a time outside her own culture and returned with a fresh viewpoint—sometimes thought to be a third culture which keeps the best of both. We are called as Christians to grow up and to live on earth as is suitable for citizens of heaven: offering God-pleasing service and acceptable worship with godly fear (12:28).

According to S. Verney, one crew on a boat found that although there's a time to row, nothing compares with the power and progress that hoisting the sails brings. We have a part to play in maturing as believers, but only the Spirit of Christ can fill the sails and help us move on to new horizons and challenges as we set our faces toward His promised unshakeable kingdom.

SOMETHING TO THINK ABOUT

1. How can we grow old in our faith without actually growing up?

2. What benefits are derived from God's discipline?

3. What are the signs of Christian maturity? Of immaturity?

4. How do Christians live in "two worlds simultaneously"?

4: Acts of Faith

HOW DID YOU COME TO FAITH IN CHRIST? WAS IT THROUGH A GREAT PREACHER? A particular author's choice of words? Moving music? The magnificence of creation? God uses many different influences to draw us to Himself. But for many of us, the consistent, cheerful presence of Christians we have known and observed in daily life convinced us to commit our lives to the Lord.

One of the best-known chapters in the book of Hebrews (chapter 11) lists a dozen or so of the notable "heroes of faith" and alludes to the scores of unnamed others. The first readers of the text would have known the names well: Enoch, Abraham, Sarah, Noah, Moses, Samuel. The writer spotlights them as men and women who believed God, obeyed God and dealt with adversity, realizing their reward would come much later. In the words of General Frederick Coutts, "They refused, unlike some of us, to isolate the immediate contradictions of faith—and how vicious these can be—from the fullness of their belief in God's utter dependability." People lack the conviction that inspires persistence because, Coutts explains, "Their vision is too self-centered . . . but the true believer is homesick for God, fired to greater exploits of faith in this world because of his awareness of the next, and because he knows that his noblest hopes, though frequently postponed, are never canceled."

These heroes demonstrated endurance and a living faith. They obeyed the command or initiative of God—often in the face of great difficulty. This faith of theirs was a choice of obedience to God's Word. They staked their lives on the unseen God. As one art critic described the genius of the painter Vermeer, who deftly portrayed daily activities in heavenly light, "He was able to see the eternal in the evanescent." Perhaps that was true of the gallants of Hebrews 11, too. Certainly their simple faith-based living kept them going and won divine approval.

Faithful in Suffering

But notice the descriptive phrases tucked in among the impressive list: sacrificed comfort, left homelands, led thousands, subdued enemies, chose death over denial of faith. Put simply, their "weakness was turned to strength" (Hebrews 11:34). What a relief to some of us. Hudson Taylor, missionary to China, was asked his secret of service. He replied, "The Lord was looking for a man weak enough to use and He found me." Paul wrote in 1 Corinthians 1:27, "God chose the foolish things of the world to shame the wise; God chose the weak things of the world to shame the strong." No Christian need be disqualified for service. J. Sidlow Baxter says, "Most of us think that suffering will break us; but the fact is that suffering trustfully submitted to, and sanctified by the Holy Spirit, is one of Heaven's surest means of lifting Christian believers from spiritual immaturity and instability into spiritual mellowness and strength." India's Mother Teresa formed a group of "suffering servants" who prayed for her Missionaries of Charity. They turned their suffering into a means of grace on behalf of frontline soldiers of Christ.

God desires our obedience more than our sacrifice. "We are saved, not by the extent of Christ's sufferings, but by the depth of His obedience," wrote General Coutts. Yet obedience leads to sacrifice. Jesus is described as being made complete through suffering (2:10) and learning obedience through suffering (5:8).

When chapter 12 begins, the author argues that we too should strive to follow Christ because of this "cloud of witnesses." Some think of the patriarchs and saints of the past as mere spectators now. Yet "witnesses" are those who testify to something or someone. Their lives continue to encourage us to put our faith in God and look beyond the moment to Jesus. They may have moved off the witness stand, but they are in the courtroom affirming further testimony and awaiting the certain verdict.

The faith and faithfulness of Christians through the centuries is part of our privileged heritage. "We are like dwarfs seated on the shoulders of giants; we see more than the ancients, and things more distant—but this is due not to our own stature" (Bernard de Chartres). Who brought you to faith? We are urged to remember those people and imitate their faith (13:7).

Faith needs to be seen in the context of current community as well. It is noted that Moses chose by faith "to be mistreated along with the people of God rather than to enjoy the pleasures of sin for a short time. He regarded disgrace for the sake of Christ as of greater value than the treasures of Egypt, because he was looking ahead to his reward" (11:25–26). The climate of persecution of Christians in the first century could have tempted them to revert to the security—even governmental protection—they had enjoyed as Jews. Moses' decisive faith would have inspired the Jewish Christians to remain true to Christ. Let us join the caravan of the faithful and the full-of-faith. Jesus says to all His followers, "Let your light shine before men, that they may see your good deeds and praise your Father in heaven" (Matthew 5:16).

SOMETHING TO THINK ABOUT

1. Who helped influence you or introduced you to Jesus?

2. Who will be in the stands as your "great cloud of witnesses"?

3. What are the qualities of a true hero? How can you become one?

4. How is faith essential to the Christian life?

5: The Path of Prayer

PRAYER, A RECURRENT THEME THROUGHOUT SCRIPTURE, IS HIGHLIGHTED IN THE BOOK of Hebrews. The Word of God and prayer are chief resources for the Christian seeking a fresh, living faith. In Hebrews we learn of the privilege of communion with God, which the cross opened for us. As our perfect High Priest, Jesus is qualified as our great Intercessor. He sacrificed Himself "once and for all" on our behalf and His grace is limitless for all who come to God by Him. His intercession is ongoing—He "always lives to intercede" for us (7:25). We have the hope of direct access to God because Jesus has entered into His presence as a forerunner and High Priest (6:19–20). Christian prayer presupposes a prayer-hearing and prayer-answering God.

Because of Jesus' ministry as our perpetual High Priest, we are urged to come freely and often to God's throne and receive mercy and timely help as needed (4:16). A picture of the holy place in the tabernacle of the Old Testament includes the ark of the covenant with its lid, called a "mercy seat." (Martin Luther first used this poetic name when translating the Bible into German.) We sometimes use that term for a place of prayer even today. Indeed, where people come humbly before God, it is a place of mercy.

> *We seek the healing of Thy cross,*
> *The mercy of Thy grace;*
> *Here at this sacred mercy seat*
> *May we behold Thy face;*

Here may we glimpse Thy holiness,
Here on our souls descend,
Here may we meet, and talk with Thee,
Our Master and our friend.

(Doris Rendell, The Salvation Army *Song Book* #590)

Prayer steadies the Christian in life's uncertain circumstances. The Psalmist detailed his frustration with life's unfairness, then added, "but I am a man of prayer" (Psalm 109:4). He had learned the wisdom of redirecting his inexplicable predicaments to God. The author of Hebrews reminds us that on earth Jesus Himself offered petitions and tearful supplications to God (5:7). Need guidance? Try prayer. The Bible overflows with promises of God's leading. The English translation of the Japanese version of Proverbs 4:12 assures, "As you go, step by step, I will open up your way before you." And what should be our natural reflex when helped? Praise and thanks. The writer reminds us that praise also results from lips that acknowledge and glorify the name of Christ (13:15). In fact, praise is another form of prayer.

Peter van Breemen states, "To pray means to turn the spotlight on Christ." In the chapter that follows the list of examples of faith, the author of Hebrews urges us to get down to basics and run with patient endurance our own race set before us. We do this best when we are looking to Jesus, because of who He is, what He did and where He reigns (12:2).

Previously we noted that the Old Testament's Enoch was included in faith's hall of fame (Hebrews 11). He is said to have walked with God and eluded death. Or as Luci Shaw puts it, "Enoch crossed the gap another way, he changed his pace, but not his company." We, too, can enjoy walking with God, albeit in a crooked world, via prayer:

He walks with God who speaks to God in prayer,
And daily brings to Him his daily care;
Possessing inward peace, he truly knows
A heart's refreshment and a soul's repose.

(Dorothy Thrupp, The Salvation Army *Song Book* #580)

Musician Frank Boggs told of something he learned in Africa about faithfulness in prayer. In a certain area people walk away from their huts into the grassland by their chosen routes seeking privacy for prayer. If a path is overgrown, it becomes obvious that someone is neglecting his prayer life. The practice of prayer affects more than the one praying. The discipline of prayer may seem like a personal quest, but it leaves a trail for others (Proverbs 10:17).

Hebrews 12:13 talks about making straight paths so lame limbs may not be put out of joint, but cured. (Knee and hip replacements of our day were not even dreamed of in the first century.) The need for preparing paths would be understood literally and figuratively. God promised, "They will come with weeping; they will pray as I bring them back. I will lead them beside streams of water on a level path where they will not stumble, because I am Israel's father, and Ephraim is My firstborn son" (Jeremiah 31:9).

In expectation of the Messiah, Isaiah's prophetic words echo over the centuries; Luke reverberates, "A voice of one calling in the desert, 'Prepare the way for the Lord, make straight paths for Him. Every valley shall be filled in, every mountain and hill made low. The crooked roads shall become straight, the rough ways smooth. And all mankind will see God's salvation'" (Isaiah 40:3–5; Luke 3:4–6). Part of that preparation is a personal repentance of sin and turning to God.

We can also help to remove obstacles for the sake of others—to prepare the way without being in the way. We can help do this by praying for people. Note that the writer of Hebrews asked his first readers to pray for him (13:18). If Jesus intercedes for us, how much more should we intercede for others? Dr. Sam Shoemaker asserted, "People should walk through our prayers in droves." Taking time for prayer in our harried lives is a choice; good intentions cannot take the place of praying. The physical strain of clearing a road takes effort, but brings results. The spiritual work of praying for others takes discipline, but yields long-term benefits in our lives and in the lives of others. With the poet we ask the Lord's help:

> *O Thou by whom we come to God,*
> *The Life, the Truth, the Way!*
> *The path of prayer Thyself hast trod:*
> *Lord, teach us how to pray!*
>
> (James Montgomery, The Salvation Army *Song Book* #625)

SOMETHING TO THINK ABOUT

1. How do we have direct access to God?

2. How do we pray? What do we pray for?

3. How are those prayers answered?

4. When we pray, how can we "make crooked paths straight"?

6: It's All about Jesus

HAVE YOU EVER STARTED TO WATCH A VIDEO OF A MUSIC CONCERT, ONLY TO SEE THE screen filled with rolling images or hear music at erratic speeds? You know that the original performance was flawless, but the poor taping does not do it justice. The distortions do not come from the musicians but from the tape through which the concert is conveyed. Similarly, the voice of God came through men in the Old Testament, but with some distortion due to the human instruments. It is the same message in the New Testament, but when it comes through Jesus, it is clearer and we can understand it better.

Men and angels worshipped Him in heaven, yet Jesus, in obedience and faithfulness to God, stooped to become human to save us. On earth Jesus spoke to the people on God's behalf—as a

Prophet. After His sacrificial death and resurrection, He resumed His place in heaven. As a Priest, He speaks to God on behalf of the people. The writer of Hebrews tells us that Christ holds His priesthood unchangeably because He lives on forever (7:24). The word "unchangeably" signifies a nontransferable quality—He is unique and without successor, and He ministers in heaven perpetually as our kingly High Priest (7:25). Jews who had been reared under the priestly system would have needed this reassurance of a better high priest than those in the line of Moses and Aaron. Last spring a visiting speaker from Jews for Jesus explained Christ in the Passover. Later we asked the Russian Christian, who was a Jew, "What do you think of the book of Hebrews?" He replied with a glowing smile, "It's my favorite book of your testament!"

We require Christ to mediate between God and us because of God's consuming holiness and our need of grace. By Jesus' finished work on the cross we have forgiveness for sin. Because of the character of our Priest-King, the covenant He makes with us is better than the old one under which men obeyed the Law in fear. The author quotes the Old Testament prophet Jeremiah, who was inspired generations before to tell of a new covenant God would write on hearts instead of stone (8:7–13). Miraculously, Jesus comes into our hearts by His Spirit when we choose Him as our singular and all-sufficient Savior. Then by His intercessory priesthood we are kept in constant fellowship with God. Jesus' first High Priestly request when He returned to heaven resulted in His Holy Spirit being given to the believers at Pentecost. Through His abiding presence we are enabled to live victoriously.

Genuine Belief

The author of Hebrews reminds readers to be content and without fear because of God's promise to absolutely never leave or fail those who genuinely believe in Him (13:5,6). Jesus is "the same yesterday and today and forever" (13:8). Artists through the centuries depicted Christ in genres according to the visual customs and biases of the day. Does this tendency carry over to man's perception of the character of Christ? General Frederick Coutts warns us to resist the temptation that worms into each age to create Christ in our own image and distort His true nature: "But how can we ensure we see Him truly? First, by recognizing how prone we all are to mold a 'Christ' after our own desires. Then by a constant recourse to the Gospels, read imaginatively and with open mind, relating each passing episode to that central revelation of His character, the cross. Lastly, by allowing the Spirit of Christ Himself to clarify our vision."

Hallelujah for the timeless Christ whose throne is forever (1:8). In His teaching, Jesus often referred to the kingdom of God or the kingdom of heaven. Hebrews also speaks of the heavenly kingdom. Sometimes it is as explanation of faithful believers' motivation through trials (11:14–16). Other times readers are encouraged to persevere by a reminder of our heavenly citizenship and future home (13:14). Chiefly, heaven is portrayed as the place where God reigns, judges and is worshipped fully by men and angels (12:22–24). Through Jesus, the Living Way, we may enter God's presence with assurance. Further, we hold our hope of salvation in Christ confidently, because He who promised is faithful to His Word (10:19–23). Because this unshakeable kingdom is our inheritance, we want to offer God pleasing service on earth (12:28) while leaving to God the timing of the King's return. The author injects the succinct reminder, "For in just a very little while, 'He who is coming will come and will not delay'" (10:37).

Everything's better in Jesus—His coming kingdom and the heavenly city, our inheritance and life of hope, our citizenship, our spiritual covenant and growth toward maturity, access to the Father, opportunities for faithfulness on the way. It's not about us; it's all about Jesus.

SOMETHING TO THINK ABOUT

1. How is it possible that Jesus can be Prophet, Priest, and King?

2. Why is Jesus superior to Moses, Aaron, or any other mediator between God and man?

3. Why is Jesus' priesthood unchangeable? How is God's kingdom unshakable?

4. What is our inheritance in Christ? When do we receive it?

A Portrait of Redemption

While redemption is woven into the tapestry of Scripture, some portraits more clearly reference this ultimate design of the Creator to save His people who have fallen victim to sin's deception. The Apostle Paul skillfully defines the scope and power of our inheritance purchased with the blood of the matchless Son of God.

THIRTEEN

THE POWER OF HIS WILL

SHARON M. ROBERTSON

Lt. Colonel Sharon M. Robertson is assistant chief secretary for the Western territory. A special interest of hers lies in the science of sacred hermeneutics. Lt. Colonel Robertson gained the inspiration for this study through an appointment as assistant territorial legal secretary.

Six years in the territorial legal department can totally color one's view of the world—even the biblical world. After reading thousands of wills to identify and analyze The Salvation Army's interest and responsibility under each, it is second nature to probe and question. A simple statement may include complex shades of meaning vital to understanding the intent of a benefactor. That legal department experience helped me rediscover the richness of the inheritance which is ours through the sacrificial death of our beloved brother and Savior, Jesus.

1: The Power of His Will

IT WAS ONE OF THOSE "AHA!" MOMENTS—THE SUDDEN DISCOVERY that in reading chapters 13 to 15 of John's Gospel, I was virtually reading Jesus' "last will and testament." They are the bequests He meant us to receive upon His death. And what breathtaking bequests—at least sixteen separate testamentary gifts, not one trivial or inappropriate!

As beneficiaries of Jesus' estate, we have the right to accept and use the gifts He left us. To do that, we must study the wording of the bequests. We need to determine not only the gift, but any terms and conditions to be met. Who would be foolish enough to let a little effort and midnight oil stand between him and such treasures!

Jesus' first bequest: Servanthood (John 13:13–17). Servanthood? Is that a let down, or what! Who in his right mind wants to be a servant? Jesus, the most dynamic leader of all time, who set the eternal standard for Christian leadership, laid aside His good clothes and washed the tired, dirty feet of His subordinates. No simple ceremony, this. If you think those feet weren't tired and dirty, you try walking in sandals—no socks—through the dust of rutted dirt roads and the filth of city streets. Jesus saw a task—a dirty, even demeaning job—that needed doing, and He did it. And then He took advantage of the shock and consternation of His disciples to impress on their hearts and minds the value of the most persuasive spiritual ministry they would ever have—the ministry of servanthood.

Innumerable books, from pamphlets to exhaustive tomes, have discussed the implications of Christ as the suffering Servant. Jesus, in a simple action and a few masterful words, went straight to the heart of the matter: "You call Me Teacher and Lord; and rightly so. Now that I, your Lord and Teacher, have washed your feet, you also should wash one another's feet. For I have set for you an example that you should do as I have done for you. . . . Now that you know these things, you will be blessed if you do them."

Servitude is not something to which one would naturally aspire. We have been trained from infancy to describe success in terms of wealth, social acceptance, recognition, and of the power these things bring. Jesus, by His example, frees us from the entanglements of unsatisfying goals and shows us how to realize the satisfaction and empowerment achievable only through effective servanthood. Jesus' servanthood was characterized by humility, but not humiliation. Humiliation is the result of shame, and Jesus saw no shame in responding to a need.

Jesus' servanthood recognized that ministry to physical needs opens the door for ministry to the needy spirit. No task is demeaning when we realize that it may lead to the healing of a soul. Jesus exemplified the sensitivity of the servant-spirit, which sees that attention to the little things sets the stage for the big. He challenged us to take advantage of insignificant tasks to teach life's most important lessons.

What an incredible treasure, this bequest! Servanthood—the key to effective ministry.

2: What's New About Love

THE WILL OF JESUS WAS DECLARED IN HIS LIFE, VALIDATED BY HIS DEATH, WITNESSED to by the Spirit, and probated through His resurrection. He did this because of His love for His heirs and His intent that we should benefit through our relationship to Him. And what extraordinary bequests He made! Reading chapters 13 through 15 in the book of John is like exploring an old, long-forgotten box overflowing with treasured keepsakes. You get so excited that you dig right through to the bottom, tossing aside valuable pieces with only a comment in your haste to see what else is there. Finally you get to the bottom, where you find—the bottom. Only when you go back and look again at each item do you recall its meaning and value.

One of Jesus' bequests which we tend to bypass in our excited search for treasures of greater worth is found in John 13:34,15:12 and 15:17. The bequest? A new commandment. "Love one another," Jesus said. "As I have loved you, so you must love one another."

So what else is new? What would you expect Him to say? Jesus knew the Scriptures. He even quoted Leviticus 19:18, "Love your neighbor as yourself." He commended the expert who included it in summarizing the teachings of the law (Luke 10:26–28) and called it the second greatest commandment (Mark 12:31). So why now is it a new commandment?

What's new is the quality of love. Jesus upsets our whole understanding of the standard for love. As His disciples, it is not enough to love our neighbors as we love ourselves. Jesus didn't stop there. He said, "As I have loved you, so you must love one another."

Releasing the Gift

So now I'm supposed to love as God loves? Lord Jesus, as much as I love You, You ask more than I can give! Well, hardly. Jesus never asks the impossible. With every gift, He gives both the power and the responsibility to realize its potential. As John wrote, "Dear friends, let us love one another, for love comes from God" (l John 4:7). My love is not to be an imitation of Christ—I am to love with His love. This is a gift—no strings. God is love. He lives in me. I don't have to try to imitate His love: I have the real thing. I am to release it, use it, let it work the way it's supposed to work!

Jesus' love was expressed in implicit obedience to His Father. And He promised, "If you obey My commands, you will remain in My love, just as I have obeyed My Father's commands and remain in His love." You can't express the love of God if you don't dwell within His love.

Jesus' love was expressed in sensitivity to unspoken need. He recognized the desperation behind Peter's declaration of loyalty, "I will lay down my life for You," and provided a reality check that helped Peter learn to better understand his own weaknesses. He saw the despair that prompted Thomas to say "Lord, we don't know where You are going, so how can we know the way?" With both gentleness and firmness, He revealed Himself as the only Way.

Jesus' love was expressed in His willingness to sacrifice His life for my sake—to bear the incredible weight of my guilt, though He had never experienced guilt of His own—and to pay the penalty that should have been mine.

I am not Jesus, but as I abide in Him, and His love abides in me, He empowers me to love with His love: "As I have loved you, so you must love one another." I can do that. Through the love of God which gives insight, and through the Spirit of God who gives power, I can look around me to identify need and let God's love through me meet it. I can do that! So can you.

JESUS LEFT MANY BEQUESTS FREE AND CLEAR, REQUIRING ONLY THE ACCEPTANCE OF the beneficiary. However, He left one special gift in the form of a testamentary trust (a trust formed under the terms of His will). Jesus' testamentary trust was carefully designed to provide for His beneficiaries until it is finally terminated and the assets fully distributed as we, His heirs, enter into the place He has prepared for us.

Jesus looked into the troubled eyes of His disciples and responded to their unspoken grief with sympathy and reassurance. "Do not let your hearts be troubled," He said. "Trust in God; trust also in Me. . . . I am going . . . to prepare a place for you. And if I go . . . I will come back and take you to be with Me" (John 14:1–3). This promise, the Christian hope, is the basic asset, the *corpus*, which funds Jesus' testamentary trust.

But, you ask, how can an abstract promise "fund" anything? There is nothing abstract about the Christian hope. The writer to the Hebrews tells us that "faith is the substance of things hoped for, the evidence of things not seen" (Hebrews 11:1 KJV). The Christian hope is not a wish or a nebulous desire. It has substance. We can depend on it. Faith is personal, an attitude which we can choose to have—or not to have. The Christian hope exists independent of our attitudes.

If there is one distinction which separates the Christian faith from other religions, it is the Christian hope. Without what the Church fathers called "the sure and certain hope of the resurrection," the Christian faith crumbles. It becomes a lovely, impractical dream. When Jesus presented Himself as the hope of the world, and proved the validity of His promises through His resurrection, He made it possible for the common, unremarkable person to live an uncommon, remarkable life. This is a life of victory with the sure and certain knowledge that our Lord has not forgotten us, but will one day return to claim us as His own.

Beauty for Ashes

What does this mean to us now? How about "beauty instead of ashes, the oil of gladness instead of mourning, and a garment of praise instead of a spirit of despair"? How about being known as "oaks of righteousness, a planting of the Lord for the display of His splendor" (Isaiah 61:3)? These are but a few of the continuing distributions which Jesus arranged for the well-being of His heirs. As a beneficiary, I am able to draw from His trust freely, day by day, even moment by moment whenever the need arises, without diminishing the assets. This daily draw–down on the Christian hope makes it possible to move ahead in faith, knowing that God can fashion beauty from the ashes when they are given over to Him.

The Christian hope rescues us from grieving over what might have been—or what we might have done better—and challenges us with all that God has yet for us to accomplish. The Christian hope keeps us from wrapping ourselves in the encumbering robes of self-pity and despair. It sets us free to praise and honor the Lord in word and works despite what happens in the world.

4: The Power Is Passed

JESUS' POWER OF ATTORNEY? AS A TESTAMENTARY GIFT? HOLD IT! THE POWER OF attorney doesn't survive the death of the grantor! Unless, of course, the grantor isn't dead.

To say that Jesus is unique is a truism. He is the one and only begotten Son of God. One of a kind, Incomparable. The singular nature of His life and death is equaled only by the uniqueness of His resurrection. As Hebrews 9:16, 17 reminds us, "In the case of a will, it is necessary to prove the death of the one who made it, because a will is in force only when somebody has died; it never takes effect while the one who made it is living." Jesus' will took effect at His death—but because He lives, His power of attorney is in effect also.

As He spoke with His disciples during those last few hours before His arrest, Jesus was well aware that His earthly mission was nearing an end. He knew that very soon the friends who surrounded Him, asking anxious questions, would be called upon to accept responsibility for publishing the message of the gospel to the world. And He knew that they were worried, confused, even frightened, though they did not yet understand how much was at stake.

"I am going to the Father," Jesus said, "and I will do whatever you ask in My name, so that the Son may bring glory to the Father. You may ask Me for anything in My name, and I will do it" (John 14:12–14). "Then the Father will give you whatever you ask in My name" (15:16). "In that day you will no longer ask Me anything. I tell you the truth, My Father will give you whatever you ask in My name. Ask and you will receive, and your joy will be complete" (16:22–24).

If your boss gives you an order, not just once, but repeatedly, you can pretty well depend on the fact that he or she means it. Jesus did not suggest that His disciples come before the throne of God asking for favors for Jesus' sake. He repeatedly directed them to come to God in His Name, representing Him, with the full authority of His name behind them. In other words, Jesus presented His friends with His power of attorney, the power to act on His behalf, to draw His assets, backed by the full authority of His name. And who are the friends to whom Jesus gave the power to act in His name? "You are My friends," Jesus said, "if you do what I command." Exciting, but a bit intimidating? You'd better believe it!

With the power to come to God in Jesus' name comes the responsibility to use His authority wisely. After all, Jesus did not transfer His authority to us; He authorized us to act in His name. The power, the assets which have been placed in our care are not our own; we represent Him, the living Lord. When a power of attorney is executed, the empowered individual is legally bound to use the delegated powers in the best interests of the grantor. He is to avoid frivolous or wasteful transactions which would squander the available assets. He is to refrain from seeking personal gain through improper use of the powers granted him. Fulfilling the intentions of the grantor must remain his supreme objective.

"You do not have, because you do not ask God. When you ask, you ask with the wrong motives, that you may spend what you get on your pleasures" (James 4:2,3). Jesus honored us with His power of attorney, the power to come before God in His name, His authority. Nothing has greater credibility with God than the authority of Jesus' name. God grant us wisdom to use it well.

IT WAS ONCE SAID THAT THE STREETS OF CALIFORNIA WERE PAVED WITH GOLD. NOW they seem to be paved with lawyers lying in wait to file complaints on behalf of money-hungry clients. Lawyer jokes aside, in a litigious society you and I depend on the intellect, training, honor, and integrity of lawyers to secure our benefits and constitutional rights. They counsel, defend and advise, mediate on our behalf, act as advocates—sometimes even prosecute us. That's their job.

That was Jesus' job, too, but on a grander scale than that offered by any legal system. "If any man sin, we have an advocate with the Father, Jesus Christ the righteous" (1 John 2:1, KJV). As Jesus prepared to leave His disciples, His heart was touched by their neediness. They were immature in faith and facing trials greater than they could have imagined. He could not allow them to think they would now be totally on their own—they couldn't handle it!

So He made a promise: "I will ask the Father, and He will give you another Counselor to be with you forever the Spirit of truth. The world cannot accept Him, because it neither sees Him nor knows Him. But you will know Him, for He lives with you and will be in you" (John 14:16, 17 NIV). Jesus promised that the Counselor would teach us all things and would remind us of everything He had said (14:26). "When the Counselor comes, whom I will send to you from the Father. . . . He will testify about Me. And you also must testify" (15:26,27).

"Unless I go away," Jesus continued, "the Counselor will not come to you; but if I go, I will send Him to you. When He comes He will convict the world of guilt in regard to sin and righteousness and judgment. . . . But when He, the Spirit of truth, comes, He will guide you into all truth. . . . He will bring glory to Me by taking from what is Mine and making it known to you" (16:5-16). This is how Jesus introduced to His disciples, through the declaration of His will, the Advocate who would be ready to take over their defense after His death.

The world of the law is so intricate, so diverse, that attorneys tend to specialize. There are those who specialize in tax law, tort law, or labor law. There are defenders, prosecutors, and attorneys who do nothing but research for other attorneys. The Advocate, the Counselor sent by Jesus, is also a specialist. He specializes in representing the down-and-out, the person who can't make it on his own, the one who is guilty and the whole world knows it. The Counselor Jesus sent specializes in representing folks like you and me.

And what a task this Spirit of truth has. The Counselor is to stick with us forever. He is to live with us, in us. Besides teaching us all that we need to know to win our suit, He reminds us of all that Jesus taught as well. He testifies the truth about Jesus, so that we in turn can testify the full truth before the world. He counsels us on how to respond to the accusations of the world and provides the support we need to speak out boldly. He provides strength to lean on and a shoulder to cry on, and never ducks out when the going gets rough. He convicts the sinner of sin, and shows him the righteousness of God. He makes the guilty face up to the inevitable consequences of his own guilt, and points to the only Way to escape a lifetime of guilt and shame—through the shed blood of Jesus Christ. If you haven't met Him yet, let me introduce you to my Counselor. He'd like to represent you, as well.

6: Straight When We Want Curls

AT THE HEIGHT OF THE ROMAN EMPIRE, MEN SPOKE OF THE *PAX ROMANA,* THE TERMS of peace (i.e. the lack of war) that Rome imposed over the nations it had conquered. During this period there were few uprisings, making it possible to travel and communicate freely to the ends of the empire. Rome performed a vital role in preparing the world for the birth of Jesus by opening avenues of communication. The gospel message spread quickly, as good news should.

The same Rome that set the stage for Jesus' birth was on hand to bring about His death. Jesus knew the deceptive nature of the kind of "peace" governments could provide, just as He was aware of His own role in the great conflict between right and wrong. He knew His coming would bring schism, not peace, to a world determined to live by its own rules and interpretations of the perfect Law of God. And He knew His disciples would be in the midst of the conflict. They had to be armed with superior weapons, weapons that would not fail them no matter how great the opposing forces. So Jesus armed His disciples with a legacy of peace. "Peace I leave with you; My peace I give you. I do not give to you as the world gives. Do not let your hearts be troubled and do not be afraid" (John 14:27).

"Lord, don't You know there's a war on?" Jesus knew . . . but He also knew God's priorities. And He knew that for anyone who appropriates God's priorities as his own, victory is assured.

Jesus gave new meaning, depth, and dimension to the word "peace." Where the world's peace is transient, Jesus' peace is stable. Where the world's peace comes through compromise and treaty, Jesus' peace is based on the only absolute certainty the world has ever known, the Word of God Himself, and cannot be compromised. Where the world in desperation cries "peace, peace" but finds none, Jesus' peace is beyond human comprehension. It comes in quietness and confidence to His heirs, who know that in Christ victory is inevitable, and peace is secured.

Yet the number one cause of work-related health problems in today's world is stress. The pressures of living in a high-intensity environment, bombarded on every side by the demands of employer, family, friends, society and self are enormous. Violence rages in the streets, and we are afraid to walk alone. Bills pile up, while we panic and compensate by buying even more. We are too fat—or too thin. Our hair is curly when we desperately want it to be straight—or straight when we want curls. Instead of having bad hair days, we seem to have perfected the bad hair life!

Jesus said, "Peace I leave with you."

You did, Lord? Maybe so, but if You left it on my desk I'll probably never find it under all those papers! Of course, maybe I haven't really been looking for it, either.

Lord Jesus, there's a war on. You've enlisted me as a soldier in Your cause. I don't want to let You down. Help me sort out my priorities—starting with Your priorities. Help me accept the peace You offer, the perfect, indefinable peace that will allow me to step back and get a clear perspective on what is happening around me. Teach me to apply the healing gospel of peace to my neighbors.

And help me to remember that "God's gifts and His call are irrevocable" (Romans 11:29). Your bequest of peace comes to me in perpetuity. Grant me the wisdom to take advantage of it to bring honor and glory to Your name.

THE 1912 CHILDREN'S CLASSIC *POLLYANNA*, WRITTEN BY ELEANOR H. PORTER, IS NOT the sort of book that I joyfully embraced, even as a child. I read it at the insistence of my mother, who was firm in her belief that it was the best of all fictional works for children. One bit, however, made a lasting impression on my young mind: Pollyanna, talking to the discouraged minister, spoke of her father identifying over 800 "rejoicing texts" in the Bible—verses or phrases which invited us to "rejoice in the Lord," "be glad and rejoice," "shout for joy" and so on. Pollyanna's father had taught her that "if God took the trouble to tell us eight hundred times to be glad and rejoice, He must want us to do it!"

In His last words to His disciples, Jesus clearly stated His intention to leave a bequest of joy. "I have told you this so that My joy may be in you and that your joy may be complete" (John 15:11). How could a man facing the agonies Jesus knew Himself to be facing speak of His own joy, let alone of bringing to completeness the joy of His disciples? What kind of joy was this, that it could enable Jesus to look at future pain and humiliation, even death, and feel a sense of joy so great that He desired His friends to share in it?

What kind of joy? The real kind—deep and abiding. Jesus was not speaking of the glow of happiness that comes and goes, or even of the pleasure that can come from knowing that in spite of one's present circumstances one may feel good about what has been accomplished. Nor is it relief that what is past is past.

Jesus' joy was the joy to be found only in abiding in God's love. He found joy in knowing that He had been responsive to God's instruction. He had been obedient to God's commands, even though that obedience meant sacrificing His own life. He found joy also in the confidence that His disciples would remain in His love, that they would obey His command to love one another as He loved them. And He finds joy in my love and in my obedience. He has confidence in me. Just think of that!

Jesus gifted His heirs with the joy of abiding in His love. Abiding in the love of God encompasses all that Jesus has spoken of in this "will" of His. It implies surrender, vision and appropriation. We surrender any need we may feel to accomplish on our own, any desire we may have to present God with the honorable fruits of our own laudable labors. We have the vision to recognize the tremendous potential for ministry that awaits the one who is willing to accept what God has made available. We appropriate and put to use the incredible resources Jesus has made available to us.

Jesus gifted His heirs with the joy of perfect obedience. "Perfect" anything is a scary concept. Jesus' obedience was perfect, but how can mine be? Peter, a man who had reason to despair of his own imperfections and could be critical of the imperfections of others, was told, "Do not call anything impure that God has made clean" (Acts 10:9-17). God can take the imperfect "best" that I have to offer and render it clean, holy, perfect in His sight. Like Peter, I must not consider imperfect what God has made perfect. To do so is not evidence of my humility—it is evidence of my lack of faith. Without faith, it is impossible to please God (Hebrews 11:6); through faith, it becomes possible for me to experience the joy of perfect obedience.

8: Righteous Discomfort

IF THE GOSPELS WERE REWRITTEN IN THE CONTEXT OF A MODERN–DAY MOVIE SCRIPT, Jesus would doubtless have an impenetrable cape or a supercharged ultra–spear. He would have taught His disciples to "do unto others *before* they do unto you," and to "*blast* those who persecute you." Thank God, the gospel is not among the works of sensational fiction. Jesus didn't charge in like Rambo or Hercules—but then neither did He sit on the sidelines mouthing platitudes, blind to the mounting hostility of the world around Him. He knew His enemies—better than they knew themselves.

Jesus knew there was another legacy that He must leave to His disciples. The world hated Jesus and His message and would hate His followers. They had to recognize the real enemy, understand the source of the animosity they would face. To meet the challenges of ministry in a hostile world, they would have to take advantage of every incomparable bequest bestowed upon them as Jesus' heirs. In the Upper Room Jesus said to His disciples, "I have set you an example that you should do as I have done for you. I tell you the truth, no servant is greater than his master" (John 13:14, 15). Later, Jesus reminded them of that moment: "Remember the words I spoke to you: 'No servant is greater than his master.' If they persecuted Me, they will persecute you also" (15:20).

Jesus was persecuted, arrested, tried, and put to death because He had committed righteousness, a crime that society could not forgive. The holier the life, the more uncomfortable the observer who is forced to evaluate his own life in comparison to the holy one. No one likes to be made uncomfortable.

A Standard Set by Christ

"If they persecuted Me, they will persecute you also," Jesus warned His disciples. But all that was two thousand years ago. Christianity is big business these days. Politicians prove their earnestness and integrity by publicly thanking God for His blessings. The evidence of the success of religious leaders is published to the world as they dress in designer outfits, drive designer cars and live in designer homes. Successful ministry sometimes seems to be measured by the number of luxury cars in the parking lot. Looks like warnings to guard against worldliness have passed our generation by. Or have they?

Why has the modern American Church seemed to suffer so little persecution? Has Christianity become so accepted and admired by the world that the world no longer has to fear or be uncomfortable in the presence of true righteousness?

Has the world become so accepted and admired by the Church that the Church no longer sets an example of righteousness and holy living? Just a thought—don't let it bother you. Unless, of course, you really believe that the standard for holy living is the standard set by Christ.

Jesus' legacies were devised to equip His heirs to model His holy standard in a hostile, non-Christian world. He has provided what we need to be winners! He set the example of servanthood. He taught us to love as God loves. He gave us hope through His promise to come back for us, so that we may live with Him forever. He authorized us to come before God in His name. He sent the Counselor-Advocate-Comforter to dwell with and in us. He gifted us with a profound peace beyond all human understanding. And He made it possible for us to experience the unquenchable joy found in obeying His commands, and abiding in His love.

What joy, what delight, what responsibility—to be named as friend and heir of Jesus. "You are My friends," Jesus said, "if you do what I have commanded you."

SOMETHING TO THINK ABOUT

1. What can you do to serve someone this week that will show your love for them and for the Lord?

2. How is it possible for us to love others as Christ has loved us—even those whom we don't really like or who have hurt us?

3. How does hope have substance since it all seems so "other-worldly"? What is that hope based on?

4. What does Jesus' "power of attorney" mean for us within the discipline of prayer?

5. How does Jesus represent us as our counselor and advocate?

6. Is it possible to live at peace in a world of chaos and violence? What has to change within to make that peace a reality?

7. How many ways can you find to use your bequest of joy?

8. Have Americans accepted Christ's legacy of persecution? Are there greater challenges coming?

FOURTEEN

THE GOSPEL FOR SAINTS: HOLINESS IN THE BOOK OF ROMANS

JOHN G. MERRITT

Major John G. Merritt retired as director of the Southern Historical Center, Atlanta, in 2001. His work has appeared in Army publications, the *Beacon Dictionary of Theology,* and the *Wesleyan Theological Journal.* Major Merritt is also editor of the *Historical Dictionary of The Salvation Army* to be published by Scarecrow Press.

1: Preparing for the Journey

> *I am not ashamed of the gospel, because it is the power of God for the salvation of everyone who believes: first for the Jew, then for the Gentile. For in the gospel a righteousness from God is revealed, a righteousness that is by faith from first to last, just as it is written: "The righteous will live by faith"* (Romans 1:16–17).

THE ANNOUNCEMENT OF CHRIST'S SAVING ACTIVITY PROVIDES THE structure for Paul's Letter to the Romans. In this passage, Christ's saving work is defined as the revelation of what Professor Don J. Kenyon calls a "God–kind of righteousness that produces deliverance for the person who trusts His Son." The God–kind of righteousness is not only who God is in Himself, but also what He does in Christ. Through the death and resurrection of Jesus Christ, God "rights" people of faith—He straightens them out into a relation with God's righteous nature in a way that sets them free from all sin. This revelation, Paul exclaims, is "good news"—it is the gospel! But why is this news so good? Because of its stark and transforming contrast to some bad news.

The Bad News

The bad news is that God must, by His righteous nature, respond with "wrath" (1:18) to humanity's moral condition and action. Paul defines this reality as "sin" and describes in Romans 1–8 its three basic components.

The first component (1:8–5:11) is sin as a specific and deliberate moral choice by a person who is responsible for his or her actions. One of the words for "sin" in the Greek language is *hamartia*. Throughout 1:18–5:11, Paul uses *hamartia* in a plural form to emphasize sin as a deed or act. This surfaces in his statement in 3:23 that, in its very expression, demonstrates the meaning of sin from the standpoint of willful acts: "For all have sinned and fall short of the glory of God."

"The glory of God" is the divine standard that defines sin as an act. This standard is the mark which humankind fails to reach. Paul does not mean, however, for this image of "missing the mark," first established in the Old Testament, to be rationalized as the "I-can't-help-it-if-I'm-a-bad-shot" sort of excuse.

The essence of sin as an act is to suppress the truth (1:18) and willfully embrace the wrong (1:19–22). It is to "put the truth in a box and sit on the lid!" From the standpoint of sin as act, Paul reaches the verdict of universal moral guilt for the suppression of the truth: "We have already made the charge that Jews and Gentiles alike are all under sin." He makes it clear that God has left humankind to the emptiness and evil it has chosen.

Why does this situation exist? This question brings us to the second component (5:12–8:17): sin as a dynamic force or principle in both Jews and Gentiles. Sin is the source of deviations from the divine standard. But in contrast to the plural use of *hamartia* (sins) Paul employs the term in singular form joined with the Greek definite article "the," which translates from Greek to English as "the sin." The late Colonel Milton S. Agnew in *More Than Conquerors* explains that this represents a focal shift from the commission of sinful deeds to the possession of a sinful nature.

The third component (8:18–39) of sin is not sin as self-inflicted wound (act) or moral disease (inward nature) but sin as "scar." This can mean the effects of Adam's sin on humanity, such as death, mental and physical infirmities, proneness to error. Sin as scar can also refer to the mental and physical effects of personal sins.

The Good News

Paul does not leave the reader at the mercy of sin's three-fold assault. He unfolds the remedy for the total sin problem in the comprehensive deliverance which he calls "salvation" (1:16–17). Christ saves us from:

1. Sin as Act: Justification

2. Sin as Principle: Sanctification

3. Sin as Scar: Glorification

Looking Ahead

As we journey down the "Highway of Holiness"—Paul's gospel for saints—we will learn why Romans is crucial to the Wesleyan interpretation of entire sanctification by faith as a second work of grace. We will come to understand why this second work of grace is a vital experience within God's providential righteousness, coming as it does after the reality of justification before God.

SOMETHING TO THINK ABOUT

1. The good news that Paul writes about stands in contrast to the bad news of sin. What are the three basic components that the author uses to describe sin?

2. How does salvation cure sin's three-fold problem?

2: The Panorama of Redemption

WHAT KIND OF DELIVERANCE IS PAUL ANNOUNCING? WHY IS IT NEEDED? HOW IS IT received? When can it be received? The answers we uncover will explain why the faith-deliverance the gospel produces is such good news. Once you have been able to look across the panorama of redemption in 5:1-11, you will have sharpened your vision to penetrate its depths in chapters 6 through 8.

Introduction into a New Realm of Life

> *Therefore, since we have been justified through faith, we have peace with God through our Lord Jesus Christ, through whom we have gained access by faith into this grace in which we now stand. And we rejoice in the hope of the glory of God.*

These two verses (5:1-2) mark out the horizons of the breadth of salvation that is in part explicitly expressed and in part hinted at in the rest of the passage. Salvation is in a new sphere of life: "this grace in which we now stand." It is a realm of spiritual existence in which grace is the basis of operation for the Christian life from start to finish. As a result it is characterized by "peace with God."

This realm of grace is "entered" by justification—the act of God whereby He declares the believer to be in right relationship with Himself—through the "door" of faith. Thus we are "justified by faith." Our "access . . . into this grace in which we now stand" is by faith which justifies. It is brought to ultimate fulfillment through glorification, when believers are finally united with Jesus and liberated from the "scars" that Adam's sin and our own have left in our minds, bodies and personalities. Thus "we rejoice in the hope of the glory of God" (5:2). In harmony with the rest of the New Testament, glorification will take place at the second coming of Jesus Christ (see 8:18-39). Consequently, this aspect of salvation is still in the future. Anticipation of it fills the expectant believer with "rejoicing"!

The Operation of the New Sphere of Grace

Since the believer has entered a new realm of life called grace that is bounded on one hand by justification and on the other hand by glorification, we conclude that, as Professor Kenyon suggests, there is a period of existence—a redemptive interim—between these two points of salvation. This is laid out in 5:3–5, 10:

> *Not only so, but we also rejoice in our sufferings, because we know that suffering produces perseverance; perseverance, character; and character, hope. And hope does not disappoint us, because God has poured out His love into our hearts by the Holy Spirit, whom He has given us. . . . For if, when we were God's enemies, we were reconciled through the death of His Son, how much more, having been reconciled, shall we be saved through His life.*

In these verses Paul pictures the redemptive interim as a rigorous life. Because of the severity of these disciplines, believers may be tempted to doubt whether they really have entered the realm of grace. They may conclude that their hope of the glory of God is an illusion, their rejoicing a psychological deception. The antidote, Paul tells us, for such misgivings is the inner presence of the Holy Spirit who comes to live in us at the moment of justification—at the time we enter the realm of grace: "God has poured out His love into our hearts by the Holy Spirit, whom He has given us."

This is not our love of God, which is perfected through the infilling of the Holy Spirit. Rather, it is God's atoning love for us (5:6–8), which is made known to us by the indwelling of the Holy Spirit. Thus the Holy Spirit assures believers that what God has promised in bringing salvation to its complete fulfillment is actually true; it will really happen; God will not let us down. Thus, "hope does not disappoint us" (5:5). All this identifies Christ through the Holy Spirit as the source of life during the redemptive interim. This is the process of sanctification. However, at this point in his discussion, Paul is only hinting at sanctification as he refers to being "saved through [or in] His life" (5:10). Not until chapter 6 does the Apostle consider this truth in detail—as the deeper dimension of salvation in Christ.

The Network of Redemption

As our view of the panorama of redemption gains sharper focus, we begin to see how justification, sanctification and glorification are the three dimensions of the liberating good news that Paul announces in 1:16–17. Because each component is so inseparably bound up with the content and meaning of "salvation," no aspect of the redemptive process is optional. This is because of the nature of our solidarity with Adam or Christ.

SOMETHING TO THINK ABOUT

1. The author speaks of salvation as introducing a "new sphere of life." Recall the moment of your own salvation. How did it affect you?

2. What surprised you or worried you as you began to live in your new standing with God?

3: The Radical Road to Holiness

PAUL TAKES US ON A RADICAL JOURNEY THROUGH THE BOOK OF ROMANS—A JOURNEY that goes to the root of things. He brings us to two points in history that focus on the experience of solidarity with Adam and with Christ. He makes involvement inescapable and places an old realm of life (5:12-19) in stark contrast with the new realm (5:1-11). This juxtaposition alerts us to a variety of crucial contrasts throughout the remainder of our study of Romans 1 through 8— the essential one being between the old and the new in relation to the present.

Adam and Christ: A Sharp and Persistent Contrast

When we look back at Romans 5:12-21 through two thousand years of history, we, in effect, look through one or more lenses which give different perspectives on how each of us was involved in Adam's sin in the Garden of Eden. The theories of original sin which tend to gather around a Calvinistic center teach, in various ways, that each one of us is condemned for something of which none of us is personally responsible—Adam's own sin and/or the possession of a sinful nature received in some way from him. The Arminian approach—reflected in this series on Romans—recognizes the solidarity of the human race with Adam and his sin (as the Calvinistic theories also do), while maintaining personal moral responsibility in relation to original sin.

The nature of humanity's relationship to Adam cannot be known apart from discovering the nature of our relationship to Christ. Thus, we must try to discern two things: First, the meaning of the terms "in Adam" and "in Christ"; second, the nature of the interaction of these two concepts with each other. By making these discoveries, we will be on our way to understanding the relation of original sin (in 5:12-21) to the experience of sanctification (6:1-8:17). This tells us that Romans 5:20-21 is a center around which Paul's thought revolves: "But where sin increased, grace increased all the more, so that, just as sin reigned in death, so also grace might reign through righteousness to bring eternal life through Jesus Christ our Lord." In 5:12-21 the Apostle moves from his emphasis on sin as a deed to sin as an indwelling nature. This passage shows the inseparable relation between these two aspects of sin and their respective redemptive remedies of justification and sanctification.

The structure of Paul's emphases in Romans 5:12-19 is discerned by noting the controlling principle which guides the flow of his thought. First, there is, as John Murray calls to our attention, "a complete and consistent contrast between Adam and Christ." Growing out of this arrangement is Paul's emphasis on the nature of humanity's relationship to either Adam or Christ. This is indicated by the concepts of in Adam and in Christ. A first reading—or maybe even a second and third!—may not uncover this double-decker principle with much clarity.

Second, the emphasis which emerges out of the relation of humanity to either Adam or Christ is that of potentiality. In these verses, Paul points out that the apparent justification of all persons in Christ is potential rather than actual. For the potential to become actual, a believing act of the will must be exercised to appropriate the provisional effects of Christ's justifying obedience. And in keeping with the consistent contrastive pattern of the passage, the condemnation of all persons in Adam is potential rather than actual. The apparent actual condemnation of all persons in Adam because of his disobedience is really potential; it only becomes actual when willfully appropriated by an act called sin.

An Ethical Relationship

It is the act of sin that results in guilt and condemnation. This may be called an ethical relationship. Used in this sense, ethical does not refer to what is good in distinction from what is bad. Rather, ethical here speaks of a relationship or condition that centers in the response of the human will, rather than referring to a situation that automatically exists. So Paul is calling our attention to a solid involvement with either Adam or Christ, the effects of which require human response. Such involvement does not automatically occur whether we personally respond or not. This understanding of the potential and the ethical will become increasingly important and clear.

The effects of Paul's ethical approach to solidarity with Adam or Christ involves two important factors. First, it answers the question about the nature of humanity's relation to Adam's sin. The answer is that "many were made sinners . . . by one disobedience" in the sense that "one man's trespass led to the condemnation of all men" (5:18). Thus, when a person by an act of sin endorses, so to speak, his or her sinful nature inherited through solidarity with Adam—sin as a specific and deliberate moral choice—he or she becomes personally responsible for his or her depravity.

Second, it reveals the connection between the experience of holiness and being in Christ, which, as we shall see, is the central emphasis of chapter 6.

SOMETHING TO THINK ABOUT

1. Christ's death on the cross provided potential cleansing for all people. Consider the difference between potential cleansing and actual cleansing.

2. If grace increases all the more where sin increases, is there any sin that is too deep for forgiveness?

4: Why All the Conflict?

THE MORAL TRANSPARENCY IN THE FOLLOWING HYMN BY CHARLES WESLEY SPEAKS a language that is foreign to the many worlds of human existence in which Adam calls the shots. Wesley framed the hymn by bringing together the vocabulary of redemption and the grammar of grace, making it untranslatable for those in open rebellion against God and those who seek a relationship with Him based on their moralistic achievements.

I want a principle within
Of jealous, godly fear,
A sensibility of sin,
A pain to feel it near.

This hymn, which celebrates "a principle within" rooted in holiness, would have been home country and native vernacular for Paul. His spiritual passions and theological thought were shaped by principles that were matters of life and death to him—and to us.

In the brief compass of Romans 5:20–6:1 three principles or dynamic forces are brought into contextual relation with the *sin principle* which Paul introduced in 5:12–19. These are the *death principle* and the *grace principle* that are displayed against the backdrop of the *law principle* throughout chapters 6 through 8. We get a foretaste of the variety of conflicts in which these three principles will be engaged as Paul, in 5:20–6:1, sets the sin principle and the grace principle in complete opposition to each other in reference to the law.

How Does the Law Operate?

We know that Paul structured the first eight chapters of Romans around three aspects of sin—deed, principle, and scar—along with the three-fold remedy of justification, sanctification, and glorification. Now we begin to see details on the function of the law in relation to the problem of sin as act and as principle. In 5:20, Paul shows us that the law increases our awareness of the persistent tendency of humans to commit acts of sin. The fact that the law makes us aware of sinful deeds points us to the root cause of such acts: the presence of an inbred sinful nature.

This shift in moral awareness—from acts to principle—is in connection with the explicit mention of the grace principle in 5:20: "But where [the] sin [principle] increased, grace increased all the more." This is a factor that points us back to Paul's panoramic structuring of that principle in 5:1–11. "You see, at just the right time, when we were still powerless, Christ died for the ungodly. Very rarely will anyone die for a righteous man, though for a good man someone might possibly dare to die. But God demonstrates His own love for us in this: while we were still sinners, Christ died for us" (5:6–8). Out of this line of thought, Paul calls our attention to the function of grace.

How Does Grace Operate?

In zeroing in on the function of grace, Paul again reveals his tendency to express his thought in a structured manner. Here he arranges his emphases in a pattern that involves problem, provision and process. Each time Paul relates the law to an aspect of sin in order to reveal the need for the appropriate redemptive provision, he always places the relationship within the framework of grace. Thus, Paul in Romans never speaks of the law outside the context of grace. The significance of this is that the divine works of grace are not disconnected events—and no aspect of salvation is optional since each is a part of the realm of grace.

How Does Grace Confront Sin?

Grace has entered human existence in Jesus Christ to deal decisively with the sin principle. Beginning with chapter 6, Paul uses this truth as a corrective measure and as an introduction to the meaning of holiness. This he does in 5:20–6:1 by declaring that although grace is magnified by an initial, heightened awareness of sin as a principle, it is not magnified by the continuation of that awareness throughout the duration of the believer's life. Commencing with 6:2, Paul tells us why grace is not magnified by the unthinkable suggestion "to continue in [the] sin." This he does by a detailed discussion of the nature and quality of the life that is to be lived throughout the time which extends from justification to glorification. This life is that aspect of the grace principle that is being "saved in [Christ's] life" (5:10 RSV), defined as sanctification, and is God's provision for sin as an inner principle.

SOMETHING TO THINK ABOUT

1. Christians often sing "I am not under law but under grace." What does this mean?

2. Does living under grace mean we will never need to confront sin in our lives again?

5: The Imagery of Full Salvation

THE HIGHWAY OF HOLINESS IN ROMANS SIX THROUGH EIGHT RUNS ALONG A ROUTE marked by three images of human experience. Paul brings this imagery together, riveting our attention on a specific moment within the process of sanctification that he elsewhere calls entire sanctification (see 1 Thessalonians).

The first marker is the image of death (6:1–14), and standing at the center of this imagery is the cross. This centrality provides angles of vision that shape the way Paul moves from 5:1–11 through 5:12–21 into 6:1–14. Until now, Paul has emphasized that Christ's saving work on our behalf has been done apart from us. This is the objective domain of Christ's death and resurrection, providing the justification that delivers from sin as an act (3:9–5:11). Having now brought us into the context of sin as a principle, Paul expands Christ's redemptive activity to include that in which we are inwardly involved. This is the subjective domain of His death and resurrection (6:1–14). Paul uses these complementary dimensions of Christ's atonement to tell us that not only did Christ die for our deeds of sin (5:6–8), but we also died with Him on the cross to [the] sin as a principle (6:3–8).

Subjective Identification

Paul's emphasis on subjective identification with Christ in His redemptive work is the grounds for his answer of "Horrors!" to the question asked in 6:1 (RSV) about our relation to indwelling sin: "Are we to continue in (union with) [the] sin?" Paul responds by prompting a further question: "We died to [the] sin; how can we live in (union with) it any longer?" (6:2). W. T. Purkiser observes that with this counter-question, Paul points out that our death to indwelling sin may be viewed from three interlocking perspectives.

First, we died with Christ in profession (6:1–5). This is introduced by the figure of baptism. Water baptism generally has been understood as a term of initiation because of its frequent association—in Acts, in several of the epistles, and throughout Church history—with beginning the Christian life. This is true whether one understands baptism to be the sacramental means for receiving salvation or to be a confessional witness to the earlier reception of new life in Christ. But how does Paul use this expression in relation to sin as a principle? This is a crucial question since baptism, interestingly, does not surface in Romans until after Paul concludes his discussion of the commencement of the Christian life through justification as the solution for sinful acts.

The late arrival of baptism in Romans is due to Paul's comprehensive redemptive purpose in the letter. This is reflected in the shifts of vocabulary and the explanatory interpretations around which 6:1–7 is built. The pronounced use of "baptism" in 6:2–4 is abruptly replaced in 6:5–7 with the terminology of redemptive union: "united with" and "crucified with." Since, as Professor Don Kenyon has suggested, baptism drops out of the picture in 6:5–7 as Paul explains what is going on in 6:2–4, it is quite likely that baptism in 6:2–4 is a metaphorical expression for union with Christ rather than a physical, ceremonial reference. This possibility is increased by the attention Paul gives throughout the remainder of Romans to union with Christ as the source of holiness.

Potential and Provisional Inclusion

Within this framework Paul uses "baptism" to point to the potential/provisional inclusion (important concepts for Romans 6 that Paul introduced in 5:12–21) of all humanity in the subjective domain of Christ's atoning sacrifice. As Professor Oscar Cullmann calls to our attention, two of the gospel writers record that Christ metaphorically referred to His impending death on the cross as a baptism (Mark 10:38 and Luke 12:50). Because of the unlimited scope of the atonement, Christ's death involved what Cullmann calls a "general baptism" of all humanity. This focus on a universal atonement, at which Mark and Luke only hint, finds detailed expression in Romans 6 through Paul's emphasis on being "baptized into Christ's death" (6:3). A metaphorical approach to baptism is foundational for the potential/provisional interpretation that will be drawn from death with Christ in 6:6–11.

Even if this metaphorical function of baptism does not exclude literal baptism in water, the contextual flow subordinates the literal to the metaphorical. This makes physical baptism a visible embrace of the implications contained in the metaphorical expression of baptism. Baptism, therfore, carries with it an obligational understanding that is rooted in grace.

In effect, then, Paul is saying that entrance into the realm of grace at justification, figuratively and/or literally symbolized by baptism, involves believers in a commitment that obligates them eventually and ultimately to go on within the continuum of grace, to the experience of entire sanctification at some point beyond the moment of justification.

This crisis orientation is embedded in the term baptism itself for, as Dr. Purkiser has noted, baptism is moment-specific; it is a "crisis word," not a "process word." This enables Paul to indicate that the meaning and scope of baptism extend beyond the commencement of the Christian life in a way that structures the total process of salvation around specific crisis points by which the three-fold problem of sin is cumulatively remedied by particular applications of "this grace in which we now stand" (5:1–2).

Consequently, we must keep in mind that it is the moment of entire sanctification for those already converted or justified, not baptism either as a sacramental or confessional ceremony, that is Paul's central concern in Romans 6. We will miss the whole point of what Paul is saying if we conclude that his main purpose in Romans 6:1–14 is to construct a doctrine of water baptism. This will become more evident as we continue with death with Christ in provision.

You need to read Romans 6 only once to discover that Paul describes your death with Christ to indwelling sin as something that has already taken place:

> "We died to [the] sin" (6:2).
> "All of us . . . were baptized into [Christ's] death" (6:4).
> "For we know that our old self was crucified with [Christ]" (6:6).
> "Now if we died with Christ" (6:8).

But when you shift your attention from the past tense verbs of the biblical text to the present tense of your own heart, it does not take much observation to discover that your relationship to indwelling sin may be far from "dead!" As you proceed further in Romans, you may find it difficult to reconcile the victory of the past tense of death to the sinful nature in 6:1–14 with the bondage created by its present activity that Paul autobiographically describes in 7:7–25. So, when did we die to inbred sin? How are we connected with that past event and how does it impact our present experience?

The answer is, as Dr. W. T. Purkiser has observed, that we provisionally died with Christ to the sin principle at Calvary (6:6–11). It is movement toward this death to which we have committed ourselves in profession at the time of justification (6:1–5). This takes us back to 5:12–21 which describes the nature of our solidarity with the disobedience of Adam and the obedience of Christ in ethical rather than nonethical terms. This has nothing to do with "good" or "bad." Rather, it indicates the part played by the response of the human will. Being in Adam means that although we have inherited a sinful nature from him we are not automatically held guilty until our wills endorse that sinful nature by sinful acts of our own—the kinds of deeds which Paul in 1:18–3:23 affirms we all commit.

Even as being in Adam does not automatically make us sinners apart from a rebellious response of our own wills, so being in Christ does not automatically impart to us all the benefits of Christ's saving work—including holiness in its fullest sense—until they are embraced by a believing act of will. The consequences of our solidarity with Adam or Christ are completely and consistently conditional.

This is why our understanding of original sin shapes our understanding of holiness, particularly in the root of entire sanctification in death with Christ to inbred sin. Theories of original sin that make persons sinners without personal response set the stage for making all believers holy without personal response. This exclusion of the conditional factor from sin and salvation manifests itself in two conceptual areas that will distort our understanding of holiness in Romans 6.

Holy in Christ and Standing and State

A non-ethical view of original sin leads to the emphasis that all believers are holy in Christ because of actual, rather than potential or provisional, participation in Christ's redemptive deed. Its formula is: "Christ is holy . . . I am in Christ . . . thus I am holy." Perfected holiness is declared to be true of all believers, even when they may be quite spiritually deficient in present experience.

Dr. Purkiser calls to our attention that the resolution of the obvious moral contradictions in the Holy in Christ approach is attempted by the Standing and State theory. On the one hand, the believer's standing is one of perfect holiness because of being in Christ who is perfectly holy. On the other hand, the believer's state is his or her actual spiritual condition at any given moment. Within this context, spiritual growth is conceived in terms of gradually bringing one's state into greater conformity to one's standing in Christ. However, any lack of such conformity does not at all disturb the believer's essential and eternal relationship with God.

Positional Holiness

This biblically-based expression, unfortunately, is frequently misused to mean that even as the guilt of Adam's sin is legally imputed to all humanity apart from personal response, all the redeeming benefits (including holiness) of Christ's saving deed are ascribed to all believers, again apart from personal response. Thus by virtue of being in Christ, the perfect holiness of Christ is automatically and unconditionally ascribed to all believers. Hence, all believers are positionally sanctified. This position, however, does not have any essential relationship to the believer's present spiritual condition; the believer's actual condition cannot alter his or her position in Christ.

These two areas of distortion are inconsistent with the root of chapter 6 in the provisional/potential/actual orientation of chapter 5. They also displace experiential sanctification in favor of positional holiness as an essential and indispensable component in the redemptive process, since nothing can alter a believer's perfect standing in Christ. This pits entire sanctification as illustrated by death in 6:1–14 against entire sanctification as illustrated by slavery in 6:15–23. The result is the injection of discord to Paul's logic in Romans 1 through 8.

These discordant factors are removed by recognizing that the complete and consistent contrast between Adam and Christ and the relationship that we have with either one (5:12–21) is the key to understanding holiness as presented by Paul in Romans 6. Thus, what can and should be ours by virtue of being in Christ is not actually ours until we make it our own by faith, through the experience (6:12–14) of the death and resurrection of Christ to which we are committed by profession (6:1–5) and related by provision (6:6–11).

1. Death is the first of three images Paul uses in Romans 6–8. How does death relate to our full salvation?

2. Paul describes the source of holiness as union with Christ. How would unity with Christ look in your life?

6: Images of Full Salvation—Death: Its Experienced Reality

"IT IS DIFFICULT TO GO THROUGH A CRUCIFIXION WITHOUT KNOWING IT." THAT IS how General Bramwell Tillsley answers the question, Can a person go through the experience of entire sanctification without knowing it? That response squares with Paul's approach to the believer's death with Christ to indwelling sin in Romans 6.

Like physical death, the prelude to death with Christ may be extended or brief. Regardless of the duration, the death itself always happens in a distinct moment of time. However, death with Christ is not the automatic end product of a natural movement reflecting some vague spiritual flow. Rather, it is a turning point, which is what is meant by "crisis," reached by a climactic exercise of faith. This is made possible by full surrender to the subjective dimensions of the cross which center in our death with Jesus at Calvary. This is why Reverend Albert Lown said that entire sanctification is a crisis experience within the larger process of sanctification that moves from justification to glorification. This is reflected in the terms with which Paul describes the total commitment that the profession (6:1-5) and provision (6:6-11) of death with Christ requires us to make, through grace, for dying with Him in experience (6:12-14).

Christ's Death as Actuality

Beginning with 6:11, Paul reveals how the provisional and potential factors rooted in the historical moment of Christ's death can become actual and contemporary realities. The believer is to "reckon . . . [himself or herself] to be dead indeed unto [the] sin—the sinful nature—but alive unto God through Jesus Christ our Lord" (KJV). The "reckoning" begins by considering the historical provision of death with Christ. It means to account as factual the historical provision of deliverance from inbred sin. Response to this historical provision occurs when we "present [ourselves] to God as those alive from the dead, and [our] members as instruments of righteousness to God" (6:13 NASB). The expression, "alive from the dead" refers to the historical provision in 6:1-10. This is the basis for the believer's presentation of himself or herself to God for the reception of the experiential reality of death to inbred sin. The seeker of holiness, realizing that historically or provisionally he or she died with Christ to [the] sin, now responds to that fact by "yielding [his or her] members to righteousness for sanctification" (6:19 RSV), so that the Holy Spirit (as Paul later tells us in Romans 8) can actually make him or her "dead to [the] sin and alive unto God in Christ Jesus" (6:11).

Indwelling Sin Displaced

Paul calls us to pray, "Lord Jesus, I realize that when You died on the cross You provisionally included me in that death. . . . I realize that when You walked out of the tomb on Easter morning, You provisionally included me in that resurrection. . . . I potentially rose with You from the grave. On the basis of these facts, I totally yield myself to You so that the Holy Spirit can make real in me what You provided for me on the cross and in Your resurrection: The displacement of indwelling sin and its replacement with the fullness of Your resurrection life." The sanctifying consequence of this identification with Christ is assured to us by Paul's affirmation that "[the] sin shall not be your master, because you are not under law, but under grace" (6:14). It is here that we begin to see how historical event (profession and provision) and present, inner reality ultimately come together in the believer's experience of entire sanctification within the realm of grace (5:1–2).

Holiness Not Mechanical

This convergence is neither automatic nor mechanical. In harmony with Paul's consistent contrast between our solidarity with Adam and Christ, and how personal response is central to such solidarity (5:12–19), we are not automatically holy simply because we are "in Christ." Because we are not automatically holy "in Him" through justification (as indispensable as that relationship is), holiness in the fullest, experiential sense is not mechanical. This mechanical view proposes that entire sanctification is waking up to what has actually been mine since I was justified: an "I–got–it–all–at–conversion" kind of understanding, and then living in the light of it without any reference to an unnecessary second work of grace.

This stands at odds with the imagery, focus, and context of Romans 6. We only move with Christ from death to indwelling sin in profession and provision to death with Him in experience through a passage built around the cross. That is why rearranging theological furniture in our minds to create non–experiential space for holiness is so wide of the mark of God's sanctifying purposes for His children. There must be distinct, present action by God Himself. This is why, in the Wesleyan perspective, entire sanctification is a "second work of grace." This does not mean that grace is compartmentalized or that Christ's atoning work is not all encompassing. Rather, entire sanctification as a second work of grace involves the specific appropriation of God's specific redemptive provision for inbred sin which is the environment of the total Christian life.

Entire sanctification is a relationship that includes more than a response to Christ's provision for believers as detailed in 6:1–10. This is properly called "consecration" and is secondary within the realm of grace. God's grace expressed in our provisional death with Christ makes possible our response to that same grace which brings experiential death with Christ to indwelling sin. We are only able to respond to justifying and sanctifying grace because of prevenient grace—the dimension of grace which is one step ahead of us in God's ongoing call to increasing Christlikeness. When holiness is approached from this perspective, the intensity that characterizes the seeking of entire sanctification will change from human struggle to a child's receptivity of a gift from a loving Father who longs to extend His holy nature through our redeemed personalities.

1. Contrast being "dead to sin" and "alive to Christ."

2. "Prevenient grace" means God is always one step ahead of us, wanting us to succeed. He gives us His character rather than expecting us to struggle to be good. How does this make you feel as you consider your life as a Christian?

7: Images of Full Salvation—Slavery

SLAVES HAVE NO OPTIONS! THAT IS WHY PAUL CHOOSES SLAVERY IN ROMANS 6:15-23 as his second image of entire sanctification as he gradually unfolds the meaning of full salvation throughout 6:1-7:6. But how does this metaphor connect with the image of death in 6:1-14? They begin to connect as we recall that in 6:1-14 Paul says we died with Christ on the cross and rose with Him from the grave (6:1-11).

Yet the Apostle urges us on to a crisis point in which we die to indwelling sin (6:12-14). In 6:15-23 Paul moves from the decisiveness of this moment to a demand which is spread across an extended relationship that is inseparable from this crisis. By doing this, Paul tells us that the implications of the cross are perpetuated in the obligations of slavery. Thus 6:15-23 is an environment devoid of options. It is the natural habitat of slaves. Paul calls us to commit ourselves to slavery—again, in a crisis experience. And solely on the basis of grace.

This (initially) apparent contradiction of affirmation and command is part of a pattern that runs along parallel tracks. The first track starts with the emergence in 6:1-16 of the obligatory implication of "baptism." This implication is that in the occurrence of justification we commit ourselves to move on to entire sanctification. Now, in 6:15-23, Paul tells us that submission to Christ's Lordship in conversion obligates us to commit to His Lordship in entire sanctification.

The second parallel track starts in 6:13 with a grammatical contrast, in the Greek text that Paul wrote, between continuous action (present tense) and completed action at a distinct point in time (aorist tense). By means of this contrast, as Dr. Wilber Dayton calls to our attention, Paul says to the believer that in justification you began a process of committing yourself to enslavement to righteousness in contrast to holiness. Up to this point your committal has been "piecemeal" (6:16-19a). Now make it complete by embracing a slavery that is total (6:19).

Pursuing Holiness

This is serious business, Paul tells us in 6:20-23. The movement from incomplete to total slavery is not a "take-it-or-leave-it" option! This is because of the way "eternal life"—used in 6:23 as a synonym for final salvation points to glorification: "For the wages of [the] sin is death, but the gift of God is eternal life in Christ Jesus our Lord." This applies, in this setting, to converted persons. The problem of sin as an indwelling nature (not acts of sin) is addressed here—a problem that can only be resolved after a person becomes a believer. Paul makes it clear that this resolution is an urgent matter for believers because the ultimate goal of all God's redemptive work in believers is eternal life or final salvation: "But now that you have been set free from [the] sin and have become slaves to God, the benefit you reap leads to holiness, and the result is eternal life" (6:22).

One consequent implication is that justified persons who do not pursue holiness after receiving the light concerning their union with Christ are in danger of being overcome by inbred sin. This truth is suggested in Hebrews 12:14 (KJV): "Follow peace with all men, and holiness without which no man shall see the Lord." This does not mean that unsanctified persons cannot go to Heaven should they die in that condition. Rather, it means that they must be living up to all the light they do have, which is always expanding as our obedience continues. This will lead them up to and across the threshold of entire sanctification.

Dr. Richard S. Taylor proposes that Hebrews 12:14 does not so much describe a distinct work of grace as it means that "the minimum measure of grace acceptable [for entrance into Heaven] would be an intense desire for the maximum measure of grace available." That intensity of desire spells "pursuit" and that maximal availability of grace embraces entire sanctification as a distinct moment within the holiness that is pursued between the past moment of justification and the future moment of glorification.

If the pursuit stops, it is possible that a believer will forfeit salvation. This is because refusing to follow light given is the beginning of backsliding—something which has ultimate consequences far more serious than simply being "out of fellowship" with Christ. The grace that Paul is laying out before us in Romans is the environment for deliverance from sin that is both radical and demanding—radical because it can only be imaged by death; demanding because it must be illustrated by slavery. This is the logic behind the ninth and tenth Doctrines of The Salvation Army:

> We believe that continuance in a state of salvation depends upon continued obedient faith in Christ.

> We believe that it is the privilege of all believers to be wholly sanctified, and that their whole spirit and soul and body may be preserved blameless unto the coming of our Lord Jesus Christ.

Consequently, the image of holiness as "slavery" means that God's redemptive purpose offers no option for spiritual detours on His map of grace.

SOMETHING TO THINK ABOUT

1. Once redeemed from the slavery of sin, we become willing slaves of God. Why would Paul suggest such an image for salvation?

2. Paul instructs us to pursue "peace and holiness without which no one shall see the Lord." The author of the series suggests that the beginning of backsliding happens when we stop following the light we are given—when we no longer run after peace with God and others. Consider examples of this either from your own life or that of others.

"SOMETHING OLD, SOMETHING NEW; SOMETHING BORROWED, SOMETHING BLUE." So runs the old marriage counsel for a bride on her wedding day. "Something borrowed, something blue" might have puzzled Paul. But he resonates with "something old, something new" as the dual emphases around which he shapes his metaphor of marriage as an image of full salvation (Romans 7:1–6), identifying both "oldness of the letter" and "newness of the Spirit" (7:6).

Something Old

The "something old" is the law. Although present in each segment of the metaphorical trilogy that illustrates entire sanctification in 6:1–7:6, it ascends to dominance in 7:1–6 where eight references are made to law within the brief scope of six verses. This is in contrast to two occurrences of the term in 5:20–6:14 and one in 6:15–23. The shape which this legal dominance takes is a contrast between bondage to the law and release from the law. This brings together several crucial emphases that look back to the provisional death motif in 6:1–14 and forward to the potential future victory-now motif in 8:1–17.

As we turn toward 6:1–14, we hear in 7:1–6 two important echoes of entire sanctification illustrated by death. The first echo is the subjective approach to Christ's redeeming work. In both passages the believer's death is based on involvement in the death of Christ: "You also were made to die . . . through the body of Christ" (7:4). The purpose of death with Christ is two-fold: Instrumentally it is "that you might be joined to another, to Him who was raised from the dead." Vocationally it is "that we might bear fruit for God."

Although the two segments complement each other at the point of death and resurrection, it is [the] sin to which we die in 6:1–14, whereas in 7:1–6 death focuses on the law: "You also were made to die to the law" (7:4). And even as death in 6:1–14 means separation from indwelling sin, death in 7:1–6 means that "now we have been released from the law, having died to that by which we were bound" (7:6). This is the application of the legal principle in 7:2–3 that is illustrated by marriage: "If [a woman's] husband dies, she is released from the law concerning her husband. . . . If her husband dies, she is free from the law."

The parallel relationship of 6:1–14 and 7:1–6 shows the theological interdependence of inbred sin and the law. But with all his emphasis on the law, Paul does not speak of *release* from it until 7:1–6. This raises two questions:

- Why is "release from the law" in Romans mentioned only in reference to severance from inbred sin?

- Why is "release from the law," in relation to liberation from inbred sin, not mentioned until 7:1–6?

Simply, release from the law in relation to [the] sin could not be considered until release from that aspect of sin itself, through atonement, had been adequately detailed as it is in chapter 6.

The second echo is the element of time. This arises from the subjective perspective which relates 7:1–6 and 6:1–14. Consequently, chronological matters in 7:4–6 are to be understood in terms of a historical past that is provisional rather than causal in effect. Since 7:4,6 speak of death to and release from the law as something which apparently has been accomplished, it is appropriate to ask: At what point in the past did it occur? The root of 7:1–6 tells us that death to and release from the law is a historical provision in the redemptive work of Christ rather than an automatic happening at the beginning of the Christian life.

Within this line of argument Paul incorporates his treatment of the problem of "flesh" in 7:5—a condition which, in 7:7–25, is closely linked with Paul's discussion of the law: "For while we were in the flesh, the sinful passions, which were aroused by the law, were at work in the members of our body to bear fruit for death." This chronological orientation in 7:5 suggests that the problem of the flesh has been solved, although the present tense context of flesh in 7:7–25 strongly implies it is still a problem. Although this is a contextual and interpretive difficulty with which we must grapple, this much is clear: Release from the law and the flesh are to be understood as potential, in line with the potential/actual pattern that surfaced in the "in Adam/in Christ" contrast in 5:12–21. Consequently, release from the law and the flesh in relation to inbred sin is an ethical event. That is, it is a moment of chosen response by persons who are already believers that makes potential release from the law and the flesh a present, actual liberation. This is an issue which is integral to understanding Romans seven and eight, for even as 6:1–14 provides the interpretive key to grasping the relationship between chapters 5 and 6, 7:1–6 contains the interpretive key for discovering the relationship between chapters 7 and 8.

This latter linkage is grounded in the vocational purpose of the marriage metaphor: "bear[ing] fruit for God" (7:4) through "serv[ing] in newness of the Spirit and not in oldness of the letter" (7:6). This is why Paul's marriage metaphor of entire sanctification includes something new.

Something New

The newness which the Holy Spirit provides is a reality that has its feet planted in two worlds: The Present Evil Age, in which deliverance from sin as an act and as an indwelling nature are so desperately needed; and the Age to Come, which is already reaching back into the Present Evil Age to give us a foretaste of the fullness of redemption that awaits Christ's return.

As George Eldon Ladd has pointed out, the breadth and content of Paul's theology is built around the overlapping of these two "ages." By using "newness of the Spirit," Paul lets us know that this is the perspective which undergirds his gospel for saints about full salvation. The foretaste of the Age to Come that we can have within its "overlap" with the Present Evil Age consists of justification and sanctification (and its pivotal center of entire sanctification). The redemptive fullness within the Age to Come will be glorification. Thus, Paul in 7:1–6 is looking at release from the law and the flesh in relation to indwelling sin from two perspectives—the provisional past (6:1–14) that reaches forward to, and the anticipated future (8:1–17) that reaches back into the experiential present.

But why does Paul choose marriage as the metaphor by which to reflect the cosmic framework of full salvation? Since union with Christ is the source of the believer's holiness (6:1–14), Paul uses marriage in order to concentrate on the concept of union in relation to law. This sets the stage in 7:7–25 for Paul's analysis of what happens when we try to make law the basis for holiness within the realm of grace.

SOMETHING TO THINK ABOUT

1. Consider something old (from your life prior to coming to Christ) and contrast it with something new (after you gave your life to Him).

2. From the marriage union comes offspring. What fruit have you been able to produce from your union with Christ?

9: How Can I Get Off This Spiritual Roller Coaster?

WHEN PETER SAID THAT THE LETTERS OF HIS APOSTOLIC COLLEAGUE PAUL "CONTAIN some things that are hard to understand" (2 Peter 3:16), he must have been thinking of chapter 7 of Romans! At least the terrain over which Paul's "Gospel for Saints" passes suddenly gets very bumpy in 7:7–25. We hit this rough place in the road because Paul now begins to positively affirm as "holy" (7:12) and "good" (7:16) the law that he has placed in such stark contrast to grace. He wraps this affirmation around two important questions.

What Happens If the Law Becomes the Basis of Holiness?

Paul does not raise this issue to exclude the relevance of the law from the Christian life. Rather he does so in order to vindicate the law in a way that points to its true function within the realm of grace. Thus in 7:7–13, Paul vindicates the law's goodness in the face of death. The function of the law from this perspective is to give the painful awareness of [the] sin (7:7). Paul personalizes this truth by showing how inbred sin, in his experience, used the very commandment against covetousness to prompt lust into conscious operation (7:8–11).

Thus Paul asks, "Did that which is good become a cause of death for me?" (7:13). The answer is "No!" For by using such a holy thing as the law to effect spiritual death, indwelling sin reveals its true and horrible nature (7:13). For this reason, Paul states that the positive moral character of the law (7:12) stems from its specific function or use (7:7), not its misuse. This explanation is expanded and deepened in 7:14–23 as Paul vindicates the law's goodness in the face of bondage.

The basic components in 7:14–23 that Paul uses to vindicate the holy nature of the law by means of revealing its function are (1) moral failure and (2) the tragic collision between the law and [the] sin which give rise to that defeat. As in 7:7–13, so in 7:14–23, these components are fleshed out autobiographically. Thus, even as the conflict in 7:7–13 results in death, in 7:14–23 it

197

produces bondage. And it is from this perspective that Paul continues with his explanation of the function of the law in the life of holiness.

However, Paul identifies the antagonists of the conflict in somewhat different ways: In 7:7–13, the conflictive contrast is between the law and inbred sin. But in 7:24–23, it is the law and the "flesh." This latter configuration points to the reason and location of the conflict that produces bondage. The focus of the conflict in Paul is "the flesh." The reason for condemnation is not because the law is sinful—it is because Paul is sinful; he is "of the flesh."

> When I want to do good, evil is right there with me. For in my inner being I delight in God's law; but I see another law at work in the members of my body. . . . Who will rescue me from this body of death? (Romans 7:21–25)

But what is "the flesh"? Sometimes it is simply a term of our humanity. But here it has a moral focus: It is, as William Barclay suggests, a condition that is both "pre-Christian" and "sub-Christian." It is in this sense that Paul locates his focus on "the flesh" after the historical provision of 6:1–14 and places it within the framework of the future victory—now deliverance of 8:1–17. Thus we may define "flesh" as an inner, dynamic, moral condition which is carried over from the pre-conversion life into the regenerate state. The difficulties arising from this "carry over" are autobiographically portrayed in 7:14–23. Placed within the contrastive relation of law (7:14–23) and grace (5:1–7:6) and viewed from the perspective of contingency (7:1–6), we begin to see why the conflict of 7:14–23 arises in believers' lives when they, in the condition of "flesh," stand between the collision of the law and inbred sin.

This points us to the nature of the release from the law within the realm of grace: It is not release from the law as the norm of holiness. Rather, it is release from dependence upon the law as the means for reaching the standard of holiness which the law embodies. This factor may help us address the vexing questions hovering around the issue of when Paul experienced the conflict he describes in this chapter, to which his other epistles or Acts provide no clues:

· Was it before or after his conversion?

· If before, is he describing himself, and us, as awakened but not-yet-justified sinners?

· If after conversion, is he describing the most that can be expected throughout the Christian life, or is he tracing the inner dynamics of the unsanctified believer?

If this is an issue to which Paul intended to point us, then, in my judgment, the placement of 7:7–25 between the past and future victory-now of 6:1–7:6 and 8:1–17 most naturally leads to a description of the believer following justification but before entire sanctification. Most Calvinists will not agree with this proposal, nor will some Wesleyan-Arminians.

But as important as this question is, does it reflect the central thrust Paul is making in this controversial passage? I suspect it may not. Following in some ways the lead of W. T. Purkiser and Watchman Nee, I suggest that Paul may be describing what happens whenever we make the law the basis for living a holy life: The inner conflict generated by the sinful nature/flesh will not be resolved along the radical lines of 6:1–23 and 8:1–17. In fact, it will return at any point we depend on law rather than grace as the basis for holiness—or any other dimension of Christian life.

Thus, 7:7–23 is not an uninvited guest that rudely interrupts the flow of Paul's message of full salvation. Rather, Paul drops it in here to say that we stay on the highway of holiness the same way we entered it (6:1–7:6)—on the basis of grace—and that we will reach the end of the journey (8:1–17) that same way we commenced it—on the basis of grace. This leads us to the second major question that Paul raises in Romans chapter 7.

What Happens When Grace Becomes the Basis of Holiness?

By the time we come to 7:24, 25, Paul has reached the point of utter despair and complete spiritual exhaustion. He now realizes his impotence to find holiness on the basis of the law and, in doing this, brings together the motifs of death (7:7–13) and bondage (7:14–23). He has also recognized that the condition (identified in 7:7–13) existed before he was ever aware of the conflict, which he has been painfully relating in 7:14–23. This is why he describes his condition as "Wretched man that I am!" This is why, in his wretchedness, he cries out for deliverance from indwelling sin: "Who will set me free from the body of this death?" (7:24). This is why the faith-locking of his confession of utter weakness onto the sanctifying intentions of God's grace calls forth the triumphant cry: "Thanks be to God through Jesus Christ our Lord!" (7:25).

SOMETHING TO THINK ABOUT

1. Sometimes Christians experience a sort of rollercoaster ride in their spiritual lives. What do you think causes this kind of struggle?

2. How can we embrace God's grace each day and live above sin?

10: Future Victory—Now!

AS WE COME TO THE END OF OUR JOURNEY, PAUL LEADS US IN SOME "VISION CASTING," bringing together the past and present victory-now dimensions of his message of full salvation in chapters 1–8 of Romans.

The Vision of Victory

Paul wants us to catch the vision of victory by articulating the need for it as he moves from chapter 7 into chapter 8. This is heard in the cry for deliverance from inbred sin: "What a wretched man I am! Who will rescue me from this body of death?" (7:24). Paul agonizes for this deliverance because of the conflict that indwelling sin creates when we misuse the law through trying to make the law the basis of holiness (7:14–23).

Paul wants us to catch the vision of the victory that comes through making grace the basis of holiness. For in crying out for deliverance from [the] sin, Paul sees Christ as the Source of victory: He is both the Instrument of deliverance "through Jesus Christ our Lord!" (7:25)—and the Location of liberation—"in Christ Jesus" (8:1).

By intersecting chapters 7 and 8 at the point of affirming Christ as the source of victory, Paul points us to the realization of the vision: "Therefore, there is now no condemnation for those who are in Christ Jesus" (8:1). The basis for stating that "no condemnation" is the result of deliverance through and in Christ is rooted in 7:7–25.

Thus the reason for condemnation, from which Christ sets us free, is traced back to the law that both defines inbred sin and provides the norm for holiness. However, the law does not condemn because it is evil—for it is good, not bad (7:12). Rather, the law condemns because it cannot deliver from that which it defines (indwelling sin) and cannot enable the believer to attain the norm (holiness). But once one is released from the law through dependence on grace so that the law no longer condemns, "requirement of the law [is] fulfilled in us, who walk not according to the flesh, but according to the Spirit" (8:4).

The Conditions of Victory

Following the pattern that has been consistently maintained since 5:12–21, Paul establishes in 8:1–4 that the experience of "no condemnation" is conditional and contingent. It does not automatically occur simply because one is "in Christ." Rather, it is contingent upon liberation from "the flesh" and conditioned on response to God's action of the Age to Come which has invaded the Present Evil Age.

This response is expressed in a new orientation of the redeemed self (8:5–8): It is to be "set on the Spirit," not "set on the flesh." Such a radical reorientation requires an equally radical basis. And, as Paul tells us in 8:9–13, that basis is the cross to which the believer must conform. However, since this takes place within the new realm of grace ushered in by God's justifying act that the Holy Spirit validates through His indwelling presence (5:1–5), this death-dealing conformity to the cross is accomplished through grace, not grit. It is "by the Spirit."

In saying this, Paul demonstrates that the Holy Spirit is the dynamic who translates the threefold imagery of full salvation in 6:1–7:6 into ongoing, present-moment reality. It is for this reason that Paul concludes laying the foundation for entire sanctification in Romans by announcing "newness of the Spirit" (7:6) in anticipation of the future victory–now superstructure he will build on that foundation in chapter 8. Because 8:1–17 connects with 6:1–7:6 in this way, Paul is emphatic that cross-centered reorientation of the redeemed self is not an option left open to the believer's discretion. Consequently, there is the obligation for victory.

The Obligation for Victory

Because the indwelling of the Holy Spirit interlocks the provision of past and future-victory-now, God's ultimate purpose to deal completely with sin is brought to bear on the "now" of the believer's experience within the realm of grace (5:1–2). As a consequence, Paul asserts in 8:12 that the believer is no longer obligated to remain locked into a mindset that conforms to this pattern of the flesh. Rather, the indwelling presence of the Spirit obligates him or her to sever relationship to the flesh.

Thus in 8:5–11, Paul is saying that the orientation of 8:4 is necessary for the fulfillment of the law as the standard of holiness (8:4) because the realization of this norm requires separation from the flesh or sinful nature. This severance is made obligatory (8:12) by God's consummated purpose, which centers in glorification—deliverance from the "scars" of sin at Christ's return. Paul does this by placing the promised foretaste of this consummation within the area of the believer's present responsibility—a responsibility inherent in the indwelling of the Spirit.

Thus, the believer's possession of the Holy Spirit from the moment of entering the realm of grace at justification (5:5) does not rule out a crisis experience with the Spirit in a "second work of grace," which some interpreters propose through a misuse of 8:9: "But you are not in the flesh, you are in the Spirit, if in fact the Spirit of God dwells in you. Any one who does not have the Spirit of Christ does not belong to Him."

On the contrary, it is the fact of the Spirit's indwelling, which begins with justification, that requires such an experience after conversion for the purpose of fully resolving the problem of inbred sin as the debilitating "carry-over" from the pre-Christian life. This points us to the movement toward victory.

The Movement Toward Victory

Lest we think that the obligation of holiness injects a foreign element into the realm of grace, Paul places his treatment of indwelling sin within the context of a child walking with his or her Father toward full salvation (8:14–17). This becomes clear as we see how he links together the phrases "walk . . . according to the Spirit" (8:4) and "led by the Spirit of God" (8:14)—particularly as they interact with 8:12,13. Being "led by the Spirit" focuses on sonship. "Walk[ing] . . . according to the Spirit" centers in holiness through liberation from the condition of flesh carried over from the old life into the new life of sonship. Therefore, the Holy Spirit leads God's children along the path of grace to the crisis of entire sanctification. This is a way-station, not a stopping point, for the Holy Spirit leads beyond this indispensable moment to glorification when we will fully realize God's ultimate intention of our sonship: complete conformity "to the image of His Son, in order that He might be the firstborn among many brethren" (8:29). Until that time, entire sanctification is an expected outcome of sonship. Consequently, even sonship must be understood in the light of holiness.

All these factors unite to demonstrate that the realm of grace is a constantly flowing, dynamic movement with specific crisis points along the way. These moments are integral elements of the process which, in 8:18, is moving toward the consummation of God's purpose to fully liberate from the totality of sin, a process Paul has been tracing throughout Romans. This is why God is calling you to "grow with the flow."

Reviewing the Journey

Let's not forget the terrain over which we have passed in Romans. It's a redemptive environment of grace (5:1–11) created out of the interplay of (1) the bad news of sin as deeds, as indwelling nature, and as "scars" and (2) the good news of liberation in Christ from all the dimensions of sin through justification, sanctification, and glorification (1:18–8:17). God's justifying work at the moment of conversion deals with acts of sin in a way that points to His sanctifying intention to confront the principle of sin (5:12–19) so as to magnify divine grace (5:20–6:1).

This confrontation which exalts God's grace is so decisive it must be imaged by a "death" (6:1–5) that is provisional and potentially, but not automatically, ours through union with Christ's death (6:6–11). This potential is made actual through deliberate identification with Christ's provision on the cross in a specific moment of grace called "entire sanctification" (6:12–14). This confrontation which exalts God's grace is so demanding it must be imaged by "slavery" to underscore the ongoing extension of that crisis moment (6:15–23).

This confrontation which exalts God's grace is so deep it must be imaged by "marriage" to emphasize union with Christ, in both crisis and radical extension, as the source of holiness and liberating service through the Holy Spirit (7:1–6). The norm of the holiness which comes through union with Christ is reflected in the law. However, it is grace, not the law, which enables us to reach that standard. Whenever we use the law, rather than grace, as the basis for fulfilling God's sanctifying intentions, the result is disaster and defeat (7:7–25).

SOMETHING TO THINK ABOUT

1. There are conditions and obligations for victory, but victory implies a moving experience. Full salvation is the work of the moment as well as a work of a lifetime. Can you track milestones in your journey with Christ?

2. What challenges have you experienced in your life that were overcome by walking in the Spirit rather than in "the flesh"?

A PORTRAIT OF HOLINESS

A sinful people looking for a holy God. We can hear their longings in the prayers and praises of the Psalms. A holy God looking for sinful people and changing them into His likeness steps in and out of both Testaments—on a lonely mountain, inside an upper room, in dusty passageways, amidst the hustle and bustle of ordinary life. Once He enters, nothing is ever ordinary again, and the portrait that emerges shines with His holiness.

FIFTEEN

THE PSALMS: A CONVERSATION

BRUCE A. POWER

Major Bruce Power is an associate professor of biblical studies at William and Catherine Booth College in Winnipeg, Manitoba, and teaches at the College for Officer Training in Toronto, Ontario. His new book, *Conversations with God: Psalms as a Resource for Prayer and Meditation* (available from the Canada and Bermuda territory), expands on the ideas covered in this Bible study.

The collection of Psalms in the Bible is structured to invite participation in a dialogue with God and the community of faith—past and present. The words of men become the Word of God—unique, in this sense, in the biblical tradition—and are then used as words of men to address God.

1: A Conversation with the Almighty

THE BOOK OF PSALMS HAS BEEN THOUGHT OF AS AN INVITATION TO a conversation between God and the community of believers, past and present. As a guide to worship, it has provided generations of Christians with a resource for growth, encouragement, and reflection. The introductory chapters of the book suggest such use, inviting us to think and rethink life issues in terms of the rule of God, the pursuit of wisdom, and the desire to obey His instructions. Reading each psalm with questions in mind allows us to discover unexpected ideas and truths.

The book of Psalms begins with a simple declaration:

> *Blessed is the man who does not walk in the counsel of the wicked or stand in the way of sinners or sit in the seat of mockers. But his delight is in the law of the Lord, and on His law he meditates day and night.* (Psalm 1:1–2)

The statement is clear. People who want to be "blessed," to find purpose, meaning, even happiness in life do not spend life in godless pursuits [note the verbs: walking, standing, or sitting]. Rather, they delight in learning from God. Traditionally, the Hebrew word *torah* is translated as "law," but a more helpful rendering is "instruction." Thus the blessed person "delights in the instruction of God . . . and reflects on this instruction all the time." The instruction becomes a guide to life and living.

The first five books of the Bible are known as the Torah as well as the Pentateuch. To ancient Israel this was the constitution, the basis upon which the people of God would structure society. The Torah provided a reference point to develop principles by which a society would live in a manner that honored God. It was as much about doing as not doing, about honoring God as about prohibitions. In short, it was instruction, not a law code.

Not only does the psalm collection make reference to this instruction of God, but the formal structure of the book implicitly claims the same status! The Psalms are structured as torah. Divided into five books like the Pentateuch, the "five books" are marked by four double amen doxologies: Psalms 1–41, 42–72, 73–89, 90–106, and 107–150. Now if you are checking this out, you are about to declare: "Hey, Book Four doesn't end with two amens!" But it really does. Psalm 106:48 reads: "Praise be to the Lord, the God of Israel, from everlasting to everlasting. Let all the people say Amen." How do you suppose the congregation of believers might have responded?

While there are many other references to the instruction of God in the Psalms, a significant use of the term *torah* is made by Psalm 119, amounting to an A–Z exploration of God's instruction. It has been suggested that at an earlier stage Psalms 1–119 comprised a five-book collection.

Whatever we conclude about an earlier format, the introduction to the Psalter and the overall shape of the book invites us to read each psalm posing the question: "What is God trying to teach me?" As we explore our own experience of God using the words of ancient experience of both individuals and communities of faith, we are encouraged to rethink our values and assumptions. These words offered in worship, selected and preserved by the community of faith, speak to us as the Word of God. Are you listening?

SOMETHING TO THINK ABOUT

1. In what way are the Psalms "an invitation to enter into conversation between God and the community of believers, past and present?"

2. Other than the familiar Psalm 23, do you have a favorite? Why?

3. Have you ever used the Psalms as a hymn or song? Which psalms?

4. If the overall theme of Psalms is "What is God trying to teach me," then what does that instruction involve?

2: Making Wise Choices

"YOU CAN'T JUDGE A BOOK BY ITS COVER" THE OLD ADAGE GOES. YET WE USE COVERS all the time to decide what we want to pick up at a bookstore or the local library. In the era before bound books, it was a little different. There were no covers or title pages to consult. You had to look at the opening lines of a scroll or tablet to determine the sort of information we find today in titles and on covers. This is the case in all the materials collected in the Bible. The opening lines of a book provide the ancient equivalent of a title page.

The "title" of the book of Psalms designates it as a book about choices—about being a wise person or having your life consumed by foolishness. Psalm 1 provides paradigms of the wise and foolish person and suggests that life is about choosing one of these paths. The psalm is often termed a "wisdom" psalm. It invites us to live an examined life, to pose questions about daily living: "How can I live wisely?" or "How can I be a person of substance?" Alternately we might ask: "How can I avoid foolishness?" In Psalm 1 an ideal is set. The person who seeks to live wisely and follow the instruction of God is seen as a person of substance, an individual who will be blessed by God. In contrast, the foolish are the wicked. No matter what they do, they will ultimately fail to endure.

Is this naive? Perhaps at first glance. But if we take the invitation to dialogue seriously and read the psalms in sequence and pose such questions, we discover the seeming contradictions which our life experience suggests are mirrored by the complaints and laments of the ancient community of faith. We are faced with questions forcing us to confront the summary statement of Psalm 1 with the enigmas of daily life.

The book's introductory statements conclude: "The Lord watches over the way of the righteous, but the way of the wicked will perish" (Psalm 1:6). Psalm 3 begins the debate: "O Lord, how many are my foes! . . . Many are saying . . . God will not deliver him" (3:1–2). Hardly an affirmation of the dogma of "Life goes smoothly for the righteous!" Or consider the "How long?" questions (4:2; 6:3; 13:1–2) that dot the initial chapters. Similarly, a series of calls for God to "Arise" (3:7; 7:6; 9:19; 10:12) hardly affirms an experience of visible divine justice. And the seeming answer to the request, "I will now arise!" embedded in 12:5 doesn't resolve the question, for the preamble to this statement declares, "Because of the oppression of the weak and the groaning of the needy, I will now arise." Psalm 12 concludes with the observation that "The wicked strut about when what is vile is honored among men." And as if to answer any suggestion that suffering is ended, Psalm 13 launches with "How long, O Lord? Will you forget me forever?" (13:1).

There is a lot to think about here if you immerse yourself in the conversation. Psalm 14 observes that "the fool says in his heart, 'There is no God" (14:1) and Psalm 15 describes those who are able to enter into the very presence of God, those whose lives "will never be shaken" (15:5).

So we are confronted with the realities of life by the Psalter even as it suggests we search to understand how the pursuit of wisdom and blessing—that which theoretically leads to life and substance—really works. And as we pose the questions "How can I be wise?" "How can I be a person of substance?" "How can I keep my life from being consumed by foolishness?" we are forced to confront the tough realities of life. The psalms do not shy away from the tough questions. There is no attempt to hide behind platitudes or to escape from real life. And there is no effort to couch frustration and anger with God in flowery religious jargon. Instead, the anger and frustration that inevitably wound us in life are taken where they can be dealt with—into the presence of God.

SOMETHING TO THINK ABOUT

1. What are some of the tough questions of life and faith posed in the Psalms?

2. Some have called the Psalms a "how-to" book from God. How is it useful for learning what God expects of us?

3. Many psalms ask the question, "How long?" How do we get on the Lord's schedule and not on out own?

4. According to Psalm 15, who can live and thrive in the presence of God? How does one build those character traits?

3: Crown a King—And Sing

PSALM 2 MAY HAVE BEEN USED FOR THE CORONATION OF KING DAVID. AN ATTRACTIVE idea is that at some stage a collection of "songs of David" began with a celebration of his enthronement (Psalm 2) and concluded with a celebration of his successor (Psalm 72). Solomon was, of course, crowned toward the end of David's life (see 1 Kings 1–2). This idea is reinforced by the statement at the end of Psalm 72: "This concludes the prayers of David son of Jesse." We will return to the theme of David in a later part of our study, but before we leave this introductory thought we should note the manner in which the first two books are described by this concluding statement. These are prayers. Whatever else we might do in terms of reading and reflection, we are explicitly invited to use the psalms as prayers.

But what does all of this have to do with the reign of God? You will note that Psalm 2 no longer makes specific reference to the kingship of David, neither in the superscription or the remainder of the verses. The superscription is that bit of small print above the psalm which in English translations of the Bible comes between the chapter title provided by the translators (Psalm 1, Psalm 2, etc.) and the first verse of the psalm. For example, in Psalm 3 it reads "A psalm of David. When he fled from his son Absalom." We tend to ignore it as if it has nothing to do with the text, but in fact in the original Hebrew, the superscriptions, where they occur, constitute verse 1. So before we throw them aside, we need to take them into account in the overall shaping of the collection.

Note the shape of books 1 and 2 (chapters 2–72)—they are organized around David and his court. But Psalm 2 serves at least a double purpose. (Triple if we consider how often Psalm 2 is quoted in the New Testament to affirm the status of Jesus! For example, verse 7 is often used in the gospel accounts. In Mark 1:11 and 9:7, God uses these words, and a theme is set which is further elaborated by Mark in 14:62 and 15:39.) In its current shape, the Book of Psalms invites us to celebrate the kingship of God by an inner frame comprised of Psalms 2 and 149. This theme is given more intense focus by the fourth book of the collection (90–106) with its theme "The Lord reigns" (93:1; 97:1; 99:1). Book 4 resonates with the theme "whatever happens—God is King!" and invites us to read the entire collection in light of this affirmation. The inner framing of the entire work makes this explicit.

In Psalm 149:2 Israel is encouraged to "rejoice in their Maker." "Let the people of Zion be glad in their King," the poet extols. The king referred to is clearly the Lord (149:4), and is identified by his personal name, YHWH. He is the king of the nations, and the world's states need to discover this truth. The warning provided in Psalm 2—"Therefore, you kings, be wise; be warned you rulers of the earth. Serve the Lord with fear and rejoice with trembling" (2:10–11)—echoes in Psalm 149. The praise of the Lord of the universe is sufficient to bring destruction to His enemies. Psalm 149 implies: "May the praise of God be in their mouths and a double-edged sword in their hands, to inflict vengeance on the nations and punishment on the peoples, to bind their kings with fetters" (6–8). Whether or not the King of the world uses human forces or the power of His command, He is in control. Rethink each psalm in light of this truth. Ask yourself: "How do I see the kingship of God at work in the world? How do I see God as ruler of my life?"

SOMETHING TO THINK ABOUT

1. If Psalm 3 were written for the coronation of King David, what did that scene look like?

2. David includes times of great personal tragedy and adversity—times when he was not at his best. What was the context surrounding Psalm 3?

3. Consider some of the superscriptions to the Psalms. How do they set the context for what follows?

4. Read Psalm 2. Are there any parallels in the New Testament gospels?

4: Coming into His Presence

THE BOOK OF PSALMS IS ONE OF THE MOST POPULARLY USED SOURCES IN PERSONAL devotions and formal liturgy. Historically, Psalm 23 takes a place of honor in the worship "hall of fame." People often think of the Psalms as a hymn book used in the Jerusalem Temple and in the local synagogues in biblical days. Previous generations of Christians used the Psalms as prayers and songs in their worship. One feature of many early psalms of lament and complaint is that although they begin with a litany of anger, perplexity, and frustration, they end with a confirmation of God's love and salvation. Psalm 13, for example, begins with the poet's inquiry, "Will You forget me forever?" (13:1) but ends with the declaration, "I trust Your unfailing love; my heart rejoices in Your salvation. I will sing to the Lord, for He has been good to me" (13:5–6). Clearly, a transformation has taken place, but there is no evidence that the externals of the situation have changed. The transformation takes place in the heart of the complainer. Talk about encouragement!

The lesson is obvious. When I take my life situations into the presence of the most holy God, I realize that whatever I have is a gift, and am confronted anew with the choice between declaring "there is no God" (14:1) or believing in the character and person of God, whose ways are often beyond my comprehension.

The conclusion of the Psalter is shaped by praise, with its concluding poem echoing the refrain "Praise the Lord" (150:1, 6). "Everything that has breath" is called upon to join the hymn. All Israel is urged to join the chorus in Psalms 148 and 149. In all, Psalms 146–150 are marked as a group by the instruction at the beginning and end of each hymn to "praise the Lord!" It is a fitting conclusion to the collection, calling upon the reader to join the chorus.

While Psalms 146–150 are anonymous, Psalm 145 is attributed to David and marked as "A psalm of praise." On the basis of content, Psalm 145 could be added to the praise conclusion of the book. But it is not generic praise which anyone might intone. It is clearly designated praise which David affirms, and as such concludes all of the larger collection's "David" material with a psalm of praise. David sings: "I will exalt You, my God the King; I will praise Your name for ever and ever. Every day I will praise You" (145:1–2). The final collection (145–150) follows up this desire by having "every creature praise His holy name."

Book 5 is saturated with praise. It begins "Give thanks to the Lord, for He is good; His love endures forever" (107:1), and repeats the declaration often. It invites us to read each psalm in both this book and the larger collection in quest of reasons to praise God. The invitation is clear. Consider again as you read, think, and meditate on the ways of God, "How can I join the chorus of praise?" You'll be glad you did!

SOMETHING TO THINK ABOUT

1. How do you read and use the Book of Psalms? In your daily devotions? Worship? Personal study?

2. Read Psalm 13, then explain the transition of emotion as the psalm progresses.

3. Read Psalm 145. How is this psalm specific to David's life and situation and not just a "generic" praise psalm?

4. Choose a psalm that is personal to your own situation.

5: Songs of King David

THE PSALMS ARE CLEARLY CONNECTED WITH DAVID, THE FIRST KING TO UNITE ALL OF Israel into a political and religious community. He is credited with establishing a new capital in Jerusalem and preparing to build a Temple there. The Bible attributes to David an organizational system for temple personnel, including musicians. The Book of Psalms probably has its origins in a collection of hymns assembled or written by David for use in the Temple. An oversimplification, perhaps, but it points us in the correct direction. We have already noted that the Book of Psalms is divided into five books. Book 2 closes with the notation: "this concludes the prayers of David" (72:20). Could this statement designate these first books as prepared for use in the new Temple?

Psalm 2, in a previous form, was likely used as a coronation hymn. Imagine for a minute that the crowned king is David. The remainder of Book 1, with the exception of Psalm 33, all begin "of David." The traditional manner of translating the Psalms into English does not indicate that these words are part of the text—but they are. The words are often taken to mean "by David," but could just as easily mean "to," "for," "collected by," or "in honor of" David. The phrase "of David" connects the poem to the king whose musical inclinations are described elsewhere (see 1 Samuel).

Book 2 begins with a collection of psalms of the "Sons of Korah." These are gatekeepers and choristers for the Temple. Psalm 50 is attributed to Asaph, one of David's chief musicians (1 Chronicles 15:17). Most of the rest of Book 2 is connected to David, through headings containing biographical notations. Psalm 72 is connected to Solomon. Psalms 2–72 may therefore present a collection of hymns connected to David from enthronement to succession!

How do these passages connect to David? Read Psalm 51 without the heading. Nothing in the song allows you to reconstruct the circumstances in the life of David without the reading guide provided. To understand this, compare our own use of hymns. Our song books are compiled of truths drawn from personal experience. These words are then democratized. The specifics of individual situations or circumstances are removed, allowing the thoughts and experiences of one individual to speak to and for the community. Just as we can sing "Amazing Grace" without knowing the story of John Newton, slave trader turned abolitionist, we can sing or pray these psalms in light of our own experiences. At the same time, we are invited to read them through David's life.

Book 3 returns to the musicians Asaph (73–83) and the Sons of Korah (84–85, 87–89). This, and the attribution of Psalm 86 to David, links Book 3 to the "Prayers of David" collection. Book 3 is also linked to Book 4 by the "conversation" which takes place between Psalm 89 and Psalm 90. Psalm 89 laments the collapse of the Davidic kingdom. Psalm 90 answers by proclaiming the kingship of God. The rest of Book 4 celebrates this kingship. Psalms 101 and 103, attributed to David, forge a link to the first three books and allow David to participate in the theological reflections affirming the rule of God over and above and prior to the promise to David. Finally, in Book 5, psalms "of David" appear in critical spots and add to the chorus of praise to God. These and other links help shape the collection, inviting us to join David as we think and rethink the prayers and praises we address to God.

1. Most of the psalms are closely connected with David. Who else contributed to this collection of prayers and songs?

2. Note the superscriptions for many of the psalms that were specifically intended to be sung. Are the titles of the tunes somehow descriptive of the context of the psalm?

3. Review the suggested "book" divisions of Psalms. How do they reflect the progress of David's spiritual journey?

4. Which contemporary song or hymn closely describes your journey of faith?

6: Reflecting the Messiah

THERE ARE STILL MANY THINGS TO LEARN FROM A CLOSE EXAMINATION OF THE PSALMS. Sometimes superscriptions link units together. Small collections often exist within the larger subdivisions. Quotations are made between various units. Particular words or themes are at times grouped together, inviting comparison between individual pieces. And of course, the literary type of each unit allows further analysis. So while we can read the text of a single psalm and think about what it means to us and our lives on its own, we can also ask what it teaches about God. We can learn perspectives for His praise or His rule over events in the lives of others, and we can be encouraged to seek His kingdom in our situations.

The accounts of the gospel writers make it apparent that Jesus knew the Psalms intimately, that they contain words which came readily to His heart and mind, including when He hung on the cross: "And at the ninth hour Jesus cried out in a loud voice . . . 'My God, my God, why have You forsaken Me?'" (Mark 15:33–34). This is a quotation from Psalm 22:1, but other parts of the psalm may have come to His mind. Consider: "In You our fathers put their trust; they trusted You and You delivered them. They cried to You and were saved; in You they trusted and were not disappointed" (Psalm 22:4–5). Or, "He has not despised or disdained the suffering of the afflicted one; He has not hidden His face from him but has listened to his cry for help" (22:24). Or even, "All the ends of the earth will remember and turn to the Lord, and all the families of the nations will bow down before Him, for dominion belongs to the Lord and He rules over the nations" (22:27–28).

One third of the quotations from the Hebrew Bible found in the New Testament writings are taken from the Book of Psalms. In particular, Psalms 2, 22, 69, 110, and 118 were popular texts in early Christian use.

Prior to the composition of New Testament documents, the Psalms were an important source for reflection on Christ's divinity. As Christians read individual psalms, they were able to move from a discussion of the character and purposes of God in times past to a reflection on the nature and activities of God in the person of Jesus. This Christological reading of the Psalms—literally reading a "word about Christ" in the text of the psalms—continues to illumine and inspire.

We can read and reflect upon Jesus' life and teaching in each psalm and apply it to our own situation. In this way, we join in praising and worshipping God for who He is and how He is at work in our world. Far from exhausting our possible approaches to the Psalter, we are only at the beginning as we conclude our study. This collection of words reflecting human experience has been compiled and edited for community use and, by the time of Jesus, had become a means of both speaking with God and hearing His responses. Each subsequent generation discovers the truth that when our own words fail, the Psalms may speak eloquently for us and lead us to the answers we long to receive.

SOMETHING TO THINK ABOUT

1. List some quotations from the Psalms that were spoken by Jesus.

2. In what context or situation did these quotations arise?

3. What references to Christ's divinity and mission are found in the Psalms?

4. What psalm most closely resembles your life to this point?

SIXTEEN

BEATITUDES: LIFE UNDER GOD'S GRACIOUS RULE

BRAMWELL H. TILLSLEY

General Bramwell H. Tillsley (Retd.) was the Army's international leader from 1993 to 1994 and has written extensively for Army periodicals. General Tillsley's cogent biblical teaching continues to be a hallmark of his life and witness.

The Sermon on the Mount is perhaps the best known part of the teaching of Jesus. It is also the least understood and certainly the least obeyed. Here we find Jesus giving instructions to the disciples. Many consider it the "Ordination Address" to the twelve.

1: "His disciples came to Him, and He began to teach them."

THE SERMON ON THE MOUNT IS REALLY A DESCRIPTION OF WHAT Jesus wanted His followers to be and do. Only a belief in the possibility and necessity of a new birth keeps us from reading the sermon with either foolish optimism or hopeless despair. It describes an ideal that can never be reached by human strength alone. Incorporated into the sermon are "The Beatitudes." If you ask the general public to name the ingredients that make for happiness, you will likely hear such things as money, fame, success, or popularity. How different was the response of Jesus. In the Beatitudes (Matthew 5:1–12) the word "blessed" is employed nine times—a translation of *makarios*, referring to the bliss that belongs to the gods. It is thus an experience independent of outward circumstances. It is a joy which has its secret in itself.

J. B. Phillips paraphrased the Beatitudes as the world would render them:

Happy are the pushers, for they get on in the world.

Happy are the hard–boiled; for they never let life hurt them.

Happy are they who complain; for they get their own way in the end.

Happy are the blasé; for they never worry over their sins.

Happy are the slave–drivers; for they get results.

Happy are the knowledgeable men of the world; they know their way around.

Happy are the troublemakers, for they make people take notice of them.

Just a cursory glance at the New Testament indicates that it is a book of joy. The verb *chairein* which means "to rejoice" occurs seventy-two times and the word *chara*, meaning "joy," appears sixty times. In the Beatitudes, "happy" is a poor substitute for "blessed," for the root of happiness is "hap" meaning chance. Happiness is dependent upon the chances and changes of life. It is an experience which life may give and take away. Joy, on the other hand, is found in the Lord. That is why Jesus could say "no man will take away your joy" (John 16:22). This explains the discourse of Jesus in the Upper Room. Though aware of His approaching death, He used the words "joy" and "rejoice" eight times. He was obviously aware of resources about which the world knew nothing.

Of course, we are, to some degree, affected by our environment. At the grave of Lazarus, Jesus wept. He was also deeply moved over the condition of Jerusalem. It is, however, one thing to be moved by events, another to be mastered by them. In our study of the Beatitudes, we will consider a "blessedness" that exists in spite of events around us. This blessedness is completely untouchable and unassailable. In the Greek, there is no verb in the Beatitudes, making them not so much statements as exclamations. They are not promises of future happiness but congratulations on present bliss. In essence they are saying, "O the bliss of being a Christian."

In the Beatitudes we have a description of what human life and human community look like when they come under the gracious rule of God. It has been said that "rejoice" is the standing order of the Christian. We will consider the conditions for experiencing this gift of God—joy!

SOMETHING TO THINK ABOUT

1. Compare the Beatitudes as the world might phrase them with the actual teachings of Jesus in Matthew 5. How would you describe the essential differences between the two?

2. How do the words happiness and joy compare?

3. What does the word "blessed" indicate in the Beatitudes?

4. We sometimes view the Beatitudes as promises contingent upon certain actions, that is, "Blessed are you (if) you do . . .". But viewed as exclamations, they describe the human community under God's rule. Write one exclamation about your life as a personal beatitude.

2: "Blessed are the poor in spirit, for theirs is the kingdom of heaven."

WE MUST NOT INTERPRET THIS BEATITUDE AS MEANING THAT MATERIAL POVERTY IS a good thing. Jesus would never have called "blessed" a state where people live in slums and do not have enough to eat. One aim of the Christian gospel is to remove such poverty.

There are two dimensions to the meaning of poor. The word *penes* means to have nothing left over. Such a person is not rich but neither is he destitute. He has enough for basic needs. *Ptoches*, the word translated as "poor" in the Beatitudes, describes absolute or abject poverty. It describes the person who has nothing at all. Because such a person has no earthly resources whatever, he puts his whole trust in God.

To be "poor in spirit" does not mean to be poor-spirited. It does not describe people with little or no self-esteem. It rather acknowledges our spiritual poverty, indeed our spiritual bankruptcy before God. John Calvin wrote: "He who is reduced to nothing in himself, and thus relies on the mercy of God, is poor in spirit." This proper estimate of ourselves is beautifully expressed in verses by General Albert Orsborn:

> *I have no claim on grace;*
> *I have no right to plead;*
> *I stand before my Maker's face*
> *Condemned in thought and deed.*
>
> *But since there died a Lamb*
> *Who, guiltless my guilt bore,*
> *I lay fast hold on Jesus' name*
> *And sin is mine no more.*
>
> (The Salvation Army *Song Book* #290)

Being poor in spirit means we look to God for everything we need. It sets us free from people and circumstances. This Beatitude could be paraphrased: "Blessed is the man who has realized his own utter helplessness, and who has put his whole trust in God." Jesus said, "Apart from Me you can do nothing" (John 15:5). The Apostle Paul then added, "I can do everything through Him who gives me strength" (Philippians 4:13).

Being poor in spirit is placed first in the Beatitudes because until we are aware of our need, we can never receive what God has for us. We remain in the state of the Church in Laodicea. "You say, 'I am rich; I have acquired wealth and do not need a thing.' But you do not realize that you are wretched, pitiful, poor, blind and naked" (Revelation 3:17). Being poor in spirit means knowing yourself, accepting yourself and being yourself to the glory of God.

"Theirs is the kingdom of heaven" or "yours is the kingdom of God" (Luke 6:20). The kingdom of God is a society upon earth in which God's will is as perfectly done as it is in heaven. Being poor in spirit, we experience something of the bliss of heaven while still here on earth.

Being poor in spirit does not mean to deny or repress your personality. In Romans 12:3 the Apostle Paul wrote: "For by the grace given me I say to every one of you: Do not think of yourself more highly than you ought." But we must also not think of ourselves less highly than we ought. There is a false humility that is as sinful as pride. We need to use our strengths to overcome our weaknesses, and our weaknesses to discover new power. "For when I am weak, then am I strong" (2 Corinthians 12:10).

"Assert yourself" is the world's slogan. "Humble yourself" is the challenge of Jesus. Thus to be poor in spirit means yielding to God and allowing Him to make us all He wants us to be. Remember, God always gives His best to those who leave the choice with Him.

SOMETHING TO THINK ABOUT

1. According to the true meaning of "poor in spirit," is there anyone to whom this beatitude does not apply?

2. Why do you think this beatitude was placed first on the list?

3. Does the beatitude's promise that the Kingdom of God is ours refer to heaven?

4. What strength do you possess? What weakness do you recognize in yourself? How might you use your strength to overcome that weakness and your weakness to discover new powers?

3: "Blessed are those who mourn, for they will be comforted."

IF YOU WANT TO FIND A PERSON'S CHARACTER, FIND OUT WHAT MAKES HIM LAUGH and what makes him weep. The higher you go in life, the more vulnerable you are to sorrow. You can escape sorrow by isolating yourself from other people and from the affairs of life. At the same time you will also be escaping joy.

In this beatitude we have a real paradox, for it speaks of the "joy of sorrow" and the "gladness of grief." The word that is used for mourn, *penthein,* is one of the strongest in the Greek language. It was employed when speaking of mourning for the dead. It spoke of a sorrow that pierces the heart, not just a passing sadness. This beatitude, however, embraces much more than mourning for the dead.

Our Sin and Sins

We need to mourn over what we are as well as what we do. "For I confess my iniquity; I am troubled by my sin" (Psalm 38:18). The way to God is always the way of the broken heart. We must be sure that it is sin and not the consequences over which we mourn. Nothing leads to defeat in the Christian life like a surface dealing with sin.

One of God's saints, David Brainerd, missionary to the Native Americans, wrote in his journal in 1740: "In my morning devotions, my soul was exceedingly melted, and I bitterly mourned over my exceeding sinfulness and vileness." That does not mean we must wallow in self-reproach and condemnation, for there is always the danger of spending too much time looking at ourselves when we should be "looking unto Jesus" (Hebrews 12:2 KJV).

Yes, there is a place for genuine mourning for our sin and sins, but let us also remember that God forgives and forgets. Leslie Weatherhead reminds us that "forgiveness is the most powerful, therapeutic idea in the whole world."

The Sin of the World

We also need to mourn over the sin of the world, as Jeremiah wept over the sins of the people and as Jesus wept over Jerusalem. Dr. Michael Ramsey wrote: "It is doubtful if any of us can do anything at all until our hearts have been very much broken." Perhaps this is why a church leader challenged his denomination with these words: "More than we need anything else today—more than money, better buildings, better choirs, social respectability—we need men and women who will tarry before God for a baptism of love. Then warmed by its fire, and gripped by its passion, they will carry this love to a needy world."

"They will be comforted." The word *parakelein* implies more than sympathy or the drying of tears. It includes comfort and consolation, summoning to one's side as an ally or helper and encouraging or giving strength. "When I called, You answered me; You made me bold and stout-hearted" (Psalm 138:3). The word "comfort" comes from two Latin words (*con fortis*) meaning "with strength." Our God is the God of comfort and the Holy Spirit is referred to as the Comforter. The promise of comfort may not always be available. "Weeping may remain for a night, but rejoicing comes in the morning" (Psalm 30:5).

Dr. Roy Allen's translation of this beatitude is this: "Blessed are they that mourn, for they shall be comforters." Paul wrote of "the God of all comfort, who comforts us in all our troubles, so that we can comfort those in any trouble with the comfort we ourselves have received from God" (2 Corinthians 1:3–4).

SOMETHING TO THINK ABOUT

1. Think of a time when you experienced a deep sorrow. How were you comforted?

2. What does it mean to mourn over sin? When that mourning is genuine, what comfort can be expected?

3. Comfort, according to the Beatitudes, implies more than sympathy. How has God done more than say "I'm sorry," to despairing people?

4. Based on the example in the Beatitudes, what comfort might we offer a sorrowing friend?

TO MODERN EARS, "MEEK" DESCRIBES A WEAK, SPINELESS CREATURE UNABLE TO STAND up for himself or anyone else. This is not the biblical concept of meekness. The noun *prautes* and the adjective *praus* indicate strength or power under control. No one could accuse Moses of being weak or timid. No spineless character could have brought Israel out of Egypt nor have led a band of ex-slaves through their years of wandering. Moses was fiery and passionate, but he is referred to as meek. The meek man may be the strongest in the company, but his meekness resides in the fact that he does not make a show of his strength.

On three separate occasions the word "meek" is directly linked with Jesus (Matthew 11:29; Zechariah 21:5; 2 Corinthians 10:1). We would never describe Jesus as being weak. Think of the occasion when He cleansed the Temple. God's house of prayer and praise had been turned into man's house of purchase and profit. In such a setting, Jesus blazed with indignation.

Aristotle defined a virtue as the mean between two extremes. Meekness is the mean between excessive anger and excessive "angerlessness." We are thus angry at the right time and never angry at the wrong time. "Be ye angry and sin not" (Ephesians 4:26 KJV). Anger is like fire. When under control it is our servant and accomplishes great things, but when out of control it becomes our master and results in destruction. There is a godless anger that destroys and a godly anger that builds. In history, it has always been those with the gift of self-control who have been considered great. "He that rules his spirit is better than he who takes a city" (Proverbs 16:32). Alexander the Great conquered the world at an early age and wept that there were no more worlds to conquer. He conquered the world but could not control himself, for in a drunken rage, he threw a spear and killed his best friend. No man can truly lead others until he has mastered himself.

We must ask the question, "Am I exercising self-control?" It is the spirit in which opposition must be met. "In meekness, instructing those that oppose themselves" (2 Timothy 2:25 KJV). This applies to our relationship with people who disagree with us. We must not try to batter or bludgeon them into thinking as we do. There must be nothing discourteous in our manner. Meekness is not something we can manufacture, for it is part of the "fruit of the Spirit." It must, however, be cultivated by submission to God's mastery.

The meek "will inherit the earth." Its origin, Psalm 37:11, speaks of the conflict between the wicked and the righteous: "A little while and the wicked will be no more . . . but the meek will inherit the land." The meek need not be afraid of anything for God is in control of both them and their circumstances. Since meekness means power under control, when you can control yourself, everything belongs to you. To inherit the earth means to reign as king over yourself and your circumstances through the power of the Holy Spirit.

William Barclay summarized this beatitude as: "O the bliss of the man who has so committed himself to God that he is entirely God-controlled, for such a man will be right with God and with man and will enter that life which God has promised and which God alone can give."

O arm me with the mind,
Meek Lamb, which was in Thee,
And let my earnest zeal be found
With perfect charity!
With calm and tempered zeal,
Let me enforce Thy call,
And vindicate Thy gracious will
Which offers life to all.

(The Salvation Army *Song Book* #568)

SOMETHING TO THINK ABOUT

1. Imagine yourself in control of that part of your character or personality that you find hardest to control. How would such control be expressed in your life?

2. Can you recall other occasions in Jesus' life when He exhibited power under control?

3. Anger is an emotion that often disrupts our lives. Consider a time when your anger flared. What caused this anger? Could it be considered "godly anger"?

5: "Blessed are those who hunger and thirst for righteousness, for they will be filled."

IT TAKES MORE THAN A DICTIONARY TO DEFINE A WORD OF HUMAN EXPERIENCE. For example, pain is quite different to the person who has never had a day's illness than to one who has passed through the furnace of physical agony. So it is with the experience of hunger. When we say we are hungry, we mean it is 1:00 pm and we are accustomed to eating at noon. In this beatitude, however, we are speaking of the spirit of Psalm 42:1—"As the deer pants for streams of water, so my soul pants for You, O God." To be hungry is not enough; we must be starving. When the prodigal son was hungry, he went to feed on the husks, but when he was starving, he went to his father.

The Christian must not simply say, "I am interested in Christ" but rather, "For me to live is Christ" (Philippians 1:21). It is a fact of life that if a person desires something sufficiently, he will likely receive it. The greatest barrier to obtaining fullness of life is not wanting it badly enough, or what Robert Louis Stevenson called "the malady of not wanting."

The presence of hunger and thirst in life is a healthy thing. To begin with, hunger and thirst are evidences of life. Dead people have no appetites. It is tragic, however, when people hunger and thirst for wrong things. "And God gave them their request; but sent leanness into their soul" (Psalm 106:15 KJV). Jesus tells us to hunger and thirst after righteousness.

220

There is no greater evidence of progress in spiritual life than a hearty appetite for righteousness. Righteousness speaks of a right relationship with God and man. Blessed is the man whose most passionate desire is to love God and to love men as he ought. Food and water are necessities, not luxuries. Righteousness, too, is not a luxury but a necessity. Doctors tell us we are what we eat. This is true not only of the body but also of the soul. Jesus is the bread and the water of life (John 4:13-14, 6:35). Thus, the source of righteousness is God—"All my springs are in Thee" (Psalm 87:7).

Already in the Virgin Mary's song, the *Magnificat,* the spiritually poor and spiritually hungry have been associated, and both have been declared blessed. "He has filled the hungry with good things but has sent the rich away empty" (Luke 1:53). For those who truly hunger, the promise is that they will be filled or satisfied. This is illustrated in the story of the woman at the well (John 4). Looking at the well of natural water Jesus said, "Everyone who drinks this water will be thirsty again" (4:13). He then added, "But whoever drinks the water I give him will never thirst" (14). This represents a spiritual paradox, for there is a sense in which we continue to be hungry and thirsty. In one case the source is external, while in the other it is internal. We do not need to get more and more of God but rather allow Him to have more and more of us.

It is not in the multiplying of activities but in the simplifying of life that we experience the deepest satisfaction in Christ. This does not mean we do less, but rather what we do is centered in Christ. In the context of externals (food, drink, clothing) Jesus said: "But seek first His kingdom and His righteousness, and all these things will be given to you as well" (Matthew 6:33). William Barclay paraphrased this beatitude in these words: "O the bliss of the man who longs for total righteousness as a starving man longs for food, and a man perishing of thirst longs for water, for that man will be truly satisfied." How encouraging that the one who achieves this goodness is not necessarily the one who is blessed but the one who longs for it with his whole heart!

SOMETHING TO THINK ABOUT

1. How do you know when you are hungry for God? Is it always clear and recognizable?

2. Does hunger for God increase as you walk with Him?

3. What practical steps can we take to increase our appetite for spiritual things?

4. Mary's song in Luke 1 indicates that it is better to be hungry (poor in spirit) than to be rich. Why do you think this is so?

6: "Blessed are the merciful, for they will be shown mercy."

IN THIS BEATITUDE WE COME TO THE VERY HEART OF THE GOSPEL. *CHESDH* IS TRANSlated as "mercy" ninety-six times in the Authorized Version. It means to get right inside the other person's skin until we see things with their eyes, think things with their mind, feel things with their feelings. This requires a deliberate effort of the mind and will. It is to deliberately identify with the other person.

The Roman world did not admire mercy. The philosophers called it "a disease of the soul." Our world is not too far removed from this spirit. In many instances, people are still treated like things. Power is the supreme deity. Success is the most important thing in life. Mercy on the other hand is literally going through what the other person is going through. It is quite possible, however, to profess and even feel a large love for mankind in general while at the same time to find the claims of an individual nothing more than a nuisance.

In his book *Life Together,* Dietrich Bonhoeffer writes:

> We must allow ourselves to be interrupted by God. God will be constantly crossing our paths and cancelling our plans by sending us people with claims and petitions. We may pass them by, preoccupied with our more important tasks. It is a strange fact that Christians frequently consider their work so important that they will allow nothing to disturb them. They do not want a life that is crossed and balked. But it is part of the discipline of humility that we must not spare our hand where it can perform a service and that we do not assume that our schedule is our own to manage, but allow it to be arranged by God.

Mercy is linked with forgiveness. The New Testament is insistent that to be forgiven we must be forgiving. After speaking about mercy in His Sermon on the Mount, Jesus says: "For if you forgive men their sins, your Father will forgive you your sins" (Matthew 6:14–15). We need to keep this in mind when we pray, "Forgive us our debts as we forgive our debtors" (12).

"Blessed are the merciful, for they will be shown mercy." This does not mean that you earn mercy because you extend mercy. The beatitude is simply saying that when you experience and share mercy, then your heart is in such a condition that you receive more mercy to share with others. "Give and it will be given to you" (Luke 6:38). The person who refuses to forgive his brother destroys the very bridge over which he himself must walk. The most miserable prison in the world is the prison we make for ourselves when we refuse to show mercy.

It is an awesome thought that when I show mercy I am practicing an attribute of God. The narrative of the woman taken in adultery (John 8) indicates various ways we can respond to sin and hurt. The way of *man* is to find and expose the sinner, using the sinner to accomplish your own selfish purposes. The way of the *law* is that such a person should be stoned (John 8:5). But the law can never cleanse, it can only condemn. The way of the *Master* says, "Neither do I condemn you, go and leave your life of sin" (11).

Jesus did not deny the fact of sin, but in Him mercy and truth came together and the outcome was forgiveness. God in His grace gives me what I do not deserve and in His mercy does not give me what I deserve. It is mercy that pities and grace that pardons.

Depth of mercy! Can there be
Mercy still reserved for me?
God is love, I know, I feel
Jesus lives and loves me still.

(The Salvation Army *Song Book* #286)

SOMETHING TO THINK ABOUT

1. Mark Twain once said, "I love mankind; it's people I can't stand." How do you think this concept is shown in some churches and in some people today?

2. Being merciful sometimes means that our schedule is interrupted. In a task–oriented society, individual needs are often ignored for reasons of busyness. Recall examples of interruptions in Jesus' life. How did He handle them?

3. Consider three ways to respond to sin and hurt in John 8. What was the way of Jesus?

4. We often want justice for others and mercy for ourselves. When were you last in the position of needing mercy? How did you feel?

7: "Blessed are the pure in heart, for they will see God."

THE WORD *KATHAROS* OR "PURE" IS USED IN CLASSICAL GREEK TO DESCRIBE PURITY in the physical sense. For example, it describes clothes that are clean or animals without blemish. It would be employed when speaking of metal that has no impurity or alloy. In the Old Testament it appears 150 times to describe ceremonial purity. For Jesus, however, purity was an inner experience, an attitude of the soul which indicated moral purity. In this beatitude, "pure" means clean or unmixed.

Our English word "cathartic" comes from *katharos*. A cathartic is an agent used by a doctor for the cleansing of the physical system. A psychiatrist uses catharsis to cleanse on the emotional level. There is also a spiritual catharsis for the cleansing of the inner man. God "purified their hearts by faith" (Acts 15:9).

What do we understand by the "heart?" The Bible sometimes employs "heart" to indicate emotions. "Let not your heart be troubled" (John 14:1 KJV). On other occasions, the Bible uses heart to indicate the intellect. "Why reason ye these things in your hearts?" (Mark 2:8 KJV). Sometimes heart refers to the will. "But Daniel purposed in his heart that he would not defile himself" (Daniel 1:8 KJV). Putting it all together, the heart means the master control area of life. "Keep thy heart with all diligence; for out of it are the issues of life" (Proverbs 4:23 KJV). The ungenerate heart is the source of all our problems. "The heart is deceitful above all things and desperately wicked; who can know it?" (Jeremiah 17:9 KJV). We can thus understand why Jesus said, "blessed are the pure in heart." What then did He mean by "they will see God?"

It is a fact of life that what we see depends not only on what is in front of our eyes but also what is within our minds and hearts. To "see God" is the highest blessing possible to man. In Isaiah's vision, seeing God was a condition to serving God (Isaiah 6:1). There is of course a sense in which God cannot be seen. "No man has ever seen God" (John 1:18). On the other hand, Jesus also said, "anyone who has seen Me has seen the Father" (John 14:9).

The Christian looks forward to seeing Jesus when He comes again. "We know that when He appears, we shall be like Him, for we shall see Him as He is" (l John 3:2). But there is a sense in which we can see Him in the here and now. The condition of course is that we have a pure and clean heart. As we have seen, this means unmixed or unalloyed. The truth is, seldom do we do even our finest deeds from absolutely unmixed motives. We thus cry out with the Psalmist, "Create in me a pure heart, O God" (Psalm 51:10). This cleansing is an ongoing process. "If we walk in the light as He Himself is in the light . . . we are being cleansed from every sin by the blood of Jesus His Son" (1 John 1:7 NEB). "Who may ascend the hill of the Lord? Who may stand in His holy place? He who has clean hands and a pure heart" (Psalm 24:3–4).

The experience of seeing God through the eyes of the heart is not simply a momentary experience but one that is constant and growing (2 Corinthians 3:18). Physically our eyes tend to deteriorate, but spiritually our eyes ought to become keener and our vision brighter. The pure in heart have nothing to hide; nothing to defend; nothing to explain—their eyes are unveiled. When you see God, you begin to see what God sees. You not only see yourself in a new light but you also see others in a new light. The beginning of the fulfillment of this promise commences in the here and now but the completing of it will take all eternity.

> *Blest are the pure in heart*
> *For they shall see their God;*
> *The secret of the Lord is theirs,*
> *Their soul is Christ's abode.*
>
> (The Salvation Army *Song Book* #411)

SOMETHING TO THINK ABOUT

1. What is meant by "the heart" in this and other Scriptures?

2. If the heart of man is desperately wicked, and only the pure in heart will see God, what hope is there for us?

3. When He appears "we shall see Him as He is," we read in 1 John 3:2. Is there a sense in which we can see Him now? How is this experienced?

4. "Seeing God through the eyes of the heart is not simply a momentary experience but one that is constant and growing." What do you see of God now that you didn't see five years ago, or ever yesterday?

8: "Blessed are the peacemakers, for they will be called the sons of God."

THE BIBLE IS A BOOK ABOUT PEACE. IT HOLDS NEARLY FOUR HUNDRED REFERENCES to peace—peace of God; peace with God; peace among men both on national and individual levels. There is hardly an experience more sought after than peace. Peace is employed eighty-eight times in the New Testament and is found in every book. Paul begins each of his letters with a prayer that grace and peace may be upon the people to whom he writes. Peace in the Bible is more than the absence of war. It is a positive experience and signifies the presence of all that is good and wonderful. The word "shalom" contains in it the desire for all the goodness that God can give—a total well-being of body, mind and spirit. It is much more than "may you have no battles." Peace is a creative force and a peacemaker is a person who releases this creative force to change his world.

The source of peace is God. Six times in the New Testament, God the Father is referred to as the "God of peace" (Romans 15:33). Jesus is revealed as God's peacemaker. "He is our peace" (Ephesians 2:14). John 14:27 has been called the last will and testament of Jesus. "Peace I leave with you, My peace I give you." The Holy Spirit is the spirit of peace. "The fruit of the spirit is peace" (Galatians 5:22). Yes, the source of peace is God.

The enemy of peace is sin. People are at war with each other because they are at war with themselves. They are at war with themselves because they are at war with God. According to James 4, the enemies of God are the world (4:4), the flesh (1) and the devil (7). This explains why "blessed are the pure in heart" precedes "blessed are the peacemakers."

This peace thus involves a man's relationship to himself. Robert Burns wrote: "My life reminded me of a ruined temple; what strength, what proportion in some parts; what unsightly gaps, what ruin in others." It also involves man's relationship to his fellow man. We begin by making peace with our brother (Matthew 5:21-26) and then extend it to our enemies (38-48). A false peace is more dangerous than open war because it gives the impression that the problems have been resolved when they have only been covered over. The quieting of the surface when the depths are still stormy is no lasting solution. "Peace, peace when there is no peace" (Jeremiah 6:14).

The minister of peace is the Christian. In the beatitudes, the people who are blessed are not the peace lovers but the peacemakers. You can, for example, know something is wrong but, in order to enjoy a shallow peace, do nothing about it. Thus you may be a peaceable man without being a peacemaker. The peace of this beatitude does not come from evading issues but by facing them. Dietrich Bonhoeffer spoke of "cheap grace," but there is also cheap peace. Perhaps this is why Jesus said: "Do not suppose that I have come to bring peace to the earth. I did not come to bring peace, but a sword" (Matthew 10:34). Jesus knew His very presence would divide people.

The blessing of peace is godliness. "They will be called the sons of God." God is the author or establisher of right relationships. When we become involved in this, we take on something of the nature of God. What a potential for good we then possess. A Chinese proverb reads: "When there is righteousness in the heart, there will be beauty in the character. If there is beauty in the character, there will be harmony in the home. If there is harmony in the home, there will be order in the nation. If there is order in the nation, there will be peace in the world."

Peace in our time, O Lord,
To all the people—peace!
Peace surely based upon Thy will
And built in righteousness.

(The Salvation Army *Song Book* #827)

SOMETHING TO THINK ABOUT

1. Peace in the Bible is more than the absence of war. It signifies a total well being of body, mind, and spirit. Why do we see so little evidence of peace in our world?

2. "Blessed are the pure in heart" proceeds "blessed are the peacemakers" in the Beatitudes. Why do you think this order was chosen?

3. Sometimes we suppress conflict so as not to ruffle feathers. Can such action be dangerous to real peace?

9: "Blessed are those who are persecuted because of righteousness, for theirs is the kingdom of heaven."

THE NEW TESTAMENT SPEAKS OF THE INEVITABILITY OF PERSECUTION. "EVERYONE who wants to live a godly life in Christ Jesus will be persecuted" (2 Timothy 3:12). One of Jesus' attributes was His absolute honesty. He made it clear that He had not come to make life easy but to make men great. The English words "witness" and "martyr" derive from the same word *martus*. In the early church, to be a witness often meant to be a martyr.

In this beatitude, the blessedness is for those who are persecuted for righteousness' sake. We must thus distinguish between persecution and punishment. We are punished by good men for doing evil. We are persecuted by bad men for doing good. "If you are insulted because of the name of Christ, you are blessed, for the Spirit of glory and of God rests on you" (1 Peter 4:14).

True persecution for righteousness' sake is the result of the believer daring to live in the spirit of the Beatitudes when the world's attitude is in opposition, walking in one direction while the world walks in the other. It is impossible not to collide. Jesus said, "If they persecuted Me, they will persecute you also" (John 15:20). If the Christians had isolated themselves or withdrawn from life, there may have been dislike but not persecution. But Paul does not write to the saints in the desert or in the monastery, but to those in Rome, Philippi, and Ephesus. The Christian ethic became a condemnation of the life of the pagan, for the Christian presence was a constant reminder of what life ought to be.

Without the grace of God, we would simply react, resent, and retaliate when persecution comes. But Christians are challenged to respond rather that react to persecution. We are to "rejoice and be glad" (Matthew 5:12). John Stott has written: "We are not to retaliate like an unbeliever, nor sulk like a child, nor lick our wounds in self-pity, nor grin and bear it like a stoic. We are to rejoice, for our reward is great in heaven." If we are persecuted, we belong to a noble succession. Through persecution, we identify with the prophets "in the same way they persecuted the prophets who were before you" (Matthew 5:12). Keep in mind, a man's company is a great revealer of his character. "On their release, Peter and John went back to their own people" (Acts 4:23).

There are three levels at which we can respond to people: *demonically*—Satan returns evil for good; *humanly*—man returns good for good; and *divinely*—God returns good for evil.

Why does Jesus exhort us to "rejoice and be glad"? First of all, persecution is a compliment. No one persecutes a person who is ineffective. George Bernard Shaw said the finest compliment the world can pay an author is to burn his books. Persecution also presents us with an opportunity to demonstrate loyalty. It enables us to walk the way of saints, prophets, and martyrs. It allows us to share the fellowship of Christ's suffering (Philippians 3:10).

In addition to a present reward, we are promised a reward in heaven. Paul wrote, "If we suffer, we shall also reign with Him" (2 Timothy 2:12 KJV). Moses chose "to be mistreated along with the people of God rather than enjoy the pleasures of sin for a short time. He regarded disgrace for the sake of Christ of greater value than the treasures of Egypt, because he was looking ahead to his reward" (Hebrews 11:25,26). Through the New Testament runs the conviction that to accept and endure persecution places man in a special relationship to Jesus Christ. And He still needs witnesses—not so much those who will die for Him, but those who will live for Him.

SOMETHING TO THINK ABOUT

1. We all love to read the promises of God, but we often are surprised by persecution, even though Jesus promised that we would be persecuted in this world. Why should we expect persecution?

2. Discuss the difference between persecution and punishment.

3. How did you respond the last time you were mistreated for doing something right? Were you able to rejoice?

4. Why should we rejoice in persecution?

SEVENTEEN

THE UPPER ROOM

DAVID LAEGER

Major David Laeger often contributes to Salvation Army publications. His online study, "The Church Beautiful," appeared on the Internet in 2003 (available as a compact disk from National Publications).

Judaism is a religious masterpiece whose colors are most vivid when blended in the person and work of Jesus Christ. Especially in Him every annual symbol finds its divinely intended fruition, particularly as He merges all history together in His days of passion. We shall see Him in His final converse and movements in the flickering shadows of the Upper Room at Jerusalem.

1: Holy Days at Jerusalem

ACCORDING TO ONE RABBINIC TRADITION, THE NAME "JERUSALEM" is derived from two words: *Shalem*, named by Shem, a son of Noah who settled there; and *Yireh*, the name given to the same place by Abraham after an angel intervened in the sacrifice of Isaac. Together the words *Yireh* (provision) and *Shalem* (peace) form *Yirehshalem*—the provision of peace. However the name originated, it became and remains God's favored city.

The prophet Zechariah warned, "He who touches you—Jerusalem—touches the apple of His eye" (2:8 NKJV). The Spanish translate that phrase, *la nina de Su ojo*, as "the little girl of His eye." Like a father's little girl, so Jerusalem affects the focus of Jehovah's vision.

Alfred Edersheim, in *The Temple: Its Ministry and Service*, wrote, "The world is like unto an eye. The ocean surrounding the world is the white of the eye; its [iris] is the world itself; the pupil is Jerusalem; but the image within the eye is the sanctuary." It is to the sanctuary that ancient Jews were drawn at least three times yearly to appear before the Lord whose abode was within its innermost room. In rich and beautiful fashion they celebrated their holy feasts, recalling in each the grand foundations of their faith. An overview of Israel's festival calendar is given in Leviticus, chapter 23. Though filled with joyous fellowship, each event had its very serious moments. Without fail came those sacrificial solemnities, in which prescribed animals vicariously suffered death for national and personal sins.

Details of each observance, each pilgrimage to the holy city, have changed in form over the centuries, but the basic purposes are still intact among the Jews. According to Leviticus, those holy convocations follow a prescribed pattern.

Pesach is first, reflecting on Israel's Egyptian exodus in which the death-angel passed by the homes where the blood of lambs was seen upon the doorways. Homes without evidence of such blood suffered the loss of firstborn sons. In that night of anxiety and anguish, Israel *en masse* had "exodused" the land of her slavery. It was an event for perpetual remembrance before the Lord.

Shavuot follows fifty days later as the next major holy day. After redemption from bondage, the nation of Israel moved toward Mt. Sinai. In that encampment they received divinely mandated law and order. Etched in stone, the Decalogue pronounced those fundamental oracles from which were formulated all other legal and moral facets for Israel—and all reasonable relationship for the rest of mankind.

The third pilgrimage to Jerusalem involves "high holy days" or "Days of Awe." The seventh of the Hebrew lunar months begins with *Rosh Hashanah,* the Jewish New Year's Day. The day of all days, *Yom Kippur,* follows ten days later. Even in Jesus' time, this day of atoning required an elaborate pattern of service and sacrifice, an outline of which is given in Leviticus 16. Five days later occurs *Sukkot,* a seven-to-eight-day festivity that fixes visual attention upon "booths" as memorials to the temporary brush arbors constructed for shelters shortly after the exodus.

These are but a basic sketch of the Jewish religious emphases.

SOMETHING TO THINK ABOUT

1. Why was "sanctuary" such a special place to the Jews? Is there a place like that today?

2. What is the purpose of keeping the religious festivals, rites, and holy days with such scrupulous precision and slavish obedience?

3. What is unique about the "high, holy days"? Explain the deeper, spiritual meaning to their observance.

4. How do the holy days and special observances point the way to Jesus Christ, "the Lamb of God that takes away the sin of the world"?

2: Christ's Humiliation

THE NIGHT BEFORE JESUS' CRUCIFIXION, HE ILLUMINATED IN SOME MEASURE THE spiritual significance of every major Hebrew festival. First, consider the setting on that night of nights—the fragrance of roasted lamb, spices, herbs, and wine filled the air; the apostles sat in typical fashion around the Passover meal; their Host sat second from the end of the right arm (as you face the group) of a trilateral formation; the ceremony began just after 6 p.m., the hour which signaled the beginning of a new day.

As Jesus initiated this last meal, high holy days were skillfully incorporated into His every word and move. While in the presence of that select few, He portrayed the drama of His whole life. The disciples were given a depth of revelation previously unknown to them. He prefaced His teaching that night with an act of humility. Washing their feet then led to the question, "Do you know what I have done to you?" That query is the focus of our series.

Let us see Him there, in the ceremony which preceded the question. He sat as the host of the feast. He was its ruler, ordainer of its communion, Lord of its celebration, blesser of its food and expounder of every morsel and drink. But once seated in authority, He stood up before them and with stately dignity removed His robe. Laying it aside, He followed in gracious manner by stepping into the role of servant. Their sovereign became their slave. In that movement alone Jesus demonstrated what has been called His "humiliation." It was an act already played out in His incarnation.

Consider the Scriptures (Philippians 2:5–11):

"Being in the form of God"—eternally and essentially having rights and powers belonging to the Creator, Preserver, and Governor of the universe (He is the host of His handiwork);

"He humbled Himself"—laid aside His celestially recognized glory, the outward cloak of His majesty (He is the servant to His creation);

"He took upon Himself the form of a slave"—stepped down into our human dilemma (He is the fully involved Mediator–Savior for those who will be redeemed);

"He humbled Himself . . . to death, even the death of the cross"—submitted Himself to which He could reach into the depth of our sinfulness (He washed us in the elements of His own life);

"God highly exalted Him"—raised Him through resurrection and ascension into heaven (He again took His place of authority).

Those words epitomize a number of other passages which also describe Jesus' condescension and exaltation, as in John 1:1–4, 1 Timothy 3:16, and Hebrews 1:1–3.

Such living portrayal must have gripped the disciples with profound awe. Their Lord washed their feet—not only a servile duty, but a move involving unspeakable distance and indignity. One by one they were washed by God! Each realized, however so uncomfortably, the cleansing touch of their Messiah. He was more than they expected. He always is!

Finishing His work, He laid aside the towel, put on His robe and sat down again in His rightful place. Thus He had given them a finite glimpse of His infinite act. May we kneel in admiration of Him there, not merely students of His story, but participants in His humiliation.

Something to Think About

1. Why did Jesus ask, "Do you know what I have done to you?" when He washed the feet of His disciples at the beginning of the Passover meal? What had He done to them? What had He done *for* them?

2. What was Christ's rightful place? Where had he placed Himself? Why?

3. Jesus humbled Himself to wash the disciples' feet. How can we humble ourselves to be His servants, as well?

3: Christ's High Priesthood

THE IDEA OF PRIESTHOOD RESIDES WITHIN EVERY CULTURE. THE WHOLE WORLD CALLS for an intermediary presence who would stand on its behalf before a higher power. Even humanism, with its egocentrism, relies upon some luminary, visible or invisible, to connect with a higher sense of being. Religious drive is universally inborn and is an evidence for the commonality of human origin and need. Deep within us abides a need for a mediator, one who will heal whatever is wrong or lacking inwardly.

We find that position filled effectually and unequaled by Jesus Christ. "For there is one God and one Mediator between God and men, the Man Christ Jesus" (1 Timothy 2:5 NKJV). In Him the preeminence of God and the poverty of humanity come together. As God and Man, He is a full participant in the total character and realm of each, sin being the only exception. His mediatorial position was especially portrayed within the rich formalities of the last supper. There He gave preview to His ultimate mission through the same act by which He dramatized His humiliation.

Let us look again at the act of foot washing, this time from a slightly different perspective. Such a bathing belonged first to priesthood. Even the Passover meal brought the priestly setting into

231

every Jewish home. It was an appropriate place for one like Jesus to stand before His guests as the High Priest of His people.

One of the annual religious feasts which Jesus drew into His salvation work was that of the Day of Atonement. On that day, the high priest of Israel laid aside his splendid robes and dressed in plain clothes similar to a common priest. Following an ancient pattern, he walked reverently into the house of God. Passing through the large first room, the priest carried embers into a darker, smaller room called the Oracle. There the embers created a vapor from incense, so that his eyes would not see the presence of God. Twice more the priest was to enter, carrying with him prescribed blood. Dipping his fingers into the blood, he sprinkled it upon the place where once God Himself had dwelt. This annual act symbolically covered the nation's sins. When the high priest finished his task, he laid aside his now bloody, sweaty garments and attired himself again in the magnificent robes of his office.

Other parts of the ritual serve to elaborate more upon the powerful truths portrayed there, but the fundamentals of that scene are sufficient for our purpose: to show what Jesus really did in His seemingly simple act of servanthood. In the Upper Room, our High Priest, Jesus, displayed what would in a matter of hours be hidden from human view.

Crucified, Jesus entered into holy work, alone. Darkness, like clouds of incense, veiled those intense moments. With His own blood, Jesus drew into Himself the height of heaven and the horrors of the human heart. Laying aside His majesty, Jesus clothed Himself in our vulgarity and covered with mercy the full range of our sins. When He rose from the tomb, He laid aside the dyed cloth of sufferings and stood again in the glorious power of His rightful position. Yes, we have indeed found in Him the only Mediator between God and men. Such a merciful act becomes intimately personal to every believing soul.

SOMETHING TO THINK ABOUT

1. Why do we feel the need to trust an intermediary to make a connection between God and man? Why can't we do this for ourselves?

2. How is Jesus our perfect High Priest?

3. Why is His sacrifice, and His alone, sufficient to cover sin and restore us to a relationship with God?

4: Christ's Holiness

BASIN IN HAND, THE LORD JESUS PERSONALIZED MINISTRY TO EACH OF HIS APOSTLES at the Passover table. As they reclined according to custom, it was possible for Him to wash their feet, an act that occurred during the meal, not at its ending. John's Gospel shows continual eating before and after Jesus' portrayal of servanthood. However, there must have been an awkward pause as their Host bent down before each one with His ministry of water.

We have supposed that Jesus, by that object lesson that night, taught His "humiliation" illustrating His condescension from heaven to earth as Redeemer for our sins. But that act reveals a priestly transparency, showing His mission as the eternal High Priest. While remaining within the parameters of the foot washing, we focus on the subjects of His attention.

A similar ceremony appeared in the Torah, specifically in Exodus 30:17–21, one thousand four hundred years before Christ's incarnation. Moses gave instruction to Israelite priests about the continual need for cleanliness. A great basin of water stood between the altar of sacrifice and the house of God. Before entering the holy house, a priest was to stop at the basin to wash his hands and feet; he had to be clean for worship. Before approaching the altar, he was to again stop at the basin to bathe his hands and feet; he had to be clean to help sinners with their salvation.

The Greek word for basin, *loutron,* is used only twice in the New Testament, and concerns the spiritual work of God in a believer's life. Paul wrote that we are saved through the "washing [basin] of regeneration" (Titus 3:5). Our initial salvation is like a washing administered to potential priests. Paul also wrote that Jesus Christ loved the church, giving His life for her. In His life–giving flow, He not only saves her but makes her holy. We find Him in person–to–person ministry, as if He were kneeling before His guests at Passover meal to ensure our continued cleansing.

In Ephesians 5:25–26, the literal translation should be that Jesus "sanctifies, cleansing by the washing [basin] of the water of the word." The last phrase qualifies the verb "sanctify." Sanctification includes the idea of deep heart purifying. Jesus calls for His church to be without spiritual and moral defilement or deformity (Ephesians 5:17). We are to be wholly holy (1 Thessalonians 5:23) in worship and in witness. Here is where the holiness of Jesus becomes the goal of the first disciples. Jesus demonstrated to His new order of priests His power to make them holy. That is still His work. He is our sanctifier, and we meet Him best in this blessing through reading and listening to the Word of God.

Every gathering of believers should have its spiritual bath. Every message from God should become the hands of Jesus resulting in purification from our walk and work in a dirty world. Every moment of devotion, through sincere reflection upon Christ's words, is a moment of refreshment and renewal, as the Spirit of Christ speaks His love–washing to the soul.

Our Lord condescended to save us from past sins, but toward those who receive Him as Savior now He administers more particularly His sacred washing. When the age has finished, the Church will take its rightful place in His glorious exaltation. And so shall we ever be with the Lord, as a kingdom of priests (1 Peter 2:5,9; Revelation 1:6).

SOMETHING TO THINK ABOUT

1. What does it mean to be holy? Why is washing essential?

2. Did Jesus die on the cross just to take away our sin and give us eternal life, or was there a higher plan for us? A higher goal? A higher relationship?

3. How does Christ need to keep washing us, as we become the people of God?

5: Christ and the Holy Spirit

HEAVENLY PLACES FOR SAINTS ARE SOMETIMES DESCRIBED AS "ROOMS" IN THE FATHER'S House. That designation would easily convey to Jesus' disciples the marvelous structure of the Jewish Temple. When the Bible refers to this Temple it uses two terms: Holy House (*naos*) and the entire complex of courts and colonnades (*hieron*). Jesus never entered the *naos* but did teach in the *hieron* (Hebrews 7:14).

We may remember that at the beginning (and ending) of His ministry, Jesus was angry with misuse of His "Father's house" (John 2:13–22). In the same context He stated, "'Destroy this temple (*naos*), and in three days I will raise it up.' . . . But He was speaking of the temple of His body" (NKJV). His words did not speak of self-destruction. He did not say that He would destroy it. He was predicting the manner of His death.

Though Jesus was offended by defilement of the earthly temple, His action was in reference to His own body. He Himself is the living Temple, about which the material temple existed only to teach. Jesus is the spiritual house of the Father. Often He said, "the Father is in Me" (John 14:10,11; 16:32; 17:11, 21–23), demonstrating the Father's indwelling through His words and works. At least twice He gave an exhibition of "glory" (John 2:11; Matthew 17:1,2).

Such visible glory evoked memories of ancient evidences in which God was with His people. The Jews called that glory "the Shekinah," the brilliant presence of God's Spirit shining from Moses' tabernacle (Exodus 40:35) and Solomon's temple (1 Kings 8:10,11). Now we see that power displayed in the person of God incarnate.

In the Upper Room, one of Jesus' disciples asked, "Lord, show us the Father, and it is sufficient for us." Philip wanted a glorious divine exhibition (*deiknumi*). Within moments Jesus' discourse revealed what His disciples should expect henceforth regarding God's holy glory. They would receive something better than sight could appreciate—they would personally know an inward glory. Therefore He said that He would "manifest" (*emphainizo*) Himself as an inward effulgence of holy presence.

Paul also spoke of believers in temple terms: "Or do you not know that your body is the temple of the Holy Spirit who is in you?" (1 Corinthians 6:19; 1 Corinthians 3:16; 2 Corinthians 3:18, 4:6 and Ephesians 2:19–22). This inward expression of God, as we now know, is from the Holy Spirit. Jesus promised that when He would ascend after His passion, He and the Father would send the Holy Spirit to be in us (John 14:15–17). Such an indwelling is a beautiful and wonderful assurance of God's complete residence in every believer. "We will come to Him and make our home with Him" (John 14:23 NKJV).

Yet, there remains a glory unspeakable for God's people, and for that our Lord has returned to heaven for preparations. What and how we shall be then has not been fully revealed to us (1 John 3:2,3). We only know that Jesus assumes for us the position of Temple architect. And similar to that ancient temple, housing priests in chambers around it, we shall each have our "room."

Be not troubled or afraid. Seeing we have such a glory in earthly bodies now, think of that which shall excel in eternity's greater glory.

SOMETHING TO THINK ABOUT

1. Jesus said He would destroy the temple and rebuild it. What was He really speaking of?

2. Why was the Temple in Jerusalem treated with such veneration and respect? Why was Jesus so angry that it was treated as a place of commerce and corruption?

3. Why has He chosen to come and reside in a new temple—in the heart and life of the believer?

4. Heaven is said to have many rooms or mansions. If they are to be built from heavenly supplies based on righteousness and holiness, what will your "mansion" look like?

EIGHTEEN

WHAT GOD IS LOOKING FOR

PHILIP D. NEEDHAM

Commissioner Philip D. Needham currently serves as the Army's Southern territorial commander. He often contributes to *The War Cry* and is the author of several books including *He Who Laughed First,* published in conjunction with Crest Books by Beacon Hill Press of Kansas City, Missouri.

What is God looking for in us? He's looking for the invitation to enter our lives. He looks, and in some He sees a readiness, a silent cry for wholeness—and He accepts the invitation. Jesus, His incarnate Son, could see that in the face, the cry, the touch of those who were on the brink of a divine experience. We stand in a crowd while Jesus passes by. We know that if He takes notice of us, our lives will be forever changed.

1: Outcasts and Sinners

JESUS RUBBED SHOULDERS WITH THOUSANDS, BUT I AM INTRIGUED by those He singled out. Why them and not others? Were they the ones who caught His fancy? Was the encounter a matter of chance? Was there a selection process? I think not. God doesn't become interested in us because we catch His fancy. Nor does He stumble upon us by chance. He doesn't come to us now that way, and He didn't come to us that way when He came in the flesh of the man Jesus.

Why would He single a person out? There are many reasons, but they have one common thread: there is something important God is looking for. Consider Zacchaeus (Luke 19:1–10). He had what God was looking for. God is looking for outcasts and sinners.

I am convinced that when Jesus saw the little man perched in the tree, He knew He was looking at an outcast. Jesus knew what being an outcast was like. His was the birth of an outcast, the wandering lifestyle of an outcast. When He saw Zacchaeus, He saw more than a man short of stature and long on wealth. He saw an outcast.

Most outcasts are poor, but there are outcasts at every level. Zacchaeus had worked his way up to the position of chief tax collector and amassed a small fortune in the process. Jericho was taxed by Rome, and tax collectors were locals who collaborated with Rome. Zacchaeus, a Jew by birth, was looked upon by his countrymen as a religious outcast, disowned by the chosen people of God. Jericho was crawling with priests of all kinds; Jesus chose a religious outcast as His host.

Jesus has an affinity for outcasts. He numbered Himself among them. He died in their company so anyone could claim Him as their own. If you feel like an outcast, He is your friend. If you feel like a sinner, He is your friend. But He can help you only if you want to change.

Zacchaeus no longer wanted to pretend he was something else. He was a sinner tired of sinning and eager for righteousness. Surrounded by the wealth of Jericho, this man of prosperity knew only the city of desolation within his own soul. He was a pauper of the spirit and he knew it. That's the kind of sinner God likes to single out. Jesus said to Zacchaeus: "I'm glad you know you're lost, . . . for the Son of Man came to seek and to save what was lost" (Luke 19:9–10 NRSV).

The key word of Jesus' understanding of His own mission is found in that word "lost." It encourages us to face up to reality and cry out, "I'm lost, until He seeks and finds me." That is exactly what Jesus came to do. Jesus had many things on His mind. He was nearing Jerusalem. His earthly journey was approaching its end. Events would soon challenge every ounce of His integrity and courage. He needed to be spiritually and emotionally prepared. But He stopped for Zacchaeus. He always has time for sinners.

If your life is impoverished by sin, and you know it, the One who came to save the lost has time for you. Today He passes by again, and "If you confess your sin, He is faithful and just to forgive you your sin and to cleanse you from all unrighteousness" (1 John 1:9).

Something to Think About

1. Why did Jesus choose to relate to those people whom society viewed as outcasts and sinners?

2 Why did Jesus, when speaking to huge crowds, always single out individuals for special attention and consideration?

3. How was Zacchaeus "lost"? How about you? Ever feel lost, outcast, alone?

2: Hungry People

HOW MUCH DID ZACCHAEUS ALREADY KNOW ABOUT JESUS? WHAT CONCLUSIONS had he reached about this center of a messianic storm? We're not sure. What we do know is that Zacchaeus hungered for God and saw the God he craved in Jesus. But who needs Him now? If there is a God, why would we need Him if we have come so far on our own and are capable of taking care of ourselves? It was Simone Weil who reminded us that we are in danger of starving to death not because there is no bread, but because we think we are not hungry.

"Well," you ask, "if there is such a thing as a hunger for God, how do I know I have it?" You know it when you feel an emptiness, a sensation that your life is going nowhere. You know it when you face important questions but you haven't met the source of the answers. Experiences like these are revelations of spiritual hunger, invitations to become seekers.

The good news is that hungry seekers are not turned away. God's chosen Man appeared on the scene, claiming that whoever came to Him would never be hungry and whoever believed in Him would never be thirsty. Was He for real? You have to decide. We can agree that Jesus was sure of Himself and His message: "Blessed are those who hunger and thirst for righteousness, for they will be filled" (Matthew 5:6 NRSV).

Zacchaeus was a hungry seeker. So what did he do? Try to impress Jesus with his qualifications for discipleship? Recite his accomplishments in the hope that they would make him acceptable to God? No, he put himself where Jesus could find him. He climbed a tree to catch God's eye. Jesus looked and saw a hungry man.

God is on a mission to find us. God was searching for Zacchaeus long before the man ever contemplated a spiritual journey. And so it is with us: the God we seek finds us when we turn from our futility and preoccupation with ourselves, put our pride aside, and climb up the tree of our desperation. Then things start happening quickly.

The first words between Jesus and Zacchaeus were Jesus' command for him to come down out of the tree, followed by brazenly inviting Himself to stay at Zacchaeus' house. Was Jesus forcing himself on Zacchaeus? Not if you understand what the story is really saying. He knew Zacchaeus' name, understood his heart, and saw welcome in his eyes. Zacchaeus was caught up in a whirlwind. God had found him.

Zacchaeus said, "Look, Lord! Here and now I give half of my possessions to the poor, and if I have cheated anybody out of anything, I will pay back four times the amount" (Luke 19:8). Was he trying to buy his salvation or make himself more acceptable to Jesus? That would have been futile. God accepts us as we are. Zacchaeus wasted no time in getting on with God's will for his life.

Why the urgency? When the door is open and you are invited to become the person you really are, you jump at the chance, especially if you're honest enough to admit you're not happy with who you are. The message of the gospel, expressed in Jesus' encounter with Zacchaeus, is that Jesus has the ability to make us better than we are. Zacchaeus was destined to become something beyond what he was. His hunger and thirst were righteous; he would be filled. It was his destiny.

Who were you meant to be? Find out first by getting in touch with your spiritual hunger. Then, get linked up with Jesus. You will not only discover who you really are, you will become it.

SOMETHING TO THINK ABOUT

1. We know about being hungry for food. How can someone be hungry for God?

2. Who began the search process—Zacchaeus or Jesus? Why?

3. Why did Zacchaeus demonstrate the transformation in his life so lavishly?

4. Who were you meant to be? What is holding you back from being that person?

3: People Who Want to Be Healed

FEW OF OUR ABILITIES ARE AS PRECIOUS TO US AS OUR SIGHT. ALMOST UNIVERSAL sympathy exists for one who is blind, especially since a lack or loss of eyesight is usually irreversible. When we learn that those who were in front of blind Bartimaeus (Luke 18:35–43) rebuked him for shouting out, we feel indignation. How could they blame him for his eagerness? Had they no sympathy for his plight? Didn't this man deserve his moment with the Master?

Could it be that those who were impatient with Bartimaeus had provided the alms by which he was able to live, had taken their turns leading him where he needed to go? And now, when they were eager to see the Messiah, they were in no mood to let their bothersome friend interfere. "Enough, Bartimaeus! Keep silent!"

The Eyes of Faith

But he would not keep silent. And because he would not, Jesus stopped and ordered Bartimaeus to be brought to Him. Why? Because Jesus always stopped for those who wanted to be healed. He was attracted to the sick, the paralyzed, the hungry, the repentant sinner. He was the exposure of God's compassionate heart. It is not surprising, then, that He was attracted to a man who suffered the isolation, and in those days the forced beggar status, of blindness.

Blind people often compensate for their lack of sight by developing the other senses. Bartimaeus used his ears: he could hear excitement and expectation. He used his voice to get information: he asked what the commotion meant. Jesus of Nazareth was about to pass by. His mind worked rapidly, "Jesus of Nazareth." What were the miracles He was said to have performed? Did not some claim that He was the Messiah? The beggar was blind, but he was beginning to see with his other senses.

"Son of David!" This was the only time in both Luke's and Mark's Gospel when Jesus was addressed by that title. But in early first-century Palestine, it was the popular name for the Messiah. Within a few moments, this blind man was able to see through the eyes of faith.

Jesus singled out Bartimaeus because he was blind. Even more importantly, He singled him out for his blind faith. People who think they can see their own way through this world believe Jesus is unnecessary. But Jesus singles out those who admit blindness, know they need healing and are ready to exercise blind faith.

Courage to Ask

Jesus said to Bartimaeus: "What do you want me to do for you?" It was not a superfluous question. Some people come to Jesus for signs and miracles. Others want cheap, easy forgiveness. Still others want prestige and power. What Jesus has to give is healing. Consider the consequences of healing. For Bartimaeus, healing would mean he would have to quit begging and find gainful employment. It would be almost like starting over. Asking for healing takes courage.

"Bartimaeus, do you want to continue as you are, using your infirmity as a crutch? Or do you want to be healed?" There was no hesitancy. He did not want alms from the One who could open blind eyes—he wanted to be healed. "Lord, let me receive my sight!"

Each of us is a face in the crowd until we brush up against divinity. We are tired of pretending happiness. We just want mercy. Divinity gives us courage to ask for mercy. Then the toughest question of all: "What do you want me to do for you?" Our answer reveals if we'll take the leap of faith from the blindness of a narrow, self-serving life to the vision of a liberating life with God.

Jesus singled out Bartimaeus because he wanted to be healed. Do you? You need only ask His mercy and His healing for your blindness. Then hang on (literally) for dear life.

SOMETHING TO THINK ABOUT

1. How did Bartimaeus demonstrate his faith?

2. Are there times when people are content to remain as they are and not be healed? Why?

3. What did Bartimaeus want Jesus to do?

4. If Jesus asked you, "What do you want Me to do for you," what would you request?

4: People Searching for Light

DOCTORS TELL US THEY CAN'T HEAL A PATIENT WHO DOES NOT WANT TO BE HEALED. They teach us that some people actually make the most of their illness and enjoy the attention it brings them or the excuses it affords. What a terrible deceit; portraying infirmity as desirable, darkness as light.

Bartimaeus was living in darkness, but he wanted to see the light of day, he wanted vision. So he cried out for mercy, he begged for his sight. Maybe Jesus could do something. Even if Jesus could heal him, there were already odds against it. Consider them.

First, the occasion was against him. The great Healer was near, but He was on the way to Jericho and ultimately to the waiting throngs in Jerusalem. Would He stop for a blind beggar at the back of the crowd? Second, Bartimaeus' physical condition was against him. He was blind, and blind persons aren't given to rash acts. He had never been able to see Jesus, or His miraculous works. Rumor was all he had to go on. Third, people were against him. His cries, each one louder than the last, irritated those in front of him. So they rebuked the obnoxious one.

Let's say something about stern rebukes. They have no place when the recipient feels drawn toward God and is acting on that pull. Earlier, Jesus' disciples rebuked those who were bringing children to Jesus. But Jesus intervened: "Let the little children come to me, and do not hinder them, for the kingdom of God belongs to such as these" (Luke 18:16). Yes, let those who hunger for God come. Let those who want healing come. Let those who want to see come. Yes, let Bartimaeus come.

There is a message in this story for both Christians and seekers. The message for the disciple of Christ is *never rebuke the seeker after God.* It has always been God's way to use the weak and despised of this world to manifest His saving grace. Let us never turn such a one away.

The message for the seeker is *don't let anything deter you from reaching out to God.* If you want to be healed, be a Bartimaeus—refuse to be turned away. Let your persistence equal your desire. Lay it all on the line. Take the risk. God loves it when someone is willing to risk something to get to Him. Such faith does not go unrewarded. For Bartimaeus the reward was beyond all expectation—he could see! Whether for the first time in his life or in many long years since going blind, he could now experience the miracle of vision.

How is your vision? Do you see through sin-clouded eyes a world with no purpose, a life with no meaning? Or do you see God at work, a Kingdom coming? Do you see God inviting you to become part of that Kingdom? The good news is that clear vision is at your fingertips. Cry for mercy, plead for spiritual vision and He will stop for you, He will pay attention to your cry and He will invite you into the Kingdom of Light.

Notice what Bartimaeus did: he came when he was called. Are you ready to do the same? Are you ready to leave the darkness behind? Are you ready to step out in blind faith to receive clear vision? Then Jesus is ready to say to you what He said to Bartimaeus: "Receive your sight; your faith has saved you." Are you ready to see?

SOMETHING TO THINK ABOUT

1. Did Jesus ever heal someone against his or her will? Why or why not?

2. What obstacles to healing did Bartimaeus have to overcome?

3. What would you be willing to risk in order to be the person God created you to be?

4. Are you blind to attitudes of heart that are holding you back? What are you going to do about it?

241

5: People Behind Barriers

HERE IS A STORY OF DISCOVERY. A STORY ABOUT A WOMAN WHO, AT THE WELL OF HER ancestor Jacob, discovered the Kingdom of God (see John 4:1–42). It's about a colorful but shallow person who found in Jesus the real meaning of her life and who was consequently able to abandon the sham and begin her journey of authenticity. John included this incident in his Gospel because there is something in it for all of us. If God's Kingdom can be discovered by a woman of dubious character by a well, then it can be discovered by you and me in unlikely places and ways. So I'm inviting you to hear this as your story.

Breaking Barriers

Jesus' mission was to bring the Kingdom of God within our grasp. Are there barriers? Yes. For some of us those barriers seem substantial. Consider what the Samaritan woman was up against.

The first barrier she faced was *national*. Although Jesus was a Galilean, He was a Jew identified with Jerusalem in Judea. Samaria and Judea were remnants of the earlier kingdoms of Israel and Judah. Israel, in the view of the Jews of Judah, had become paganized. Judah, on the other hand, saw itself as the faithful remnant of a great nation. It looked upon Samaria as a despicable mongrel. In Jesus' day, when a Jew and a Samaritan met, not much good came of it.

The second barrier was *religious*. According to the Samaritans, it began when Eli set up the sanctuary at Shiloh. The "chosen place" prescribed in the law of Moses was Mt. Gerizim—the very mountain at the foot of which was Jacob's well where Jesus and the Samaritan woman met. The Samaritans believed that the center of Jewish worship should have been there.

Samaritan and Jewish doctrines were more similar than different. Both nations believed in one God and one immutable law. Both awaited a God-sent Messiah who would usher in the new dispensation. But the Samaritans accepted only the Pentateuch (the first five books of the Old Testament) as sacred writ. They believed Mt. Gerizim existed before creation and escaped the flood; it would escape the destruction of all things on doomsday; and the Ark of the Covenant, somehow hidden in it now, would be revealed.

So it wasn't just a passing comment when the Samaritan woman said to Jesus: "Our ancestors worshipped on this mountain; but you say that the place where people must worship is in Jerusalem" (John 4:20). It was a subject of bitter religious debate. Religion was a serious barrier.

Another serious barrier was *sexual*. There were strict codes about relationships between the sexes in public places. The rabbis taught that a man was not to converse with a woman in public. That's why the disciples were astonished. Jesus was breaking rabbinic convention.

We can identify a final barrier against the success of this encounter. It was a *personal* barrier: they had little in common. She had a seamy past; her eyes were full with the tears of her failures; she clung to the flimsy security of a lover. Jesus' eyes were swimming with visions; He clung to nothing, for He was secure. Her mind skimmed the surface of life. His plumbed the depths. She protected her emotions through superficiality. He went for the heart. How could they ever communicate in a meaningful way?

The Gospel does not spare us the awkward moments. When Jesus spoke of living water, she wondered how He would get it without a vessel. Then she asked if He would show her where it could be obtained. When she raised the question of worship places, He said that holy places had become irrelevant.

How to Get Through

So many differences. But Jesus still got through. He can get through to you and me, as well. It's what He's good at: finding a way to penetrate our failure and shallowness, our callousness and pride so He can release His transforming power in our lives. It happens at conversion. But it also keeps happening throughout our pilgrimage as He springs up unexpectedly, enticing us with visions of His Kingdom and living water.

God is looking for us—people who struggle with barriers that keep them from fellowship with Him, people who bring with them an imperfect past, people who thirst for the water of life. He promises that those who drink of the water He gives them will never be thirsty (14).

SOMETHING TO THINK ABOUT

1. What barriers might have prevented the Samaritan woman from receiving grace and forgiveness?

2. The Samaritan woman had a "past," but was Jesus shocked or offended? Now think of your past. Is Jesus shocked? Offended?

3. How does Jesus penetrate our defenses to get to the heart of our need for salvation?

6: People Ready to Discover God

JESUS INVITES US TO A LIFE OF DISCOVERY. "THE KINGDOM OF GOD HAS COME," HE said. "Discover it! Abandon your old ways of thinking! Get out of the ruts of your futile life!" For a Samaritan woman who lived two thousand years ago, the journey of discovery began by a well where Jesus changed her life forever. What exactly did she discover that shining day? The most crucial thing was Jesus—Jesus the Christ, the one sent from God to save His people from their sin, the one who was God. It's interesting to see how the Messiah chose to reveal Himself to her.

First, He taught her about *living water*. He wanted a drink, and in His asking there arose an interesting word interplay found in the passage. When the woman referred to the well, she used a word that denoted an artificially constructed well. When Jesus spoke of His well, He used a word that denoted a natural, spring-fed source. The water from Jacob's well was not to be compared with water from Jesus' well. The old order was not to be compared with the new. In the old order, one had to work to get water. In the new, it was a continuous, unfailing supply, ever satisfying the need: it was a gift.

Have you discovered the supply that never fails to refresh and renew? Jesus is speaking here of a daily flow from which we can partake if we are not to go dry and shrivel up. Do you ask for the gift daily?

Jesus revealed Himself to her in another way. He taught her *living worship*. She raised the question, "Where should we go to worship?" Jesus quickly made it clear that she was still in the old order in her thinking: "God is spirit" (John 4:24).

It's hard to imagine a statement so disarmingly simple yet so powerfully true. "God is spirit" says that worship is not going to this place or that to find God. Worship is knowing that God is at work in the world and in our lives. He can't be contained in our neat agendas and habits of worship, He has His own. He will make Himself known, and we will come to know and worship Him—"in spirit and truth" (24).

We must give the lady credit, for she then made the right connection. When Jesus spoke of worship, she began to think of the Messiah. She had been taught that the coming Messiah would restore worship to its purified form. So she said, "I know that Messiah is coming" (25).

Jesus the Messiah brought us worship. How well have we received that part of the Messianic package? When we come together in worship, do we in spirit and truth seek to glorify the God who came in Jesus, to know Him and obey Him? Or do we instead reduce our worship to a celebration of our own church culture—our version of Jerusalem or Gerizim exclusiveness?

Living water and living worship—what a conversation between two strangers on a hot day! Jesus never wastes time. He has a way of introducing Himself that makes us catch our breath. We look into His eyes and see eternity. We listen to His voice and hear truth. We sense His concern and learn love. Jesus invites us to discover God.

SOMETHING TO THINK ABOUT

1. How did Jesus reveal Himself to the woman at the well?

2. What does "living worship" involve?

3. How do we worship "in spirit and in truth"?

4. What did Jesus mean by "living water"?

7: People Ready to Discover Themselves

JESUS INVITES US TO DISCOVER OURSELVES. THE WOMAN HE ENCOUNTERED AT THE well was beginning to realize that He was the Messiah. But tied to this realization was another awakening: she was beginning to realize who she was. Christ not only reveals Himself to us, He also reveals us to ourselves. This should not be surprising. Are not the most saintly among us those who know themselves inside and out and, knowing the truth, therefore speak of themselves with great modesty? How well do you know yourself?

The Samaritan woman's encounter with Jesus required the moment of truth: "Go, call your husband" (John 4:16). Her response: "I have no husband." Then Jesus: "You are right in saying, 'I have no husband' for you have had five husbands, and the one you have now is not your husband." He elicited a confession of truth, and He exposed the failure of her life—her inability to sustain holy matrimony. She immediately changed the subject. When first brought to the brink of painful insight, people usually back off. Wouldn't you?

The Samaritan woman backed off alright, but the story hints that in her own way she started to come back to the truth, to face it and deal with it. Not only did she give witness that this Man told her all she ever did, but the liberation that this knowledge brought her was so undeniable that many believed in Jesus because of it (39).

Have you had your moment of truth with Jesus? Have you allowed Him to reveal the sin that stands between you and the Kingdom of God? And has your pilgrimage through this life been a journey of honest self-discovery, or has it been a journey of smug self-satisfaction? Have you been willing to expose yourself to what General Albert Orsborn called God's "kind but searching eye"?

There's a difference between brutal self-honesty when you're standing alone and brutal self-honesty when you're standing in the presence of Jesus. The one can be devastating and shame us into retreat. The other can bring courage and joy. God can do something with people who are willing to stop pretending in His presence. It is the nature of God to free us to face our tarnished selves in order to discover our true selves.

Eagles in Disguise

Ted Engstrom tells a Native American story about a brave who found an eagle's egg and put it into a prairie chicken's nest. The eaglet hatched with the brood of chicks and grew up with them. All his life the changeling eagle thought he was a prairie chicken. When an eagle soared overhead, he asked his companion what it was and was told, "That's an eagle, but don't think you'll ever fly like him!" So the changeling eagle died thinking it was a prairie chicken.

In a day when the rabbinic schools were still debating over whether women had souls, Jesus made it possible for a Samaritan woman to discover that she was an eagle who could soar. He can do the same for you. Before Him, confess that you have been living a meager and meaningless life. Then allow Him to teach you who you are and what you are capable of. He will release you with wings to fly where you never imagined your life could go.

SOMETHING TO THINK ABOUT

1. Are there things about you no one else knows?

2. Has the Lord ever revealed something in your life that needed to be changed, regardless of how painful that process might be?

3. How do you cover your faults and failures to market your best self?

4. How could you grow spiritually if you tell yourself the truth and discover yourself?

8: People Ready to Discover Their Mission

JESUS' ENCOUNTER WITH THE SAMARITAN WOMAN IS A WONDERFUL EXAMPLE OF what can happen when we meet Him. First, He breaks down the barriers keeping us from God. Then He offers us Himself, and we come to know Him as our liberator from sin. We discover, and receive the power to become, our true selves. Finally, we discover our mission.

The root meaning of the Hebrew word "to save" or "to find salvation" is "to make wide or spacious." Isn't that what Jesus does for us: opens up the world to us—and opens us up to the world? He did for the Samaritan woman. God called her to do something for Him in the world.

The Samaritan woman had no plan of action, only the contagious joy of discovery. She had met Jesus and it showed. The Gospel writer tells us, "Many Samaritans . . . believed in Him because of the woman's testimony" (John 4:39 NRSV), so convincing was the change they saw. The message is clear: our mission is to infect the world with what we've caught. The question is whether or not we've got something potent enough to be catching.

Evidently, the woman did. The story is interrupted by dialogue between Jesus and His disciples. The disciples return with food, and Jesus, refusing to eat, points to fields that are white for harvest. He tells them the Kingdom harvest has already begun. What role will you play?

An Indelible Contribution

Retired General Eva Burrows tells the story of the weavers of that great tapestry of "Christ in Glory" in Coventry Cathedral. It was woven in France and was so huge that the weavers could work on only one section at a time. When the tapestry was completed, it was shipped to England—none of the weavers having seen the work in its entirety. Some time later, the Anglican bishop brought the weavers from France to see, for the first time, their magnificent work. Each was now able to see Christ in His glory—and know he had made his own indelible contribution to it.

Christ invites you to make your own indelible contribution to His mission in the world. He has gifted you to play a part. Where do you fit in?

One night, Bramwell Booth, son of the Salvation Army's founder, passed his father's house and noticed a light was still burning. He went in to say goodnight. "General," he said, "what are you doing at this time of night? You ought to be in bed. Don't you know it's nearly one o'clock?"

The General said, "Bramwell, I am thinking about the people's sins," and then with great intensity, "What will they do with their sins?"

The Salvation Army addresses that question. What remedy is there for the sickness infecting humanity? How can people be freed from their sinful existence and the bondage of a sinful lifestyle?

The gospel is the remedy. It leads repentant sinners to forgiveness. It points the way to a cleansed life and a new future in Christ. And to those who respond, it calls to a mission.

What is your mission in life? When you discover Christ, you discover your mission. He will point you where you can effectively serve Him; and when you follow, like the woman at the well, you will find something to live for.

1. What did Jesus ask the Samaritan woman to do concerning evangelism? Was it her idea?

2. How can you contribute to the building of the kingdom of God?

3. What is your mission in life? How can you put that mission into action?

CREST BOOKS

The Salvation Army National Publications

Crest Books, a division of The Salvation Army's National Publications department, was established in 1997 so contemporary Salvationist voices could be captured and bound in enduring form for future generations, to serve as witnesses to the continuing force and mission of the Army.

Leadership on the Axis of Change

Sanctified Sanity: The Life and Teaching of Samuel Logan Brengle

A Word in Season: A Collection of Short Stories

Andy Miller: A Legend and a Legacy

Pen of Flame: The Life and Poetry of Catherine Baird

If Two Shall Agree: The Story of Paul A. Rader and Kay F. Rader of The Salvation Army

Fractured Parables: And Other Tales to Lighten the Heart and Quicken the Spirit

Our God Comes: And Will Not Be Silent

A Salvationist Treasury: 365 Devotional Meditations from the Classics to the Contemporary

Slightly Off Center! Growth Principles to Thaw Frozen Paradigms

He Who Laughed First: Delighting in a Holy God

Easter Through the Years: A *War Cry* Treasury

Who Are These Salvationists? An Analysis for the 21st Century

Romance & Dynamite: Essays on Science & the Nature of Faith

A Little Greatness

Pictures from the Word

Celebrate the Feasts of the Lord: The Christian Heritage of the Sacred Jewish Festivals

Christmas Through the Years: A *War Cry* Treasury

Never the Same Again: Encouragement for New and Not-So-New Christians

Above titles can be purchased through your nearest Salvation Army Supplies and Purchasing department:

ATLANTA, GA—(800) 786-7372
DES PLAINES, IL—(847) 294-2012
RANCHO PALOS VERDES, CA—(800) 937-8896
WEST NYACK, NY—(888) 488-4882